Trail Magic

A Physician's Journey Through the Appalachian Mountains

JoDean Nicolette

Finalist for the 2023
Kenneth Johnston Nonfiction Book Award

Nominated for the 2024
National Book Award

For my Aunt Bonnie and Uncle Don,
who took me on my first backpacking trip

And for my mother,
who said being a doctor was boring,
that I should be a writer instead

In her remarkable debut memoir *Trail Magic*, JoDean Nicolette does more than carry her readers with her as she hikes the 2,182 miles of the Appalachian Trail, section by section, over the course of a crucial decade in her life—although that would be gift enough, letting us breathe the forest air, absorb its green light, muddle through rain and fog (and worse), encounter fellow hikers who flash into life on the page and then return us to the profound and transformative experience of solitude. Nicolette weaves her adventures on the trail together with challenges she faces as a woman resident and physician, as a wife and a caregiving daughter, and as a human being discovering her own powers—and limits—by finding her place in the natural world. On top of all its other delights, *Trail Magic* is an education in the health benefits of engaging with the wilderness. As vivid and scenic as the richest novel, it takes you on a journey you don't want to miss.

> Mary Helen Stefaniak, author of three novels, most recently *The World of Pondside* and *The Six-Minute Memoir: Fifty-Five Short Essays on Life*

In this seamlessly braided narrative, a woman sets out on an adventure that exposes her simultaneously to the depths of solitude and to a kaleidoscope of characters: human and animal, tender and threatening, illuminating and comic. Through exquisitely vivid description, the reader is swept into her journey: all the way from extreme workplace burnout, through intense physical exertion, to a kind of rebirth in the shimmering green vastness of the world around her. In language that is intimate and honest—yet without ever being histrionic--she faces certain dark places within herself, confronts dangers in the world without, and exults in the wild beauty of nature.

> Noelle Oxenhandler,
> author of *The Wishing Year* and *Eros of Parenthood*

To read *Trail Magic* is to travel the 2,181-mile Appalachian Trail with an open-hearted and courageous guide. Hiking with Violet (Nicolette) brings encounters with snakes, bears, and copious bird species, as well as fear, panic, and "chest-beating pride." Physician Nicolette embraces a view of medicine that treats the whole person. Similarly, writer Nicolette moves us to open to joy and healing through the interconnection of self and nature. She deftly interweaves the field of medicine, her own emotional wounds, and the natural world from forest to mountaintop into an alchemy of magic itself.

> Carol Ann Wilson, author of award-winning
> *Still Point of the Turning World: The Life of Gia-fu Feng*, and
> *Because We Wanted To: two women, a dream, and a ranch called Singing Acres.*

JoDean Nicolette beautifully weaves together the lyrical and the practical as she traverses the Appalachian Trail and ponders the essential connections that help us to see the world and to know ourselves.

> Susanna Sonnenberg, author of *She Matters* and *Her Last Death.*

Trail Magic is about braving the woods and one's self. It is forest bathing at its fullest, exemplifying the role wilderness plays in our health and well-being. The journey of this brave and authentic woman lingers long after the last step on the Trail.

> Cristine Milton, PhD, retired Geography professor, and author of *Landscapes of the Mind*

Walking with JoDean Nicolette in *Trail Magic*, you can't help but marvel at the glory of the natural world and the way that finding our place in it—through our senses, with our minds, our spirits—expands our humanity within a society that's too often constraining and opposed to life fully expressed. Writing with care and a sharp and inquisitive mind, Nicolette explores worlds larger and vaster than those she's otherwise found familiar, and somehow finds herself, *beyond herself*, along the way.

> Scott Korb, author of *The Faith Between Us* and *Life in Year One*

They say hiking the Appalachian Trail will make you laugh, cry, confess, and grow. The same can be said of *TRAIL MAGIC*, which offers an unflinching, deeply personal window into one woman's journey to reclaim herself. Nicolette carries us, along with her rain gear, sleeping bag, and dehydrated hummus, into the human predicament of belonging and acceptance, weaving threads of healing, hardship, and humility, in a narrative that truly captures what it's like to carry a body--and all its creative intelligence--into the woods and over 2000 miles, reaching not only the northern terminus at Mount Katahdin, but the person she has been striving to become.

> Katey Schultz, author of *Flashes of War* and *Still Come Home*

Contents

Part I: Heal Thyself

Chapter One

I sat on an upturned stump among sugar maple and red oak, my palms resting on my thighs. A light breeze crept through the trees, nudging my chin, lifting it, encouraging me to open my chest to cool wet air. I breathed in.

Water smells like this. Clean. Uncomplicated.

My neck relaxed; my shoulders dropped. Muscle by muscle, nerve by nerve, vertebra by vertebra, tension dissipated into the fog. Nowhere to be but here.

I was a doctor, just finished with training. I had graduated medical school, then stumbled through three years of the on-the-job whirlwind called residency. Yesterday, my last day had finally arrived: I signed my last order, dropped my pager in a desk drawer, scrubs in the laundry chute, and listened for the swish and click of hospital doors as they closed behind me. Today, before the sun rose, my husband Ben had dropped me at an already busy San Francisco Airport (SFO) where I dodged people and luggage to catch the 6:05 AM flight to Atlanta. Once there, backpack slung over one shoulder, I navigated the complex array of terminals and traffic to a remote curb where I met a shuttle that ferried me into the hills, leaving me at the corner of forest-service-road and dirt-track-leading-into-woods.

"That's the Benton MacKaye Trail, right there," the driver had said, as she slowed, turning the SUV so headlights shone into forest. She pointed. "Take that for a mile to the summit of Springer Mountain—the south end of the Appalachian Trail." She turned to me and the glow from the dash lit half her face. "It's the closest you can get to the AT by vehicle," she added with a shrug. Her keys clicked against the steering column as I hopped out of the front seat and pulled my backpack from the hatch. I peered ahead into fog so thick it masked any break in the trees.

We'd arrived around 9 PM, after the long ride from the airport. The shuttle driver insisted on idling, shining her headlights on the flat area that cut into mountain broadleaves. Her high beams flood-lit tiny droplets in the air, spotlighting me as I scuttled about, constructing my first campsite. What was she thinking? That I looked like a tinhorn? Pale and soft after years indoors, now stomping around, snapping tent poles, and clattering as I prepared to spend the night alone in the mountains. That I should be more afraid? I weighted the end of my bear-line with a small stone, and, despite the high beams, required three lobs before I landed it over the right branch and levered my food sack up.

Unpracticed and relaxed is how I felt—two sentiments that had rarely existed together in my life. I turned and faced the headlights, nodding and waving, to signal the invisible driver that she could leave. I heard her window slide up, and she pulled away, tires crunching over dirt and gravel. Maybe I imagined it, but the truck seemed to slow just once, a brief hesitation, before it rolled again. As the tail lights vanished over a rise, I wished I'd explained that I'd be fine. I wasn't faking my calm. Perhaps I was confident because I had grown up near the Catskill Mountains in upstate New York and vacationed in the Adirondacks. But the truth was, facing a night alone in the Appalachians was nowhere near as scary as a night in the hospital as an intern, assaulted by alarms, beeps, and code blues, surrounded by my own real inexperience. Nurses summoned. Supervisors squawked. Patients moaned...a few wailed. The pager routinely hailed me to some new medical urgency in a patient I didn't know, on a hospital floor I didn't yet know how to get to.

The Appalachians—wise, weathered, ancient—seemed familiar to me. They made California's Sierra Nevadas seem like adolescents, angular and awkward... . And the Appalachians called, like ancestors, like home. *Come here...Heal...Feel safe. Walk.*

And now, in the darkness that had settled onto the other end of the day, trees cloaked me in quiet. Moisture clung to my hair and skin, and I closed my eyes, not worried about what moved in front of me, or behind, among trunks and brambles. Not feeling the tug—for the first time in years—to glance over my shoulder. I opened my ears...not listening, not with intent, but simply to receive what existed around me. A brook burbled to my left, and moist mountain air coalesced on branches, before plunking onto layers of soil and downed leaves. The forest seemed to have settled under the thick air, stilled for slumber. I opened my eyes and noticed that I couldn't see the trail running next to my campsite. Or the logging road, where my ride had dropped me minutes before. But night, snug against me, held me safe.

My tent stood close by, a brazen blue and white against muted forest tones. From inside, my sleeping bag beckoned, a warm burrow. I hoisted myself off the stump, ready for sleep. The screen's zipper softly wheezed but once inside, quiet surrounded me again. This tent was called "Clip Flashlight," and I'd purchased it because one of the Appalachian Trail how-to books listed it as reliable. It *clipped* together in a *flash*, with plastic hooks and aluminum poles that folded into a tight little bundle—and *light*, it weighed maybe three pounds. But mostly it was cheap—the demo model and only one of its kind left in the store. With a resident's salary, economy had been important. The Clip Flashlight was a two-person tent; I'd worried I'd feel claustrophobic in tiny one-person models. But out here, sliding into my nylon bag, with my backpack at my feet, it ballooned around me. It was too much space—more than I needed—the ballroom ceiling too high to make it cozy.

I'd gone from so much to so little, I thought, as I slid into sleep. Sprawling, tentacular medical center reduced to a blue and white dome. Frenetic days, bumping through rushing bodies, between flashing red lights, crushed beneath overhead announcements about patient emergencies or incoming ambulances, managing complicated patients, wondering how I'd fit it all in—reduced to here and now. But then, as my body relaxed into the ground pad, unexpected thoughts barged in: images of me glancing around corners, cringing at new phone messages, willing my trembling hands to calm. I jerked, startling myself awake as panic re-emerged, another bruise still blooming from my psyche, tender when inadvertently touched.

That was all in the past. No more unwanted attention, no more churning days. Here and now. *Here* and *now*. I rolled onto my side, putting my back to the tent flap, and to the existence I had left behind. I hoped when dawn came, and I emerged to sun reflecting off dew, a new path would be lit.

My first morning on the trail was peaceful, but not quiet. A chipmunk scurried and hopped, and a robin chirred. Wind patrolled through trees. From the warmth of my sleeping bag, I listened to gentle taps as condensation dropped onto my tent—*tik, tok, tik...tok, tik-tik, tok*—the only measure of time in the sunless mountains. Liberated from pinned, rotating arms and crisp digital displays, I lay still long after pale light hit the campsite. Stared up at silhouettes of soaked leaves and mud spatters on my rain fly: Rorschach images.

What did I see, and what did it say about me? *It says you're on the Appalachian Trail, and there's something wrong with you if you're still thinking about medicine and Rorschach tests.*

I shimmied out of my bag and reached for clothes. Shirt, pants, underwear, a sock. *One* sock. I got dressed anyway, alternating between sitting and squatting, breathing between grunts, and making a huge and foreign ruckus among gentle forest sounds. I stuffed my sleeping bag into its tiny sack and pulled the drawstring tight. Sitting on my ground pad with one bare foot, I looked around...no sock. I slipped on my flip flops, pushing the thong between toes on one socked foot. In trying to haul myself out of the tent, I fell backward onto my bottom several times and finally discovered that backing out worked better. I leaned my pack against a tree and looked around at my surroundings for the first time.

Trees, a mix of deciduous and conifer towered over me, all of us shrouded by fog. Leaves and needles hung pendant from branches, and thick layers of browns and golds covered the earth. I smelled the damp, a mix of soil and mold, teeming with life, so different from the hospital's antiseptic, which barely masked other scents: urine, stool, vomit, blood. I parted my lips, inhaling again through my nose and mouth, and fresh air filled me, this time radiating past my chest. Openness, the expanse of the forest, authenticity of life seemed to reach into my arteries and veins, swelling my blood volume and inflating my limbs past the contractures of my previous existence. I exhaled, spread my arms, and unfurled with new light, and with trillium and tiny fiddlehead fern reaching for the morning sun.

The chipmunk clicked and squeaked, watched on its hind legs as I took down my tent. Before I could start breakfast, spatter from mist became the more regular rhythm of rain. Like shoulder taps, a prod into action. My knowledge of what to do surprised me; I'd never backpacked in rain before. I reached for my rain gear—

a bright yellow poncho with Mickey Mouse on the front—and wrestled it over my head. It spread behind me to cover my pack. I pulled on my boots. My long braid hung between my pack and back in an uncomfortable bump, so I tugged it forward over my shoulder. I would walk first, then eat breakfast when I had shelter.

"I'm fleeing the jungle for the woods," I said to a red-back salamander and the chestnut saplings, just to hear my voice in the stillness. And the woods—without pressure, hours, and hierarchy—already seemed so much more hospitable, especially this first flat frontage path, leading to the AT. Was it possible that the whole 2200-miles from Georgia to Maine would be this easy? My braid swung across my chest as I marched into air so dense I couldn't see three feet in front of me, one foot snug and warm, and the other squishing naked against the bottom of my boot.

White diamonds mark the Benton MacKaye trail, not that it mattered in the pea soup hanging over the mountains that morning. Trees ushered me along. This shorter trail is 300 miles total, running in both Georgia and North Carolina, and named for the man who first conceived of the AT in 1921, as an escape from pressures of low country life. To me, its length was inconsequential since I was merely using it for access. Disoriented by jet lag, I had no idea what time it was. And that was all right by me. I didn't own a watch; residents usually told time by glancing at their pagers' digital displays. Initially, I had thought about it, considered buying an inexpensive timepiece in a local drugstore...Minnie Mouse, Winnie the Pooh...maybe Scoobie Doo to keep me company, but I decided I could approximate time by the sun in the sky.

It had never occurred to me, living in California, where rainfall is limited to winter months, that I might not see sun for days at a time in southern Appalachia. I wandered forward, floating in fog and my lack of concern. It was almost summer. Days were long. Still, squinting ahead, I was beginning to sense that a watch would have been helpful to gauge my distance...maybe twenty minutes to a mile over this even, walkable path? I hoped I wouldn't walk right past the Appalachian Trail and find myself far to the west before sun broke through and revealed my location.

I stopped when I heard a noise behind me. I barely had time to wonder about black bears when a lanky hiker whisked past, tin cup bumping against his pack, red bandana trailing.

"Hey!" he said without stopping, gear swishing with his stride.

"Hey!" *Where had he come from?*

"Can't stop, headed for Woods Hole shelter tonight. Twenty-seven miles," he said, glancing back. "Then another twenty-five to Unicoi after that. Probably won't see ya! Good job, though!"

Mist swallowed his long legs and olive pack. The same wet air condensed on my warm face, and a drop slid down my nose. The percussion of my boots dislodged it, and it fell. I imagined I heard the *plop!* For some reason, this made me giddy, and I spread my arms as if I could catch more drops, scoop them into my poncho sleeves. I skipped—something I hadn't done since...When?—celebrating the openness, lack of boundaries, absence of limitation on my body and my thoughts.

The glee surprised me, and I searched for a reason, examining what it was I'd broken free from. My attention returned to a time when life felt smaller, more constrained, wedged into a chair-desk, anonymous shoulders inches away on either side, cramped despite the cavernous auditorium. I scribbled every word the professor said into a spiral notebook. Inflammatory diseases: rheumatoid arthritis, Reiter's syndrome, systemic lupus erythematosus. The wire coil pinched my wrist, but I was unwilling to adjust my hand in case I missed a word. The professor described effects on kidneys and used the terms "B-U-N," and "creatinine," terms that measured kidney function, terms that I didn't comprehend. My classmates all nodded in understanding, hands paused from notetaking. Did they? Understand? Because I didn't have a clue. I'd felt alone and overwhelmed in the crowd, out-prepared and out-classed by other matriculating students. I was just a hard worker from a semi-rural community in upstate New York, while most of my classmates came from Ivy League legacy families, or were professional athletes, concert pianists, children of diplomats. At the time, it didn't occur to me that probably no one in that room knew much, and that they, too, felt like imposters. Instead, the struggle to keep up kicked in and drove me into late nights and less-than-healthy compromises.

Unwilling to make the same mistake on the trail, I held myself at a steady plod. Maybe that was its own form of overcompensating, but I'd recognized that ultra-hiker that charged through, went to medical school with guys just like him, happy to tell you all they had done, all they planned to do, glancing back to make sure they'd left you in the dust. And I'd read about ultra-light, ultra-long-distance hikers in the AT books. Twenty pounds of gear, thirty miles a day. Grudge kindled as I wondered how it felt, in medicine or on the Appalachian Trail, to bound straight ahead, unobstructed.

Suddenly, my almost reflex resentment morphed into something else. Maybe it was the humidity or the altitude or the fresh mountain air, or maybe it was just the first time in years that my mind hadn't been fenced by schedule lines or calendar boxes, or the need to conserve mental energy for the intense hours ahead, but my thoughts opened and blossomed, then swirled around me as if lofted by evaporating moisture. They settled in a comforting way, instead of nagging me with their pettiness. I saw my snap judgement and released it, letting wonder take its place. Was taking success for granted limiting in its own way? Lacking depth or authenticity? When the first barrier in this changing world, the first failure, rose up, would such a person have the tenacity, the skills to find a way forward?

But that was his journey, and I was navigating my own. I'd learned some things besides medicine in the last few years, and I wanted to insulate my experience from anyone else's. I imagined the ultra-hiker stretching out the space between us—practically in North Carolina already—while I practiced not-thinking-about his pace, practiced not-keeping-up, practiced simply moving forward and matching my breath with my strides.

I started the Appalachian Trail with limited experience. My Uncle Don and Aunt Bonnie had taken me on my first backpack trip when I was just out of college—three days in the Adirondack Mountains. Before we set out, I sat dumbfounded, watching them divvy up equipment: pots and pans, tent stakes, rope to hang food, stove and fuel, meals. How did they figure this all out? My then-backpack was a canvas, external-framed contraption, already years out of date. Despite its obsolescence, I used it for the Adirondack trip, but needed other things. Something besides a huge, flannel, Ho-Ho roll sleeping bag, for one. At the outfitters, I marveled at sleeping bags that scrunched into tiny sacks the length of my foot and ran my fingers over Gortex. I muddled through the Adirondack trip learning to carry weight, walk over uneven ground, tune to my surroundings. Both sounds and quiet scared me, and the pack weighed me down, rendering me unable to move quickly in case I had to. I never did.

After that, I took a few trips on the west coast with my husband Ben: Yosemite, Cascades, Lassen, Lost Coast. Each time, I hiked stronger, slept better, worried less about wildlife, as all the animals seemed to bolt from my path. Hiking distances became attainable, and I wanted to do more.

Preparing for the Appalachian Trail, I made up for my inexperience with what you would expect from a young scientist: I studied. I had gotten through medical school and residency, and I knew how to do research. I pored over AT material during free minutes in clinic, or when I finally staggered home. Ben would hover at the kitchen table as I read, leaning over my shoulder to scan maps, and playfully snagging books while I slapped at his hand.

One of the planning guides was a workbook, which I initially filled out in pen. Mistake. I changed my mind regularly about all aspects of the trip. Food, for example. *Did kettle corn, extremely light, take up too much room? Maybe Chex mix would be better. Was peanut butter too messy?* And clothing. *Not a sweater...too heavy. Three, no two, no three pairs of socks. If I turned my underwear inside out, could I get a second day?* Or about what should be in supply boxes I mailed down the line. *To chocolate or not to chocolate? That was one question. Books? Yes, books. Could I walk seventeen miles in a day? No, ten. Wait...probably fifteen.* I had transformed the pages into illegible squiggles, cross-outs, and arrows. The next day I brought home whiteout pillaged from clinic and began my ritual of planning in pencil.

I stopped short at the Appalachian Trail intersection, nondescript as it was—a couple of dirt tracks crossing in the middle of nowhere. I peered left and right, certain but uncertain as I sank into the usual insecurities born of my medical training, entertaining brief images of myself wandering aimlessly in the woods, evolving slowly into feral existence before being discovered by ground-sniffing dogs and orange-vested searcher-rescuers. But the white, two-by-six-inch rectangular trail markers (called blazes) painted on the trees tipped me off. And the small rectangular sign that said, "Appalachian Trail," over an arrow labeled "N," pointing to the right. My next steps would be my first on the 2,182 miles north to Mount Katahdin.

Instead, I turned left, encountering a bronze plaque, bolted to a rock at knee level, identifying the trail's official start on Springer Mountain summit, 3,780 feet. Chattahoochee National Forest. Maps placed the first AT shelter just south of this official southern terminus; I headed there.

The AT, I would learn over the ten years I would ultimately travel the trail, cut through federal lands for most of its journey to Maine. Some of the trail had been originally interrupted by private or local territory but was subsequently cobbled together using imminent domain laws to make the journey possible. I hitched up my step a little, felt gooseflesh spread along my back and arms as I contemplated the continuous path stretching between my boots and Maine's Mount Katahdin. Today's trail had evolved from Benton MacKaye's original vision into a challenge, a trek, a longer escape into months of simpler life. Two thousand hikers set out each year to attempt the full journey. Less than ten percent made it. How far would I get this time? I had no ambition to go the whole way, since I had to start working that summer. I had only planned on hiking until, well…until I was done.

I spied the shelter's sign and stepped into a soupy clearing, aiming for a roof under which to boil water for warm food and drink to fuel the day ahead.

"Here comes the sun, dah, dah, dah-dah! Here comes the sun!" erupted from the rustic, three-sided Springer Mountain shelter. *Someone is here.* I'd assumed I'd have the place to myself. Between fog outside and shadow inside, I couldn't see who had belted out the Beatles, but I looked up and around to see if, in fact, the sun was breaking through.

"He's talking about you," a younger voice offered as I got closer. "That yellow poncho is the only thing visible out there." *Two men. Okay.* I reminded myself that I was rolling with things out here...all the things. And this wasn't such a big deal: guys. I'd expected to see mostly men on the AT. I dropped my pack on the wood-slat floor and dug through gear for my stove. More bodies rustled as I assembled and lit the burner. I smelled marijuana and looked up in time to see a body climbing a ladder to a loft. I was suddenly glad that I hadn't walked the mile to this shelter the night before, where I would have found a party instead of quiet.

The water boiled and steam rose against my face; hot water was step one on the way to coffee and oatmeal.

"I guess a watched pot really does boil," the older man said.

When I turned, he winked. And my world tilted, slowed. Tiny droplets hung from his dark beard, and a drip from the rafters splashed onto his small pate. Adrenaline surged. Burn spread through my chest and sweat leaked across my back. I sloshed boiling water onto my thumb. I set the pot down and attempted to coordinate my fingers to get the zip-lock with my oats open. Echoes from my pounding heart surrounded me, and lifted me above the scene. Faces and voices retreated, now far away. Finally, a woodpecker rapped against a tall spruce, and I was in my body, in the shelter again. Smelling coffee. A laugh and snort dropped from the loft, then thumps and shifting gear. A lighter flicked twice.

Stupid, I thought, as medical school, now years ago, reared up again. *That's not Neeman.* We're 3500 miles away, and that's a hiker.

In a split second, I had rearranged my face into "doctorface," an expression I learned during residency to hide my reaction when patient visits became awkward or shocking. It's a mask, but it doesn't mean I'm feeling less, just that the situation calls for reassurance, wisdom, an interested but objective eye. Like when a man pulled off his sock, revealing a cold, purple foot. Or when a woman opened her shirt to show me her "rash," and instead revealed a fungating mass growing from her breast. My face remained concerned but unperturbed. *This does not alarm me; I've seen all this before.*

Picking up my pot, I turned to the older man, smiling, "Hey, smart ass. Would you like some hot water?"

A woman emerged from behind the shelter, and climbed in. Frizzy blond hair escaped from underneath her wool cap. Her eyes darted between me and the bearded man, then she sat next to him, thigh pressed to his. She nodded toward my coffee-making system. I carried grounds and tiny triangular filters which I suspended with a twig across the top of my cup. I poured water through, and *bingo!* drip coffee.

"That's quite a set up," she said, tucking toilet paper into a pocket. "I bet that doesn't make it to Katahdin. Or even past Neel's Gap."

I looked up at her long enough to tip precious coffee past my mug's rim.

"Those grounds are a lot of weight. You'll be carrying them dry and wet."

This was true. It's pack-out-what-you-pack-in.

"Especially because there's no calories," she continued. "That's a beginner mistake."

Jeez, another one from my training. Are they all out here? I stirred raisins into my oats, took a small bite to test the temperature. *Residency this time, wielding criticism like a weapon, a tool to enforce a hierarchy.*

Doctorface again.

"Coffee's a staple for me." I said, smiling at her, not wanting to seem either defensive or argumentative—not wanting to *feel* that way—I'd had enough digs and criticism in the last few years to last a lifetime. Especially being in Family Medicine.

A blackbird darted in front of the shelter, and pine scent crept back into my nostrils. I remembered the unbounded space in these mountains, red-backed salamanders and black bears, horned owls and mosquitoes, trees and brambles, sun and fog, the unfenced web of life... . It doesn't matter, what this woman thinks of my equipment and food. *My* journey. Lots of room for all of us.

"I'm not walking to Katahdin," I started to say, red in the face that I was even answering her. "I'm only walking for a few weeks..."

"We met thru hiking ten years ago," she interrupted, nodding toward the older man. She leaned her shoulder against his. "We're here to celebrate our anniversary. We're getting out at Neel's Gap. I'm Patches and this is Minuteman." She offered their trail names, handles hikers used on the AT.

Three young male voices floated down with smoke from the loft.

"I'm Cheech."

"I'm Chong."

"I'm Strider."

That seemed like my cue to get moving, so I repacked in a more organized way, finding my sock in the process. I clipped my pack around my waist, grabbed my poncho from a wall peg, and settled it over my pack.

I headed north into the clouds, toward Hawk Mountain shelter, determined to shake what remained of the panic and annoyance that seemed to have hitched a ride onto the trail with my gear. I caught myself clenching my teeth—bruxism is the medical term—and focused on relaxing my jaw. *Just breathe*...and walk.

As my boots left the clearing and hit the Appalachian Trail, Minuteman called after me, "Her trail name will be Sunshine! You can't miss her!"

Chapter Two

Violet was the trail name I had chosen for myself, for reasons I didn't completely understand at the time. It seemed right, since violet is often identified as the color of the imagination, and I'd lost mine, a sentiment echoed by people close to me. I found it devastating.

"You'll be yourself again," one friend had responded as she observed my shoulders shaking with sobs, my tears, my broken spirit. She stood then, pumped an encouraging fist and exclaimed, "You're...you're a caged bird. You'll sing again."

In the stillness, my mind had wandered to life off the trail. Patches, and Minuteman especially, had yanked my thoughts back to medicine. It ran through my head again, how it started—the avalanche into emotional disarray. I saw myself crammed into one of those desks, stacked in an auditorium, hunched over the cardiovascular medicine exam. One of the multiple-choice questions had irked me, and I was stuck on it. "Which of the following is most consistent with angina pain?" The question had an obvious answer that would drive the point home about how to recognize heart disease, identified during the course as leading cause of death for men in the United States. The instructor wanted students to pick answer B which read, "Left sided or substernal crushing chest pressure, associated with exertion." I'd finished the test but kept going back, unable to let it go.

My pencil hovered. I tapped the page, then chewed the yellow shaft. Erased the lead marks in the margin. Brushed away rubber bits. Tapped the eraser instead. Pages shuffled, and I looked at my classmates circling confidently. Blood and heat rushed to my face and a compulsion seized me: I licked the lead and circled B. Then my hand, as if someone else were controlling it, drew an arrow to the bottom of the page. "*Unless of course you care for female patients, in which case angina pain can present as exertional fatigue, center or right sided pain, sharp in nature. And P.S. Heart disease supplanted breast cancer as the leading cause of death for women in the 1970s.*" I got up and, eyes to the floor, climbed steps to the auditorium door. I dropped my test face-down in the box, cutting my eyes left and right, wondering how long before I was identified as a student with attitude.

I'm not sure how many weeks passed before a pink phone message slip appeared in my med school mail box. It was handwritten: *Please call my office so we can meet. Dean Frank Neeman.* Crap. I slid it into my spiral notebook pocket, thinking I'd call from home but couldn't shake the dread. I climbed stairs to the student computer lab and like a young Alice to the Madhatter, punched in the number on the community phone and waited while it rang.

I aimed for Hawk Mountain shelter, eight miles north. My thoughts of life off the trail faded with distance. More and more I'd find myself wondering what type of hardwood I was looking at, or why certain ferns hadn't yet unfolded. Or cataloguing the new aches and pains that emerged with my increased exertion. Events from *that other life* had a harder and harder time keeping pace with my strides. Soon the memories vanished altogether, and woodland enveloped me. I found myself rooting for the sun, which would intermittently push through, lighting up the forest, but then retreat just as quickly. It was as if we were on the same team; I was a part of it all, life dancing around me, wonder rising with dew steaming off thickets. Trees stood like spectators, watching the transformation, dropping leaves and pollen like confetti. I'd never known poetry well, but I thought of Wendell Berry and "The Peace of Wild Things." How wandering "where the wood drake rests...and the great heron feeds," I came into grace, not taxing my life with forethought, or hindthought. A stand of spruce beckoned from ahead; I counted trunks in time with my steps.

It made so much sense, that humans would find ease in wild spaces. It's where we came from. A spot in the clouds brightened, and the sun pushed through again. Rays warmed my cheeks but only for a moment. The temperature changed with the sun and clouds, leaving me alternating between a little too cool and a little too warm. It was an unfamiliar feeling, having no access to "inside" or a multitude of possessions to increase my comfort. Having no sense of time. Or place, I thought, as I looked around at vague forest shapes. Fog not only filtered the light, but also sound, muffling daily woods business. Rustles and cracks. Whistles and quivers. To soothe myself, I watched my boots strike the red Georgia earth.

Rolling hills, not tall, but numerous, made my quadriceps burn. On steep sections, I stopped too often, hands on knees, to catch my breath. I hadn't yet discovered hiking poles, and my external frame fit poorly, pulling me right and left with each step. I pictured myself waddling like a penguin, the lateral tilt of my torso propelling my gnomic legs forward. I'm not sure if penguins ever teeter over, but I certainly did.

Falling is common enough for hikers, some more than others. And many of the AT stumbles have earned nicknames. A *turtle*, for example, lands a hiker on her backpack, arms and legs in the air. A *blow-out* is a fall due to a boot malfunction, e.g., a sole breaking loose. A *glissade* is a slide down a slope, on gravel, mud, or leaves, which most often culminates in a butt-landing. And, related, a *fall-line* is the straightest path between a hill's top and bottom, independent of the trail, which when contemplated, conjures a head-over-heels type image.

That first day, I performed the most spectacular of falls, which I later learned was called a *Superman*. My launch occurred somewhere just past Hickory Flats when I tripped over a root and pitched forward, arms outstretched. I landed on my elbows, and then my chest, sparing my chin. The ground knocked the wind out of me. My pack's weight pinned my face millimeters from wet earth, my braid stretched out, floating in a puddle. I wiggled my arms and legs to roll onto my side, where I collected myself, and, despite my lonely location, cast my gaze around for witnesses.

A tangle of poison ivy occupied the trail's edge, right next to my face and my cheeks suddenly itched. I hoisted myself up, pausing when I noticed a single wild rose winding its way through the vine's center. It emerged pink and persistent, from the top.

I'd felt out of place like that, winding my way through the med school bracken. It's probably why I ended up so susceptible to the attention. When I met with Associate Dean Frank Neeman, he never mentioned the cardiovascular exam. He simply said it had been brought to his attention that I was...pause...passionate about healthcare for women.

"You might be aware," he said, leaning forward, revealing the edge of his bald spot, surrounded by tangled black hair. "That we in medical education have been focused on new information about how women might differ from men in disease and treatment." He seesawed his pen between his index and middle fingers. "We want to start a curriculum here for the students."

"I'm interested," I said, nodding. I should have stopped there, but like an eager witness on the stand, offered up too much. "The faculty seem so out of date." I cringed at myself but kept my eyes focused on Dean Neeman. My knee jiggled.

"I need help organizing faculty from different disciplines to put it together." He pointed his pen at me. "Can you act as a teaching-slash-research assistant on that?"

"Sure!" Did I sound too eager? Could I?

"I can pay you."

"What?" I slid to the edge of my seat.

Dean Neeman laughed. Laughing was good. He seemed less formal than other faculty. And I liked that he seemed to like me, to like my beginner-ness. My un-belonging...I relaxed a little.

At first, the project seemed like what I needed; it gave me a goal, made me feel as if I contributed to larger good. I didn't realize it would contribute to an already charged medical school experience. I dove in, fascinated by the history of health care for women. It was new to me, the idea that medical science wasn't objective, that it was subject to the biases of its practitioners. At that time, most doctors practiced "bikini care," as if a woman's primary health care needs resided in their pelvises and breasts, rather than their hearts, lungs, brains—the entirety of their bodies. There was the whole history of how women ended up shuttled to "specialists," as if men defined the standard, and women deviated from the norm. Researchers had begun

21

to learn how female and male bodies respond in biologically different ways to the same conditions, metabolized drugs differently, required differently engineered surgical implants like joints. I immersed myself in collecting materials and designing curriculum to teach medical students these new ideas.

On some level, I knew it was happening, the way Dean Neeman focused so much attention on me, called too much, wanted more time than I could spare between classes and labs. In crowded meetings, his attention seemed riveted on me. No one else seemed to notice; it was my secret, and I started to feel smug, important for the first time, and so different from the inconsequential student from rural New York.

One afternoon, as I stood at a screen leading a discussion about the bone health curriculum, one of Neeman's nods continued south to my legs and rested there. The feminist part of me ruffled, tempted to shift the laser pointer to his nose, but another part of me felt wildly powerful. His approval drove me. Soon, the women's health curriculum garnered increasing attention. Professors and students would stop me in the halls to ask about it, about how to be involved. We wrote articles and spoke at meetings. Faculty from other med schools emailed us for information. I received an award from the Governor's office. But that same afternoon, as I sat hunched in the computer lab, generating a conference abstract, my thoughts felt jumbled. Why couldn't I concentrate? What was this knot lodged in my chest? I brushed it off like a gnat on my arm.

"She defines frigid," Dean Neeman said about his wife, at a Friday lunch meeting. He sucked horchata from a straw, his lips an obscene pucker. A grain of rice had lodged in his beard. The restaurant's fluorescent light reflected off his pate. Neeman winked and tilted his head, but all I could do was stare at a fly crawling on the red plastic tortilla basket. In the silence, a young man with a mop squeaked by, and ice from a machine tumbled into a cup.

I rationalized: I was one of the club now, a colleague, not simply a student; I shouldn't read too much into it. After all, we were both married; after all, he was a *dean*; after all, he was at least twenty years older. But the next Monday as we reviewed an article I had written, his actions knocked me back into reality. I had inquired about his weekend conference, which I had assumed was work-related.

"...in trouble at home with Brenda," he said, locking his eyes on mine and leaning forward over his desk. "...San Diego instead of home," he said.

"Work must keep you busy," I said, on edge against his tone of intimacy. Clarity rushed in. It was the ultimate cliché. *She just doesn't understand you, right?*

"It wasn't work. It was a conference on Tantric Practice," he said, winking again.

The desk top clock ticked. A bizarre image formed in my head: two dimensional female figures— the kind we use in anatomical diagrams—standing in a row like paper dolls...then folding, contorting into a Twister game, arms and legs at odd angles and mouths morphed into "o's," with smeared lipstick.

My jumbled thoughts fell into place like lotto balls.

"I've got class," I said, collecting papers and stuffing them in my bag. I darted out of Neeman's office and down the hall, an exit sign like a beacon for the escape hatch.

Without realizing, I had started to hike faster, my boots slapping earth like an ultra-hiker. As if I could leave it all behind. But that was my goal, wasn't it? I slowed, conserving both my mental and physical energy, and my thoughts returned to the trail. Goal: Hawk Mountain shelter. Gooch Mountain shelter was seven miles farther, and I wondered if I could make the whole fifteen before dark or end up sprawled and panting in the dirt.

I thought I had traveled at least eight miles. Of course, I grossly overestimated the distance I'd hiked, something I did early in my trail experience. With the poor visibility, I became more and more certain that I had blundered by the shelter, even though my map showed it right *on* the trail. I stopped at least twice, turning around, wondering if I should walk back to look for it. Suddenly a small sign nailed to a tree emerged. "Hawk Mountain Shelter." An arrow pointed to a clear path leading away from the AT through white pine and beech. But it pointed to the west.

I looked at my map again; that was wrong. The map had the shelter in the other direction. And it should be right in front of me. Was I that bad at reading maps? Plus, I had walked *way* more than eight miles. I stood, confused, feeling a little like the Gretel, and wondering if I was being led astray, into hands of a harmful and vicious forest-dweller...who eats children. And new doctors. In the mist, I saw a younger, pig-tailed me, alarmed but safe, curled on the couch next to my mother who read from a battered *Grimm's Fairy Tales*. My pause extended... . She hadn't offered such comfort in years. *How many? How old was I then?* And no one here to comfort me now. I shrugged against the weight of my shoulder straps and headed down the barely visible opening in the trees.

The shelter loomed, entrance gaping like a mouth in the fog. I dropped my pack under the roof, unable to go any farther, floating in fog. I decided to set up my tent and hang out—read, I had brought along *The Hobbit*—or nap. Or just think. It felt like years since I had been alone with my thoughts, had unscheduled time, and the leisure to ponder how to spend it. I slid the plastic bag with the shelter's green and white Composition Book register toward me and read the hikers' dated sign-ins. I learned with relief (and a little alarm) that the original Hawk Mountain shelter had been where I expected but had burned. Other entries were more pertinent. "Coffee Bean and Water Baby in for the night. Noisy jays in pines!" Someone else had written, "Moses stopped in for lunch, headed for Justus Creek to camp." I laughed at the illustration from a few nights ago depicting lack of "doze-time" due to "Bulwinkle's epic farts." I turned pages to earlier entries. "Dumped my GPS and *Dune Trilogy* somewhere on Black Mountain in case anyone needs directions or a good read." Hikers also leave good information: you might find out about a dried up water source, or a town restaurant to avoid. I took out my purple ink pen and wrote, "Violet was here. Not sure where to next. Or when."

Chapter Three

The shelter held a collection of donated, forgotten, and discarded items. Like a magpie, I examined the treasures, out of both curiosity and interest in their utility. Could I filch any of this stuff? I was carrying so little, never knew what I might need. A ripped blue hoodie, box of matches, three tent stakes, Bible, length of yellow nylon rope, and an old Sterno can pushed into a corner. I wondered if there was a Bible at every shelter, like in hotel bedside drawers. All seemed like unnecessary weight, even the matches. Finally, I plunked down and rooted around in my pack. The hiking books insisted that regular calorie intake was important for both physical and mental endurance. The problem was, I wasn't hungry. I pulled out a baggie of trail mix: peanuts, raisins, pretzels, dried pineapple squares. My tongue simply rolled the food around my mouth between chews, but I couldn't swallow. My stomach threatened revolt if I forced it. What was it? Nerves? Fatigue? *Where was a doctor when you needed one?* I was struggling through a chocolate energy bar, practically one lick at a time, attempting to wash it down with swallows of iodinated water when Patches and Minuteman walked in.

"Haaaallloooo!" Minuteman sounded like a cartoon character. "Stopping for lunch?"

"Probably the day. Not confident I can make it to Gooch Gap."

"We're going to camp part way," he said. "Lots of water along the trail." He raised his eyebrows.

This seemed like an invitation. I had worried I seemed unsocial earlier, heading out on my own. Should I have waited for the group? What was the etiquette? I fiddled with bungy-ing my poncho to my pack. "Okay. I'll walk on."

I waited for Minuteman and Patches to eat their peanut butter and bagels. They bit large pieces of bread and licked dollops of peanut butter hanging from their fingers. White crumbs clung to Minuteman's beard and noticing me watch, he winked again, but I didn't react. Instead, I wondered if he washed his face and beard before bed, so the scent of the food didn't tempt a bear to crash their tent while they slept.

Patches and Minuteman had their "trail legs" from several days of walking and moved easily over Sassafras and Justus Mountains. I struggled to keep up, bending forward at times so my pack rested on my back. Patches walked ahead, but Minuteman intermittently waited, always with a question ready about medical training.

"How many hours a week?"

"Depends. Medical school is more manageable, but after you graduate and start residency, then it could be eighty or a hundred. Sometimes less in the outpatient rotations like rheumatology, but there's always overnight call."

"With overnights, is that daytime, too?" he asked, twirling his hiking pole. People always asked this.

"Yes, all day, all night, and most of the next day," I answered, thinking how crazy it sounded. How did the programs get away with that? Wasn't it a human rights violation? At that time, resident work hours restrictions were just coming under discussion, so the new rules got ignored or "worked around." Maximum call every third night. Minimum one day off a week, one weekend a month. *Right.*

"How can you make decisions when you're that tired?" Minutemen stopped and turned around.

I shrugged as best I could with a pack. "You do your best." Somehow, I just did it, napping in storage rooms on extra beds, the rubber mattress covers squeaking underneath me, walking up and down stairs to stay alert. Charting, I would rub my eyes and shake my head, trying to unseat the fatigue that settled behind the bridge of my nose. In the wee hours, I couldn't get warm, and wrapped myself in thin hospital blankets to round on patients and chart. Some nights adrenalin charged me up—the high I got dashing through halls, blanket flying like a cape—on my way to a code blue, a gastrointestinal bleed, or another crisis during which I could be the heroine. On those nights, I felt like I could do anything. But even then, exhaustion struck as my head nodded at a desk, my vision blurred over documentation. The next afternoon, hitting hour thirty-six, I drove home struggling to stay awake at the wheel.

And then there was the panic that had stalked me from medical school to residency, making a hard job even harder. The attacks strobed through my mind, sometimes resulting from a senior resident's harsh words toward me or my specialty ("Family Mal-Practice), other times pouncing out of nowhere. I shook my head to reorder my thoughts, allow the images to reassemble into a more tolerable scene: a healthy patient, a still life, a barnyard. Anything.

I heard myself breathe; I had stopped hiking. Minuteman had turned to watch me. I flapped my hands around my face, as if to shoo a black fly. After a moment, he started forward.

"I tried my best," I called ahead, hurrying after him. "You know—the field—it's slow to change. It's an 'If-I-did-it, you-need-to-do-it' kind of thing."

I made it to Blackwell Creek, about thirteen miles...fourteen counting the mile from my campsite along the Benton MacKaye trail to the AT. Not as long a day as I had hoped, but I assumed I would get stronger.

South of the creek, flat strips of earth lay between trees and rock piles. A bluff fell off to the east. Patches turned in the middle of the first flat spot, dropping her pack, claiming it. She unrolled the rainfly and laid out poles, back to me, striking me as impolite. But I remembered how abrasive she had been at Springer and decided it was probably every hiker to herself out here. She and Minuteman had walked in first so got first choice. I set up on the other side of a pile of boulders clambering up the hillside.

My tent almost assembled itself. Faster this time. Elastic cords wound through the segmented, folded poles and when I shook them, they straightened themselves out, clicking together. I bent them over the nylon, snapping plastic hooks onto light metal. *Voila!* My Ridgerest foam ground pad fit neatly inside, and I spread out my sleeping bag. Tent-space seemed like home already. I slid my head lamp, book, and toilet paper baggie into mesh pockets. I was developing a system. Routine made me comfortable.

I sat on an oak log stretched across the site and boiled ramen noodles, throwing in a few almonds and the mystery-flavored powder. Ramen seemed like the ideal trail food: light, tasty, cheap. Just then, anything was better than cafeteria. The concoction smelled delicious after hiking all those miles with a pack, and, when the salt hit the back of my tongue, I fought the urge to tilt up my pot and suck the broth down. Instead, I scooped and chewed. The slightly rubbery almonds added texture. Still, after a few bites, I was done. I stared at the wormy mass. It was taboo to throw food into the brush, plus I didn't want to attract bears, so I walked around the rocks and offered leftovers to my campmates.

Without a word, Minuteman took the pot and finished my dinner. He stood from his cross-legged seat in one motion, walked to the site's edge, grabbed a few leaves, and wiped my pot clean.

After only two tries lobbing the bear-line, I tied it off and crawled into my sleeping bag. The Ridgerest didn't offer much cushioning, and my lower back complained; a nagging pain shot down the outside of my left leg. I turned on my side and ignored the ground prodding my hip. I wanted to think a little, to run through my day, consider how I felt about the first thirteen miles. But hard ground or not, I tumbled rather than fell into sleep, cheek pressed into my windbreaker, sleeping bag rustling softly with my breath.

New light woke me. The morning had a distinctly pink tint to it...a *sunny* one. Leaves to my left stirred with chipmunks patrolling for crumbs. Birds chirped among branches, but I couldn't yet assign songs. I would ask Minuteman if he knew the calls. Or maybe Patches...maybe that would get her talking. I wound up my bear line and packed while my water boiled.

Coffee in hand, I opened my guidebook and ran my finger up and down mileage columns, calculating distances between peaks, water sources, and camping spots. Woods Hole shelter was about fourteen miles. Doable. I looked at my hot cereal, mixed with dried apricots and cashews. Still no appetite. The coffee creamer had a few calories but not what I needed for miles in the mountains with weight. Would it affect my miles? Cause fatigue or that "hangry" feeling we Americans made jokes about, even though we rarely felt real hunger.

"Still not hungry," I said, holding out the cereal as I rounded the boulders. "Do you guys want..."

Patches looked up, and I braced myself for her criticism about the coffee again, but instead, she slammed her bowl onto the ground and glared. "You'll get your appetite. Just get walking!"

Minuteman looked down.

"Hike your own hike," she said. She gestured to the trail with her hands. "Get moving!"

I froze, unsure for how long. Then I imagined a clock ticking from behind the boulders, the birds and chipmunks gawking at the scene. Heat crept from my neck to my cheeks. I finally found my feet and scurried to my pack, hoping they hadn't seen my burning face.

"We'll probably see you between here and Blood Mountain," Minuteman called after me.

A half-mile farther, I spit dirt, wavering on bloodied knees and abraded palms. Pebbles poked my skin. My heartbeat slowed as a beetle lolloped under my nose, heading for the cover of grass. I pushed myself up, resisted kicking the offending root, and lurched on. Sweat rolled down my back long before the exertion warranted. It was anxiety, my conditioned reaction to criticism. Or to mistakes like making myself an unwelcome tagalong, misinterpreting Patches' behavior. Or ignoring it. Too focused on the goal, getting to the next place, too worried about seeming rude, too self-absorbed to notice another person's rising reaction. Now I saw it, her terse answers, and the way she tromped ahead, despite Minuteman's fascination with medical education.

Don't personalize her behavior, I had said during my internal dialogue. *You're far away from that type of interaction.* Patches' was simply less extroverted than Minuteman, in her own head, focused on the trail. *Me: clueless.* I worked to avoid the trap, the one where I spent too much energy fending off a tide of self-criticism.

I focused outward: earth beneath boots, fabric brushing skin. For anxiety and panic, we recommend patients note sensory aspects of their environment. *Ground yourself in the present.* I examined layers on the cliff faces—whites, tans, grays, listening for the breeze through maple leaves. I ran my hands along aged and wrinkled trunks; smelled fern and wet earth, slowed to touch my tongue to salt from my fingertips. My mind defogged, ricocheting images slowed. I thought the panic from medical school and residency had fallen behind when I journeyed into the mountains, when my attention had settled onto trees and undergrowth. Disappointment eclipsed my reaction to Patches.

Above me, a few clouds stretched thinly across the sky. I watched them, letting my head rest against my pack, and allowing the panic to drag me back to the first overwhelming episode, the cycle's start, when I stared up at the ceiling in medical school. I'd felt much worse then, shaking and longing for calm. It was as if the universe needed me to relive all of it, piece by piece, in order to leave it behind with shelter detritus, among the matches, Sterno cans, and tent stakes.

"Hi, JoDean," Neeman said, as I entered the conference room. Eight senior faculty members from gynecologists to cardiologists looked up from around the table as I slid in, clammy with nerves. I had deliberately arrived late, and hated it, but I didn't want to be alone with Neeman. This was my final year of med school, the women's health curriculum nearly completed, and this group of accomplished, crazy-busy professional woman had assembled to be kept waiting. By *me*.

"Didactics ran over," I mumbled, with a close-lipped smile, and hurried to the nearest seat. I shuffled pages, certain other attendees would think I was scattered. I clutched a pen with one hand and sat on the other, so no one would see the tremble. Questions and comments darted around the small room; I felt relieved the attention was elsewhere.

"What do you think, JoDean?" Neeman asked about a proposal that students spend a morning seeing women at the cardiology clinic and an afternoon in the diagnostic area watching heart testing. He was saying my name too much.

I nodded, afraid to reveal my dry mouth. Everyone must be seeing his intense fixation on me. The meeting lasted forever. As we finished, I tried to stand quickly, blend in, moving with other attendees toward the door.

"JoDean, can you stay a minute?" Neeman asked. "Go through a few things?"

"Sorry, appointment," I said, rummaging through my bag as I shuffled out, using the cardiologist as a shield. I moved with her through the door, calling over my shoulder, "Maybe we can chat on the phone." The corridor tunneled down, voices—faculty as they dispersed, medical students at their mail boxes— hummed and swirled. A locker slammed shut. My anxiety boiled over; I began to shake. I bolted for the nearest restroom, pushing open the door, nearly falling into the last stall. I turned the lock, and fell back onto the seat, my face buried in my hands.

Sweat leaked on my brow, then upper lip, my head pounded with my pulse. Each heartbeat seemed to rise into my throat, choking me. I wondered if I would die, slump over in the stall, landing on the tiny tiles under my clogs. The thought of cool floor against my cheeks both soothed and nauseated me. The restroom door scraped open, footsteps, a stall creak then slam. I sat up, certain the other occupant could hear me quaking. How could she miss my rapid breaths? The world spun. Thoughts swarmed: I would be found out, identified as crazy. That would give Neeman the excuse to kick me off the project. I would be asked to leave. Never graduate. Career over.

Slowly, I forced inhales and exhales, calmed. I knew what this was; we'd learned this in psychiatry class. A panic attack. Boy, they sucked. I sat straighter, looked up at the particle board ceiling, the familiar flea-bitten rectangles. How could an inanimate object comfort me? If I stood on the seat and reached, could I dislodge one of the panels, pull myself into the dark, hide in vents until graduation?

The clouds spread, stretched until they vanished. I was hiking now, and under clarion blue. My hands shook slightly, and my arms tingled. But my emotional and physical reactions to the memory seemed diminished. The openness of the mountains, cool air, ripple of summits and hollows diluted the panic, and it dissipated with the clouds, rather than bouncing back like aftershocks from cramped desks, tight walls, and strangling expectations.

Sunlight blessed me and the Appalachian Trail, drying sweat that had spread across my back and shoulders, and driving away chill. I'd like to say that I enthusiastically charged forward with determination after that, but the truth was that I felt drained. And I had no option but to continue walking.

Approaching graduation, attacks seized me several times a day, starting each morning as I put my foot outside the apartment door. Some days I got to the bottom of the stairs, and then ran back up to sit shaking on the top step. As I withdrew, Neeman tried harder to make contact. I stopped answering my phone and each day the answering machine registered a message or two from him, then repeated hang-ups. I kept working, communicating only via email, and dodging private meetings. I avoided the computer lab. Neeman eventually seemed to understand the new terms. Thoughts intruded at times, about what he might do if he got defensive—pre-emptively make complaints, paint me in a negative light, discredit me, before I could rat him out. One afternoon, in a used bookstore I found a small paperback on sexual harassment and pored over it, recognizing myself on every page, especially the need to escape quietly. *Most victims of sexual harassment* (I hated that word "victim") *just want it to stop...* . That was me. No gossip. No attention. Invisible. Graduate. Leave.

As I moved north among birch and oak, blackberry and boulder, up and over hills, reflecting on my last few months as med student, I realized my daily trail runs had been how I coped. Eucalyptus and live oak had sheltered the hills near campus, and I usually had paths to myself as my sneakers hit dry dirt, and I exhausted my brain and muscles climbing the coastal ranges. During this time, my anxiety eased, and mind cleared. I thought it was the running that helped, not realizing the therapy nature provided. Later, during long residency hours, fluorescent light replaced the sun. and the lonely cafeteria Ficus failed as a substitute for the tunnel of buckeye and live oak. "Indoors" damaged me more than I knew. Life sank into gray, my time relegated between the hospital's dimness and the austere walk to and from my car across the cement parking lot.

After an hour, I veered off the dirt track into brush, reaching behind me for the pocket with wipes and tissues. Leave-no-trace policies dictated that I find a spot at least 200 feet off the trail. Picking through the undergrowth, I scanned for poison ivy, a ubiquitous component of ground cover on the eastern seaboard. Instead, another obstacle bounced me back a few steps. A snake with alternating brown and tan markings lay coiled among leaves.

Morning chill still sedated the snake. At first it appeared motionless, but then its scales rippled, spiraled along coils, the first signs of a leisurely rising. The reptile's morning stretch. Conflicting impulses pulsed. My muscles poised to spring back, retreat to the well-trodden break in the trees. But the sight of the golden scales among the muted leaves, glistening in morning light, mesmerized me. I sought the creature's hooded eyes and resisted temptation to sway.

I'm not a herpetologist, but I'd researched wildlife like I'd researched everything else about the trail and knew most of the snake species were harmless. Only two venomous varieties lived in the Appalachians: rattlers and copperheads. Rattlers, common around northern California, I could spot, but I had no experience with copperheads. And yet, though I'd only seen a suggestion of the wide angular jaw, herald of the vipers, I knew what this was. The book's copperhead photo next to the word "venom" had been enough to imprint the reptile in my mind. I sniffed for the reputed copperhead cucumber scent. Despite my urge to linger, to watch the mesmerizing, shimmering scales, I trusted my instincts and backed away. I'd learned that lesson; there's no bargaining with snakes.

To the east, a rocky ledge overlooked a valley. I climbed and sat, legs dangling. I tried to fight dejection about my hike's start. Making a pest of myself, the shadow of panic, my poor physical condition. Sun beat like a spotlight on my already red face. Was this my now-and-forever life? I pulled out my stove and cooked on the flat surface, replacing the hastily discarded coffee. Oats and raisins went down okay. I'd just begun to feel the calorie rush when I heard clicking poles. I faced forward, focused on swallowing, hoping they wouldn't see me out on the edge.

The valley spread north and south, and tree tops poked through low-lying clouds. As moisture rose, sun-rays glistened on a creek winding below. Like treasure, gems glinting. Heat from the stone ledge radiated against my thighs. The weight of my boots tugged on my ankles. The sky's warmth lifted my chin. Two raptors floated and circled, weaving across each other, dropping and rising again on thermals. Rolling summits stretched away in layers, as far as I could see, making me small among the hills where copperheads and hawks existed without "forethought of grief."

This immense place seemed to claim me, and my pulse reverberated with the land. Pride emerged in my breast at being there, forging a new way. At first, I thought that a new part of myself was breaking free, but it was an old part, buried by years of uncertainty and self-doubt. Since the start of my training, I'd only caught glimpses of that person. I felt certain she was out here, and that I would find her, among ancient hills, battalioned timber, and unfettered life.

Chapter Four

Sunlight and food bolstered my mood. My problems had shrunk against the rippling vista. Wendell Berry was a smart man. "I come into the peace of wild things/ who do not tax their lives with forethought/ of grief...For a time/ I rest in the grace of the world, and am free." I doffed my long sleeve shirt and slipped a map from a side pocket, unfolding it across my knees. Woods Hole shelter? Gear up! The trail beckoned.

Maps of the Appalachian Trail are published by local Appalachian Trail clubs (ATCs), and depict details of terrain—peaks and valleys, streams and springs—and human additions, such as shelters, campsites, intersecting trails and roads, and park boundaries. Topography lines describe slope. Most useful for me was the elevation profile running along the map's bottom edge, showing the trail as if you looked at its silhouette, like ridges of a key. The jagged line provides a visual of the inclines and declines. Using the Georgia ATC map, I studied the miles to Woods Hole shelter. The climbs didn't *look* too rough: Ramrock Mountain, Big Cedar Mountain, and Burnett Field Mountain, all only a few hundred feet in elevation. Having some information about what lay ahead comforted me.

By the time I saw the side trail signed, "Woods Hole Shelter, 0.5 miles, the blister on my right pinky toe screamed, my right shoulder burned, and my left ankle ached from several rollovers. Half a mile off the AT? Maybe I should continue north instead, find some water and tent...where? But my toe. And my shoulder. And my ankle. My body wasn't expressing an opinion, it was an all-out assault. Besides, a roof and designated gathering place seemed more inviting. Who knew what discarded treasures I might find in the shelter nooks? Or how many guffaws might seize me from the register entries? *What's a half mile out of a two-thousand-mile journey?* I turned left, heading down the red track edged by leaves and pine needles.

At the clearing, I unclipped the pack from my waist, sighing as the strap slid off my raw shoulder. I twisted my head to glimpse the red and purple splotch.

"Hey, Sunshine," the voice came from the shelter.

"Her trail name's Violet," Patches snapped from the tent barely visible among spruce trunks.

A sick feeling rose in my gut. My hello was a whisper as I bent to grab my pack. I couldn't bear the idea of intruding. I felt fragile, the smallest slight toppling my journey. Urge to flee. *Again.* If I did it quickly and gracefully enough, it would look as if I had just swung in to check out the shelter or get water. A temporary stop before I moved on to my actual, intended camping place...which was not here. *Really.*

But then I considered the half mile trudge back to the AT. With every minute, and every inch the sun dropped toward the western peaks, my exhaustion spread, now creeping past my back and shoulders, weighting my arms. A whole extra mile, and how much farther to a camp spot, maybe without water? The pause was enough for me to make the transition from embarrassed to determined. If I was supposed to be hiking my own hike, I couldn't make decisions based on anyone else. This shelter had been my day's goal; I was tired, thirsty, and done. If they wanted to be alone, they could avoid the official spots. I set up my tent in a corner of the clearing, opened the shelter register, and signed in purple ink: "Violet. In for the night."

A clear spring burbled nearby, prompting me to imagine the cool flow against my tongue and throat. *Slake* took on a new meaning, and I sank into the pure, basic need, so rare amongst our usual glut of products. Simplicity and authenticity, little known members of Appalachian flora, sprouted between pitch pine and southern red oak.

I resisted temptation to push my lips into the cool water. Culprits like *E. coli* and *Giardia lamblia* skulk in water used by humans or animals. I dropped iodine tablets into my filled bottles and waited for them to dissolve. The slightly metallic taste would tinge my experience, but it beat having stomach upset, cramps, gas, and trots in the woods. I boiled water for dinner: a prepackaged, instant meal labeled *chicken fried rice.* Add water and stir.

Patches' voice drifted, but I couldn't discern words.

I waited for anxiety, or at least some upset to emerge, as my body slowed. Instead, I felt strangely objective, observing my lean into self-blame, observing how I stretched out my arms, slid the whole misunderstanding toward me like poker chips. My reflex to bully myself, this time for contaminating a couple's backpacking trip like...like microbes in the water. An unexpected organism in the wild flow that, when encountered, had truly unpleasant consequences. I struggled to sort out responsibility in the misunderstanding: what I owned, and what I didn't.

I'd ruined my own med school graduation this way, unable to separate my initial vanity from Neeman's choice to employ systematic predation. After I'd distanced myself, and independent of his relationship with me, he had received patient complaints about his "boundaries," and had been suspended pending an inquiry. Even this information, which rang true when I heard it, failed to soothe. My self-indictment had bloated to a new scale, and at commencement, even though I knew he wouldn't—*couldn't*—attend, I suffered through what should have been one of the most triumphant days of my life.

When the speaker called my name into the microphone, I stood, then struggled to move. On stage, faculty stood in full regalia, and as I approached, one of the gowned deans leaned over and whispered to another. Panic and paranoia seized me. Bizarre fabrications emerged in my thoughts. *She must be talking about me. They all know. Surely behind every closed door, in every meeting they had discussed how I somehow entrapped one of their own. The best plan to rid themselves of the problem was to graduate me.*

Gowned classmates blurred, and ground spun as I staggered to get my diploma. Why had I worn these treacherous pumps? I forced one foot in front of the other, my heels echoing as they hit the cement. I didn't hear my achievements, list of awards, any applause. Instead, I focused on the simple task: get up to the stage, grab my diploma, shake the hand, and *flee*.

The foil dinner pouch felt warm in my hands, and well mixed. Kneaded for the memory's duration. My medical school experience followed me like a wasp—a swarm of wasps—down the trail, and I wondered if I would be saddled with constant vigilance, ear cocked for the approaching, escalating whine. Still, could I achieve some peace if I faced the events honestly and let them go? Take "a fearless inventory," as the twelve-steppers say?

I catalogued my choices. There was the initial vanity associated with the women's health project. Cause: insecurity, lack of confidence in my ability to succeed among peers who seemed more sophisticated and better prepared. And then there was my silence at Neeman's behavior which amounted to complicity. It was fear, at first, at how he might affect my career, but if I was completely honest, it was also ambition; I wanted the project to move forward, and I wanted to stay on it. I tolerated his behavior, managed it, so I could continue my success, despite the costs. I had a right to work passionately on a project without experiencing such predatory behavior, but I didn't have the courage to stand up, insist on my right to a respectful supervisor, whether it meant a more comfortable working relationship or being booted off. I accepted less than I deserved.

I spooned rehydrated chicken fried rice out of the pouch and chewed, savoring salt and warmth, toggling between self-indictment and redirecting my thoughts. Time to observe myself kindly, objectively like I might observe a patient. *And how did that work out for you?* I reached a decision to trust my skill and drive. Believe I could succeed without tolerating unhealthy situations. Like the Appalachian Trail, I'd have to believe I could travel alone.

My body sighed as I stretched out in my sleeping bag. I'd read once that you can ingrain certain notions if you hold them close while falling asleep. I thought about releasing self judgement, about existing beyond good and bad. So much easier in the wilderness, where the community busied itself with the basics: eat, drink, stretch toward the sun, sleep... . And then I was out, accompanied by the spring's bubble and pine trees' murmur in the breeze.

Climbing Blood Mountain, the highest peak in Georgia, I left the weight of uncertainty and anxiety anchored at the bottom. Was it the climbing? Or was it simply the passage of days that liberated me in increments. By the time I reached the summit, I felt lighter—exhilarated and accomplished—a feeling I would experience more and more as I travelled farther north. Lying on a stone ledge at the peak, I soaked up sun. My sweaty back and skin warmed against the rock.

As a child, after a series of cannonballs into the public pool, or a ruckus of Marco Polo, I would lay flat on the poolside macadam. I felt cold, just emerging from the water, yet the rough, black surface would be too hot on my bare soles. I hopped to my favorite spot and flattened my skin against the heat. Soon it became perfect and comforting. I imagined steam evaporating around me and with it, my cares.

This hike could be like that. Simple. Childlike. With none of my previous life's complex layers: schedules, appointments, work place politics. It could be like playing...each moment only about what I was doing just then. I didn't want to stop thinking altogether, stop working through what nagged me, stop making peace with complications of my training and my own foibles...only to feel less wounded.

When the ledge cooled, I rocked upward, cleansed. I pulled on my pack and started the walk down the mountain and toward the first rural community along the Appalachian Trail.

Chapter Five

In Neels Gap, the Appalachian Trail passes through a breezeway under the Walasi-Yi Interpretative Center and into woods again. The Civilian Conservation Core built the former inn and dining hall in 1937. It now housed a backpacking outfitter and hiker hostel. In the restroom, I peeled off everything, donning my yellow poncho and fixing a bungee cord around my hips to keep the plastic from flying up. I felt like a flasher, though I knew this get-up would be acceptable at a hiker stop. I dumped my clothes in the washer, and prayed a little that these machines could remove all that grime.

From the breezeway's payphone, I called Ben. The process for long distance calls was cumbersome, and seems archaic these days, in the age of ubiquitous cell phones and vast areas of cell coverage. First punch the 800-number on the prepaid card, next indicate English, then a ten-digit account number, and finally the phone number. Wait for a series of clicks, then the ring. If no one answered, I'd have to do it all again.

The wall's cold stone pressed against my back during the rings. I poked at my pale, shapeless legs, the ones that had carried me for daily runs in college and med school. Were those legs buried under all that marshmallow? Was the rest of me?

Ben answered. I felt goose bumps and a rush.

"Hi," I sighed into the plastic receiver.

"JoDean! Where are you?" Silence. I looked around the shaded breezeway—stains, shadows, road on one side and forest on the other. I slumped and started to cry.

"Neels Gap. And I miss you. Suddenly I want to come home."

"Are you done?" he asked.

"No." I pressed my forehead into cold metal, letting my tears run down over the silver keypad.

After I hung up, I really let myself cry. Exhaustion and fatigue, uncertainty and self-doubt bubbled, rose like the fog. I had sweat off years of defenses in the thirty-plus miles from Springer Mountain, pain radiated like rays from my small body slumped in the tunnel. An older woman who worked at the center approached.

"Lots of hikers come through," she said, "And it's amazing how they feel after a hot shower." I didn't know how to explain that I had expected to fall apart, to shed layers I had clutched and wrapped around me like animal skins to remain functional in a system that dealt daily emotional and physical blows. My tears didn't mean I was going to quit, as Ben had thought, maybe hoped. I would walk through it and come out stronger and lighter on the other side. But she was right: a steamy rinse would be great—even a lukewarm one. I imagined water hitting between my shoulders, running down my back. Soap.

The next morning, I headed north again on a fast and smooth track. Fatigue joined me, despite the newly purchased hiking poles, for the next forty miles of ups and downs through Tesnatee Gap, Wide, Low, and Hogpen Gaps, Cowrock and Tray Mountains, and Kelly Knob. And so did a new companion: hunger. I yearned for hot dinner in camp and went to sleep imagining the morning's hot cereal. I timed out my daily snacks, small amounts, to keep me going but not weigh me down as I wandered forward, wondering when to harvest fiddlehead ferns, when blackberries ripened, and marveled at trail construction and shelter design. I magpied a Raggedy Ann wristwatch discarded at Deep Gap shelter. As I watched the sunrise from Blue Mountain shelter, grandeur brought me to tears.

Waxy, hand-sized rhododendron leaves boxed in the trail and cast shadows under an already gray sky. I batted to clear the way. Gnarled branches grabbed at my clothes and pack. There was supposed to be a shelter and camping up here. My shirt clung, damp with sweat, and I felt chilled, even after twelve miles from Dicks Creek Gap. I finally stomped into Muskrat Creek late afternoon, triumphant after crossing my first state line into North Carolina.

I turned slowly in the overgrown, dim space, my pride evaporating, displaced by a brand-new sensation. A dilapidated shelter stood off to the side, reclaimed by wild birch and hemlock. Creepy. I tugged the shoulder straps tighter, snugging against my pack. It comforted me, warm against damp skin and against the chill running down my spine. Until then, I'd only known the wind to blow high in the trees, causing leafy tops to lean and wave, but not this day. On this day, the breeze slithered close to the ground, brushing my bare legs and swaying kudzu on low branches. Leaves rustled from the undergrowth.

Werewolves live here, I thought to myself, *How could I have ever thought that they didn't exist?* I glanced back the way I'd come, hoping to see another hiker emerge, but dense rhododendron had swallowed the trail. I busied myself setting up camp, cooking an early dinner and hunkering down in my sleeping bag. My tent felt safe, like a womb. But that day I pulled in a hiking pole and a large rock, just in case the full moon rose.

At the Rainbow Springs campground store, next to potted meat and lighter fluid, I found Bill Bryson's *Walk in the Woods* tethered by nylon cord to the shelf. I browsed through it as I ate Spaghetti'os from the can, leaving a bright red thumbprint on page eighty-two. Bryson shocked me with his unkind treatment of the local folks. I never met any "cyclops" in Hiawassee, or hillbillies. Or waitresses "who could scare a baby." So far, hiking alone, I had met only generosity and kindness from the trail's neighbors: my shuttle driver, the kind woman in Neels Gap, my ride in and out of Hiawassee, even Buddy and Jadene, the owners at Rainbow Springs. Truthfully, my only harsh experience had been with another hiker. And I wasn't angry with the trail, as Bryson experienced; I was in awe—a continuous footpath from Georgia to Maine. Even though I had only glimpsed the hiking lifestyle— independence, hard work, simplicity—I had been captured. By the bustle and peace, the heights and valleys, and by the embrace of the land offered up as morning chatter by chipmunks, the sun's warm rays, and the intertwined branches open wide as arms.

Approaching Nantahala, a riverside resort, I was deep into trail rhythm. So deep that I almost missed one of my most anticipated events. The colossal bear slammed me to a stop, stealing my breath. She was bolting, powerful haunches launching her like a locomotive up the ravine's far side. Astonishing, such bulk paired with such grace. Watching dust churn as her paws ate up the pine-covered hill, and her long cinnamon fur gleaming in the sun, I forgot to be afraid.

The next afternoon, I *was* afraid. I stood stone-like, pivoting eyes only, seeking the source of the acute buzzing that greeted me as I crested Cheoah Bald, a 6000-foot summit between Nantahala and Fontana. I backpedaled. Bees, I hoped. Something mechanized? I scanned the forest floor, scanned again.

When forest fell silent, I zeroed in. Almost invisible, a burly rattlesnake lay coiled and angry among pine needles. *Two species of venomous snakes, the northern copperhead, and the timber rattler.* So here's the other one. Clearly awake in the afternoon heat. A bead of sweat rolled down my cheek. A distant voice echoed from the Nantahala River, and a squirrel darted straight up a Douglas fir a few yards north. The snake stared with slit eyes, tail vibrating faster than I could see, but when it paused, the sizable stack was apparent. Facts popped up like gophers: old ones are wise, rarely aggressive, avoid confrontation, don't dump venom when they bite. But facts failed to comfort me. The snake's tongue darted, and I caught the pink flash of his mouth as he tasted air... *In case of snakebite, seek immediate medical attention.* Right. From whom? An *expert* like me? And in case of snake bite, here's what I'd do: flap my arms and legs and scream my head off, hoping someone besides wood thrushes and hooded warblers would hear...*Generally speaking, rattlesnakes do not strike unless provoked...*I took a step back; he stopped rattling. I glanced back down the mountain toward Nantahala. Not going there.

I took a step sideways. No buzz. The snake watched, mouth closed. A squirrel with an acorn rustled to my left, chewing, spectating like a moviegoer. I hesitated for one breath, two breaths, then pushed past, offering a wide berth to the rattler. I kept my focus on camp, but my back burned with images of the snake glaring as I marched away. A red bird with black wings that I eventually learned was a scarlet tanager called *wi-wi wurr, wi-wi-wi, wi-wi-wurr,* which I took to mean "nice job," and I exhaled a whistle in response.

The next day, I sauntered up to Fontana Dam, which runs across the Little Tennessee River, known as the "gateway" to the Great Smoky Mountains. I noted the Fontana "Hilton," a new shelter, constructed from finished wood. Fancy, but I was staying at the Hike Inn, owned by Jeff and Nancy Koch. They held my mailed supply box and offered information for walking through the Great Smokies.

"Now the trick is," Jeff told me, between puffs on his cigarette, "To make it to Russell Field shelter on the first day. That way you'll be set up for fifteen to seventeen-mile days and be walking out on day five." After so many years supporting hikers, Jeff gave good advice. In the Smokies, camping outside the shelters was prohibited. Hikers traveled from shelter to shelter, and the days wouldn't work out well without planning.

Sun blazed onto Fontana Dam and the Little Tennessee River as I started out the next morning. Apparently, the hills wouldn't be living up to their legendary smokiness for my hike, and the vistas were reputed to be stunning. I launched across the half mile cement expanse, seventy-five miles of Great Smoky Mountains beckoning. The clock had started on my rediscovery...*tik, tik, tik*: measured by the clicking of my poles, rhythmic and in time with my footsteps on the dam's cement walkway.

Part II: Fear Itself

Chapter Six

Tik, tik, click, click...clickclick. Stop. *Click. Clickclickclickclick. Click.* Damnit.

My hiking poles stuttered across Fontana Dam, reminding me of an abnormal heartbeat, called atrial fibrillation. "Irregularly irregular" is what we call it. The rhythm is ineffective at pumping blood, just as my faltering pace was ineffective at propelling me over the Little Tennessee River and into the Great Smoky Mountains National Park.

The first day I paced north and south over the dam for an hour, my hips and knees aching from so many steps on the cement. Fontana Dam is immense: four hundred eighty feet high, stretching about 2300 feet across, making it almost a half mile long. I never even got to the middle, where hikers typically enjoy the view, reservoir on one side, river of varying flow on the other. On the last few attempts, I barely got past the trees on the southern edge. Finally, I plopped onto the curb by the visitors' center, rattled and defeated. Two hikers appeared and asked about the Hike Inn. I took it as a sign and piled sheepishly into Jeff's truck with them, thinking I needed a rest day.

Hikers sometimes did that. "Zero-days," or "zeroes," they're called. A slight variation in the term, "nero," is a stop day near enough to zero but not a full stop, such when a hiker walks only a few miles. Reasons for either kind of day might be resupply, visiting with friends or family, or simply days off the hard work walking with thirty to forty pounds on their joints. One hiker I met needed a day to find an outfitter because his boot soles had peeled off. Surely, after a zero-day with plenty of food and a good night's sleep, I would be eager to go, as I had so many mornings before.

The next day, buoyed and brave, I glared, and then strode across the dam. But halfway, I stalled. Again. The closer I drew to those legendary hills, full of mystery, the more intensely the turbulence rose. What was scaring me? Something about those shrouded mountains? After all, fearful things do exist in the Appalachians. Venomous snakes, as I'd seen. And bears, iconic characters in the Great Smoky Mountains, had certainly lumbered into my thoughts. As I'd arrived in Fontana Dam, the local paper's headline grabbed my attention: *Fatal Bear Attack in Smokies*. Rangers hunted for a mother bear and her yearling that had purportedly killed a woman. This was the first bear related fatality in the national park's history. Local talk buzzed. *Bears this year the leanest they'd seen...scavenging in town...garbage cans tipped and scattered.*

"A young one climbed right on my porch last week." The grocery checker nodded and wagged her ponytails as she talked. "I watched it from the kitchen...Pawing..."—she made the motion with her hand—"...at the screen door." She chewed her gum faster, eyeing the energy bars on the conveyor, then punching in the price from the peanut butter jar. Woods suddenly seemed sinister and foreboding.

But as I left the store, thoughts of bears had left my mind until this attempt at crossing, until I searched my neuro-circuits for the cause of my stalled progress. And despite the hullabaloo in town, and even the recent attack, I thought about bears and everything else *less* with each attempt. In fact, I had fewer coherent thoughts each time the shaking, sweating, and feeling of doom swallowed me, like an ever-bigger wave. Finally,

53

merely approaching the dam would coat my back in sweat and bring on nausea and spins. *No way... .*

This wasn't the remnants of anxiety and panic that I had experienced in Georgia, the milder versions that felt more like tapping on a bruise. Those earlier episodes weren't the real pain of injury, just a reminder that the wound was once there, yet to be completely healed. On Fontana Dam, I was quaking as if my fear had conjured a trembler. The road rocked from side to side, threatening to launch me into the water. Emotion swelled and made me feel tossed like a clamshell in the surf. Just as bad as the first fit I had struggled through in a bathroom stall. *Why was this happening?* After two hundred miles, I had gone from stumbling along a magical footpath to being stymied by an oversized bridge. Finally, I retreated to the visitor's center, my thoughts scrambled, barely able to punch the interminable sequence of numbers into the payphone to ask for a ride back to Hike Inn.

Back at the inn, I sat alone on the porch, hugging my knees, calmed by shelter and a cup of hot tea. Like most hiker hangouts, Hike Inn had a common room. A group of young men sprawled on the battered furniture with ice cream, pizza, and beer. Typical town food. Their voices and laughter drifted out the open window. Along with their smell. I pulled at my t-shirt's neck and sniffed, hoping I wasn't that offensive. Their camaraderie floated out and around, poked me like a finger, reminded me of my failure. Tomorrow, the other hikers would be walking across the dam and back into the green tunnel. And I would be headed home, stalled at the Great Smoky Mountains. The evening's chill reached my back and shoulders as they swapped trail tales. Exhaustion, hunger, insects, and equipment failure. A few had encountered bears and snakes, and like me, found them disinterested or shy. Nantahala-bear had literally run for the hills. Even the rattlesnake I'd stumbled onto had issued a warning, and then silently let me pass. Voices faded as I watched the trees.

Branches belonging to yellow birch, mountain maple, beech, hemlock, and oak swayed hypnotically on the property's edge quieting my mind and body, allowing me to reach for the source of my fear. I couldn't blame my panic on the mountains; it had come from somewhere else. From inside me: my own thoughts and experiences posed the real risk.

An occasional chestnut sapling peeked from among the stouter trunks. Ancestors of these American chestnuts had been giants, presiding over the mountains. In the early twentieth century, a fungus had ravaged them; misguided arborists destroyed all the infected chestnuts, minimizing the probability that a stronger strain could survive and propagate. Now chestnuts existed only as youngsters, infection killing any tree growing higher than about fifteen feet. I picked out the slim trunks, bending with the wind, frailer than older maple, birch, and oak. Their leaves glistened like eyes, and I wondered if we were kindred spirits, doomed to exist only as stunted versions of ourselves.

"Good, come home," Ben said, when I called from the inn's office. "Listen to your intuition." But my intuition, my sub-cognitive pattern recognition, was inaccessible, blocked by scrambled thoughts. My eyes darted around Jeff's desk: trail guide, ancient blotter, ash tray, coffee table, bookshelf, hole in screen, phone cord. And tacked on the wall, photos of hikers who had made it to the summit of Mount Katahdin and sent postcards to people they had met along the way.

The following morning, Jeff drove me to the Greyhound station, occasionally glancing over as if he wanted to say something. I stared out the Suburban's window, images of past events mingling with blurred birch and maple: pressure, anxiety, buzz and bedlam of the hospital, peals of the pager, relentless sleep deprivation. My eventual flight to the mountains.

I had acted on instinct, seeking an unscheduled and peaceful experience, hoping simplicity would help me reconstruct myself. I had never heard of biophilia, a term describing how humans have an innate affinity for nature, and how nature affects human health and wellbeing. But I had experienced it: soothing scents, the quiet and clatter, and the trees' sheltering canopy. I rose with the sun, ate, walked, slept, and walked again, meeting the occasional hiker, but mostly accompanied by four-legged and no-legged inhabitants of the forest. The only assaults I faced were low branches that nicked my forehead, and roots prodding my back as I drifted off.

Slowly, over miles, as my mind cleared and lightened, I discarded my defenses like dented armor on the forest floor. My deepest pockets of pain boiled up, forcing me to face them. Some of my friends who meditated described a similar reaction as they dove past layers and years in their psyches; episodes of terror emerged. Does trauma lurk? I wondered...stalking a quiet mind?

What had happened at Fontana dam now seemed clearer. While my attention had been on trees and wildlife—or nothing at all—events from my training had ambushed. Swirling emotions that I had tamped down, buried to function in the frenetic residency environment, escaped while I wasn't paying attention. I'd been "triggered," common enough in people who experienced severe psychological trauma. As a resident, I had taken care of a woman who had been in a car accident on a bridge. Months after, she found that every time she crossed a certain overpass, which was nowhere near the accident-bridge, she had a panic attack.

"The road starts to move," she'd say, tucking her hands under her thighs. "It blurs like a mirage. Then it shakes like an earthquake. I stare at the cement barrier, and I know I'm going to drive off the edge."

I wish I'd known enough to suggest ecopsychology, wilderness immersion that helps patients recover from anxiety and panic, as well as depression, grief, and addiction. Instead, I sat on my stool, listening, nodding. Thinking, *But the accident was so* long *ago. You know the overpass isn't really moving—why can't you get passed this?* Along with traditional therapies, a walk in a local park, or regular gardening might have helped her heal, among petunias and roses, tomatoes and basil, curious chipmunks and wild turkeys.

My "overpass" was Fontana Dam. The straight cement walkway—so different from the meandering forest path—had transformed into an aisle, and into my interminable commencement walk. Shimmering leaves blurred like faces; cement writhed. My poles had clicked like my high heels, amidst the water's roar and wind in the trees. The images rose, then muddled, out of my grasp but catapulting me back, not only to the dam's southern edge, but also into past emotional turbulence. No amount of self-talk, or intellectualizing quelled my mind and body. There was no way I could "just take a deep breath and go," as I'd thought my patient should. Looking back, I'd been arrogant, shielded by the sterile clinic, thinking her weak-willed. And I had underestimated how much I buried and how deep, convinced instead that I had left it behind. I had inadvertently allowed panic to stalk me like a viper, poised and waiting to strike.

Chapter Seven

For the next year, I worked for the university family medicine clinic and their Half Moon Bay satellite, energized by teaching medical students in addition to seeing patients. I moonlighted when I could. Ben had accepted a position as a nephrology fellow for additional training to learn how to care for patients with kidney disease, especially transplanted kidneys. He earned less than he had as resident. The cost of living in Silicon Valley was at its peak, our 800 sq-ft, over-garage apartment costing $2400/month, a huge sum at the time. Together, our student loan payments exceeded $2000/month.

My first case as an independent physician involved a complaint listed as "personal." I tried not to assume—insert any bias—as I stood outside the door in my new white coat, with "Nicolette, MD," embroidered over the left chest pocket. Approaching a patient with a particular idea can slant what you hear, your mind assembling the history and exam to fit your preconceptions. This is a major reason doctors shouldn't care for their families...*baggage*. Early in my career, I'd learned about provider bias and chest pain. If doctors believed women didn't have heart disease, then chest pain could be subconsciously shuttled into other categories, like anxiety or musculoskeletal issues, rather than life-threatening coronary artery disease.

I secured my stethoscope and knocked with my free hand. Lisa, a twenty-three-year-old woman with spiked purple hair, sat topless on the exam table, the flimsy clinic gown tossed over a chair. I clung to my rehearsed greeting, and offered my hand. "Hello Ms. Smith, I'm Dr. Nic..."

"Take these out," she blurted, breaking our eye contact, looking down at her nipples. She pointed with her thumbs for emphasis. *I should focus on her face,* I thought, *attempt a few words of introduction.* But, instead, my gaze fell, too. Right away, I understood what she wanted. A beaded, pewter ring pierced each nipple. I doctorfaced, nodded, and backed out of the room.

"Do I do that?" I whispered to my medical assistant, pointing at the door. Let's face it, I'd trained for more cerebral practice: diabetes, lupus, colon cancer, and any combination of complex illnesses. Nipple rings—or piercings, tattoos, or any other body art—had not been covered in medical school curriculum. And I certainly wasn't prepared for immodesty. The etiquette from medical school was clear: meet the clothed patient, look the patient in the eye, take a history, then step out so they can disrobe with privacy.

My medical assistant lifted a needle driver, a sort of medical pliers, and said, "Take two of these, grab hold and twist in opposite directions." I must have stared at her a little too long because she added, "The rings, not her nipples."

Despite my inexperience, and the hectic schedule, my life improved. I worked fewer hours and slept every night. I restarted trail running, daily lacing up my running shoes already smelling sage and eucalyptus, eager for my feet to carry me through parks and mountains, especially my favorite ascent to a ridge named Windy Hill. As with Georgia's Blood Mountain, my stride lengthened as the track tilted, and I reveled in the power that sprang from my quadriceps. My breath fell into sync with steps, my head cleared, and I could process my days...financial pressure, managing Silicon Valley's traffic and crowds, practicing as a new doctor.

After experiencing nature's therapeutic effect in Georgia and North Carolina, and drawn to wild spaces at home, I did some reading, for the first time discovering the term "biophilia," coined by Harvard zoologist E.O. Wilson. According to Wilson, if we slow, listen to ourselves, we'll feel the draw whether it's to the mountains or the beach, or a nearby park. And it made sense. *Homo sapiens* evolved in an undeveloped world, unfenced and unscheduled. Our urban life has existed for only a sliver of our existence, not nearly enough time to eliminate our proclivity for natural light, open air, and unchecked flora and fauna.

Biophilia clearly resonated with other physicians because research had already been done demonstrating that pulse and blood pressure lower when we're in nature. In one study, surgery patients went home earlier and used less pain medication if their hospital rooms overlooked a garden rather than cement or brick. Some data suggested we think better surrounded by greenery, for example, remembering a string of numbers more accurately if we hear it in parks rather than offices. In the years to come, I would learn more about biophilia and its complex and varied effects.

Whatever I pondered on the way up Windy Hill, after the last steep stretch of switchbacks, I would pause, consumed with chest-beating pride at my endurance, and scan the countryside. Viewing tree tops and grassland, I reclaimed joy for the first time in years. On this ridge, I found my love for the range of patients presenting at the office. I chose Family and Community Medicine, because I believed in the philosophy—caring for whole individuals, from birth to death, and in the context of their families and communities, rather than dividing bodies into arbitrary systems and ages, separating them from their surroundings. I would head down the ridge with the sun's final golden rays, racing turkeys through grass and once spotting a mountain lion slinking, silent and powerful up the slope to the north. I grew into my own skin there, with my wild companions, and settled into my place in the world.

Chapter Eight

The next spring, I stared across Fontana Dam, pulling my pack's waistband tight, adjusting the shoulder straps. I leaned forward against my hiking poles. Morning hung gray—the hardest weather. Sun was easy. Even rain was easy, when I donned my rain gear, tugged down my rain hat—feeling armored—and marched. But gray was indecisive, drifting between two colors, lending its ambivalence to me. I straightened, inhaled, lifted my chin, and strode. My new *Femme Nikita* pack was designed for women, with a shorter frame, narrower shoulder harness, and tighter waist strap. The nylon hugged my back, and weight sat ergonomically onto my hips. It didn't sway side to side like my older, external frame contraption. Outfitters had gone the way of medicine: figuring out that women and men might have different needs.

I breathed in steady rhythm to my steps, poles clicking like a metronome. A heart in sinus rhythm. As I approached the dam's midpoint, my pulse accelerated, and my arms numbed. I slowed. Sweat popped, and I gripped my poles tighter to steady my hands. I stared straight ahead. Sun poked through clouds, and I raised up like a sapling, letting rays warm my cheeks. Clouds closed over me again. This time, the rush felt more like a trickle than a wave, and when I stepped off Fontana dam on the far side, I knew I could make it to Russell

Field shelter, as Jeff Koch had suggested my first time through. Fourteen miles. Just *go.*

The sign ahead marked the boundary of Great Smoky Mountain National Park. Seventy-seven miles from Fontana Dam to Davenport Gap. In 31.4 miles at Newfound Gap, Tennessee Route 441 crossed the AT. I doubled up on determination. Rte. 441 was the only road crossing, and the only chance to get in or out. I'd completed the first step: conquering Fontana Dam. Next step: fourteen miles and 3000 feet up and over Little Shuckstack and Doe Knob, to get to Russell Field shelter. Then I would be poised to traverse the famous park in five days.

My legs reached for the slope, like ascending to California's Windy Hill. Flat, well-packed dirt allowed me to browse the forest: brambles, carpet of leaves, conifer and hardwood trunks, tangled patchwork of branches silhouetted against brightening sky.

On the flight from San Jose, I had composed a list of subjects to occupy my thoughts in case my quiet mind invited tumult. Many of my mulling-over topics had to do with continuing as a teacher, what I'd always wanted. We had found jobs in a small city north of San Francisco. A local nephrology practice needed a transplant nephrologist, and the family medicine residency, a faculty member. From my first declaration that I wanted to teach, I had been told the only way to do it was to be a residency faculty member, so I leapt at the position. I avoided basking in our good fortune, nagged by thoughts of jinxing us, but occasionally I let out bits of excitement like a bluebird peeking out from its oak trunk nest.

Trail and life opened in front of me; I marched toward my goals. *True north,* is that what they said? Toward Maine, toward family medicine, toward viewing patients in the context of their lives and lifespan. Whole women, not just reproductive organs, and whole bodies, rather than silo-ed organ systems. Gastrointestinal system did not exist in isolation from cardiovascular system or from reproductive system. Whole families—neonate to elder—ignoring the myth that some magical physiologic transformation took place at ages like eighteen, and sixty-five, moments of life when people often sought out a new medical expert, negating everything the last doctor knew, what the last doctor knew *about them.* Our bodies and lives were interconnected, transcending arbitrary organ-system and age-related boundaries. The way the trees around me existed together, from saplings to ancient elm, roots and branches intertwined to create the forest.

Connection was so integral, altering one species could disrupt the whole system. I considered loss of the mighty chestnuts; the well-intentioned culling designed to eliminate parasitic fungus. After the great giants had been eliminated, their shade-canopy destroyed, undergrowth had expanded and escalated the fire risk. Years later, without competitors, an age-even cohort of oak expanded, inviting gypsy moth invasions. Human bodies and their environment share similar interdependence. To disrupt the web provides an opportunity for imbalance and illness... . I wanted to teach this philosophy of medical care.

My new faculty job provided an ideal ecosystem for this. The residency, being the only training program in the area, was like the Appalachian Trail, protected against encroachment; the trainees didn't compete with other specialties for interesting or unusual cases, or get scotch taped on to other services to learn "internal medicine," or "pediatrics," rather than the integrated care family medicine was designed to provide.

I sank onto a grass patch and rested against a maple trunk. A honey bee bounced on and off my thigh, then landed on a white flower to my left. Sun pushed through clouds and lit the forest floor in beams, one landing on the path in front of my outstretched boots.

64

Chapter Nine

I trucked up Shuckstack, relaxed and light. The track switch-backed through stands of straight-trunked spruce and hardwoods with vibrant fern and blackberry undergrowth. The air smelled fresh. *Felt* fresh, lighter than city air, less close. A northern cardinal flitted from branch to branch, and a downy woodpecker pecked. I ducked when a great horned owl swooped, startling me with his daytime flight. That spring, I'd bought a bird guide that included southern Appalachia to remedy my ignorance from my first trip. Time spent hunched over the book, sticking and unsticking post-it notes had been enjoyable in itself, given my tendency toward research. I tried to remember what I had read from the stack of books near the window...*northern cardinal is a large, crested songbird...male bright red, female tanner with reddish wings...the downy woodpecker is a black and white bird that doesn't sing songs, but instead drums loudly against wood or metal to achieve the same effect.* Almost giddy with my new knowledge, I glanced up and around whenever I could, to spy and identify a new set of wings.

I was searching high branches as I rounded a switchback to find an older man with a neatly trimmed gray beard and single walking stick hurrying toward me. He wore a light blue shirt with a patch sewn on his left arm. He was a ridgerunner, employed by the ATC or agency partner to cover AT sections for maintenance and to educate hikers about lowering impact.

"Did you see 'er?" He grinned with his news.

"Who?" I stopped walking.

"The mama bear and her cub! Right in front of me, lost sight of 'em." His eyes sparkled under raised eyebrows.

"Just birds," I said, feigning disappointment. I recalled the mother-and-cub fatality from last year. Before I got spooked, I asked, "Say, how's it walking to Mollies Ridge?" I indicated with a hiking pole.

"A few miles and some climbing. That where you're headed?"

"Hoping for Russell Field?" *Why was I making that a question?*

"You got an early start, should be fine. You walk from Springer?"

I nodded, not mentioning that I had walked from Springer last year.

He nodded back, "If you're lucky enough to see 'em, just let 'em be on the same side of the trail. Don't walk between. Got it?"

"Got it." I waved, pole in hand, and stepped. I was reluctant to leave this man, who obviously knew the Smokies so well, and yet reluctant to grow roots in that spot. *Go.* I stamped each foot in dirt, stirring up determination like grouse from underbrush. I knew it might be hard, facing this section alone again, that I might face anxiety or uncertainty... , but I thought those challenges would come from within *me*. Despite the long, inextricable relationship between black bears and the Great Smoky Mountains, I hadn't predicted this on day one—a mama and her cub—one of the most dangerous things out here.

I told myself they were gone. Somewhere between the ridgerunner and me, they had bolted. If she was a normal protective mother, they would be quite a distance away already. Just barrel straight ahead. Lean right into the punch.

"You're like a boxer," my father had said, over dinner. "The jab comes right for your face, you lean straight into it." He set his fork down and glowered from under Sicilian eyebrows. I looked at my grilled fillet. It lay alone and bloody. In response to both my father and my plate, I reached for the salad bowl.

"The hardest thing," he said, using his good hand to pick up his fork up again and point it at me. "You always have to do the hardest thing." He switched the fork to his left hand—the one attached to his crippled arm—and managed to stab and secure his steak, cutting off a piece with his right. He lifted the fork, using all his fingers.

"You were so scared. Why on earth would you go back there?" He paused, spreading butter on his steak. "And to where? Nowhere, Tennessee?"

I searched for a place to put my attention—well-coiffed Tempe patio surrounded by desert plants, artificial canal flowing past, hummingbird at feeder—but his ire cut through, his frustration, his reach to control what I did.

"The trail runs on the Tennessee-North Carolina border," I said. "And I wasn't scared. I had panic attacks; it was different. A flail. I can't live with that."

"Why can't Ben go?" my mother slurred. She swirled her scotch, ice clinked. This was her daily-after-5 PM routine now. The scotch, the slurring. She no longer remembered our evening phone conversations and probably wouldn't remember in-person ones either. I watched her, thinking of the contradictions. When I was younger, publicly supportive, sounding my strengths to her friends. *Smart, creative, friendly.* Things she made such a point of saying, I wasn't sure she believed them. But in private, it seemed nothing I

67

did was right, especially when my choices demonstrated independence and self-care. She had been more functional then; she had to be. My dad had been battling cancer, and they both had been working. They had since retired, moving to Arizona. Her red-rimmed eyes watched me back, then she stood to pour herself more Dewar's.

"Ben wants to go." I looked back and forth between them. "Another year. But he wants to start at the beginning, to see Springer Mountain."

"That awful trail," my dad said. "Why can't you see the Smokies like we saw it—like everyone else—by car?"

At the time, I missed it: the insecurity behind his intense gaze. I wouldn't have insight into his fear for me, his love, until years later. Then, and for the first time, I only saw an older dad. Graying sideburns, lines radiating from his eyes. Paler skin and narrowing shoulders. I was too defensive to see control as a cover. It's clear to me now, how he reacted to life—by dominating, storming in. I thought of his relentless determination to beat the bone cancer that ruined his left arm. When chemo or radiation flattened him, he raised his fists and charged. I got my drive from him: to graduate medical school despite my fear, and to finish residency. To forge north across Fontana Dam, through the mother bear's territory.

"Dad, I have to," I said, with too much edge, setting my fork down too hard. I looked right at him. "I know if I can walk into those mountains and out the other side, it will do something big for me...something I need." I looked away toward the prickly pear that grew at the patio's corner. "I can't live with quitting, with letting the thing knock me down."

Chapter Ten

"Violet," I said to the young man parked in the dirt. I paused, a little uncertain. Out here, we all sat on the ground from time to time. I halted altogether when an older man leaned from his seat behind a tree trunk. I decided it was a great time for a break, and I nodded toward the older man's chestnut log. Even in wilderness, hikers had a proprietary claim to their natural bench.

"Help yourself," the older man said, gesturing with a sneaker in his left hand. He introduced himself as "Uncle Bob." He and his friend "Draggin'" were walking a 300-mile section from Springer Mountain to Hot Springs, North Carolina. When I chinned at the sneaker, he blushed.

"I made these for camp," Uncle Bob said, waving both shoes this time. "Hoping they help. I have a heel bruise that's been bugging me."

"I'm a doctor," I said, then pressed my lips together. *Why had I offered that so soon?* Draggin' and Uncle Bob looked up at me. No one spoke. I shifted, looked at the dirt, finally, asking, "What do you mean, heel bruise? Did you bang it on something?"

"It hurts near my heel," Uncle Bob said, "When I walk. And mornings...ouch."

"Loosens up after your first few steps?" I asked. "Plantar fasciitis?"

"Yeah. Arch support helps, so I made these," he said, offering me a shoe. It was a white, modified, minimalist sneaker with a handmade insert.

"I'm an orthotic technician," Uncle Bob said. "For therapeutic footwear. Someone like you—a doctor, I mean—sends people, and I make something to help." He and his brothers had an orthotic and prosthetic business in Florida. They made more than sneakers, they made arms and legs.

"Wow," I said. I studied the shoe. I hadn't yet graduated from flip flops in camp, despite their flimsy performance. Plus: *slap, slap, slap* with my steps. These sneakers were light and sturdy. I tossed one between my hands.

"I don't save lives or anything, like you, Doc," Uncle Bob said, re-lacing his boot. "But I know how to make the right shoe."

"Violet," I said, flushing at *Doc*, even though I had announced it, and at the idea that I would judge his trade. Feet are complex. And indispensable. I knew so little about them. And I understood how it felt when other professionals scoffed at my contribution. "Cool," I said. "I never knew what happened after those referrals."

We were all heading for Russell Field shelter and shooting for Davenport Gap on day five. They asked if I was ready to continue. Draggin' strode ahead with his giraffe-legs, while Uncle Bob and I talked.

"I embarrassed you," he said, after a long period of quiet. "Calling you *Doc*."

"No. Well, yes," I thought about how to answer. "It's more about me not claiming status...our fields, I mean." I glanced at him. "Guess I have some baggage about that."

"Meaning...?"

"Family medicine," I said, wiggling my index finger at myself. "Not the most prestigious of specialties." I shrugged.

"GPs aren't smart, you mean...according to hoity-toity specialists?" Uncle Bob asked.

"Kind of like that," I said. "They don't understand what we do."

"What do you do?" he asked. People seemed so interested in the secret lives of doctors. This would be good practice, speaking about family medicine. It was one of my mull-over topics for residents. I wanted to teach confidence.

"Family medicine sees the big picture; the symptom when it first presents," I said, pausing to tighten my waist strap. Uncle Bob waited. I considered the best way to describe it. "The patient is a blank slate, hasn't been diagnosed yet. We have to sort that out. We cut across specialties, I guess." I sliced my hand horizontally in front of us.

"What does that mean?" He fell in next to me on a wide section.

"We're detectives. For every symptom, you have this list of possibilities in your head. Is it the lungs? The liver? The heart? The kidneys? Because they're all connected. By the time I refer a patient, we've sorted out that it's *that* specialist's organ-system. The specialist takes it from there." Uncle Bob studied me, as if he'd never heard this before. Was I making medicine less opaque? He turned back toward the trail.

"If they get to me, it's clearly a foot issue," Uncle Bob said. "But that's probably not hard to diagnose. There are probably more complicated situations?"

It seemed important to offer good examples. Because Uncle Bob was interested, but also so I could use them when residents needed perspective. And for when I needed it, myself.

"One time, my team admitted a patient with heart failure, which is when your heart doesn't pump blood very well," I said, gauging Uncle Bob's understanding. He nodded. "Sometimes those patients back up fluid in their belly. This guy had belly fluid, called ascites." We stepped side by side over a slim, downed fir. "This is the first time this guy had the fluid. The cardiologist assumed the fluid was heart-related—because that's what he sees—you know, when you're a hammer everything looks like a nail. But family physicians aren't hammers, they know that first-time ascites requires a work-up, to exactly determine the cause."

"More tests," Uncle Bob said, "But the heart doctor disagreed."

"We didn't ask him. We used a needle to get fluid and sent it for the tests."

"He was mad? Got his ego, huh?"

"Called it malpractice. '*Typical family mal-practice*,' he said." I noticed my edginess. "But we did the right thing." Saying it out loud had a quality of finality, as if maybe I was finally putting this case to rest.

"Who was right?"

"There's not really a *right*, only the standard of care, or what the patient needs," I said. "It turned out that the patient had fluid because of undiagnosed colon cancer. The belly tumors pull in water." File that one under *did-right-thing-for-patient* section, despite external pressure.

We walked in silence up the gentle incline toward the ridge. The sun hovered to our right, sliding in and out of the clouds. "That's what we do. Start at the base of the pyramid and narrow it." I said, watching branches ahead, arching and intertwining into the long, green, beckoning tunnel.

Chapter Eleven

The Appalachian Trail transformed into a breath-taking ridge walk, rippled valleys and Blue Ridge peaks extending east and west. As I'd expected, the sweep of the Smokies offered me peace and perspective. A sense of awe I couldn't quite explain. On the third day, I climbed the Clingman's Dome observation tower, wallowing in the 360-degree view. My landmark, Rte. 441, passes through the Smokies just north of Clingman's, sprouting the turn-off that wound up to parking and access. I took a break from wilderness, sprawling on a lawn near picnic tables, watching all the *normals* who drove to see the Smokies. I used a toilet and filled my water bottle from the un-iodinated tap.

A family of four picnicked on manicured grass nearby, complete with a red-checkered table cloth. They glanced over and shared hushed words. Finally, the father approached. He squatted and reached out, placing an apple and sandwich on the ground, then nodded and backed away, never taking his eyes off me. I pictured a sign peeking from over my shoulder: *Please Do Not Feed the Thru Hikers.*

I imagined my parents here. They would be among the normals who motored up and walked 0.2 miles to the observation tower—never leaving cement. They saw Clingman's in white tee shirts, and fragile sandals, not dressed for the same Great Smoky

Mountains. I sat alone, knowing the large space around me was caused by more than a few days' sweat and dirt. My "otherness" swaddled me. Alone but protected. As if other lives, other values, other focus could somehow influence me, distract me from the person I strove to become. I didn't feel judgmental, just separate. How did I end up so different from everyone else?

"Hey, where'd you Yogi that?" Uncle Bob asked, as he and Draggin' strode in.

"What?"

"Yogi...beg food from the tourists. That sandwich? Did you just sit here and look hungry, or did you go over and ask?"

I handed him the white bread and American cheese sandwich and pointed. "They brought it over." But Uncle Bob and Draggin' had missed their chance, because the family had viewed enough wildlife for the day and were loading into their SUV, ready to drive down the mountain.

From Clingman's, I walked down, down, down into Newfound Gap and crossed Rte. 441. When I had taken my first steps up and away from Fontana Dam, I wondered if I would be dashing toward this road, the only bailout, hoping to hitch a ride. Gatlinburg. Dollywood. Neon. *Anything* but hills, trees, and dirt. But, instead, tackling the Great Smoky Mountains had helped me gain confidence, and energized me. I escalated three miles up and out of Newfound to Icewater Springs shelter and turned in early. The next day, I would be starting the second "half" of the Smokies, and although I had forty miles left, I considered myself to be all but done.

Expectations are the archest enemy of a good trail day. Just ask any hiker who expected spectacular views, and got fog-socked, or who took for granted the last two "easy" miles. The next day, I set out early, with the goal of getting into Tricorner Knob shelter by mid-afternoon, with lots of time to claim a comfortable shelter spot, even take a nap before dinner. A decade earlier, in an effort to minimize the escalating human-bear interactions, the National Park Service had installed cyclone fencing across shelter openings and had prohibited tenting along the AT. Overnight space was tight. I hoped for a spot next to the wall, so I'd have a most-likely-male stranger on only one side as I slept.

I cruised, feeling like a skywalker on this warm, clear day, thinking I pretty much had this hiking thing down pat. My poles and boots hit dirt in regular rhythm. My eyes and mind wandered. Sometime midday, as sun beat the ridgeline between Mount Sequoyah and Mount Chapman, my pace caught up with me. I was pushing, thinking of that wall-spot, but it wasn't fun anymore. I had about six miles left and sweat poured down my forehead and cheeks and drenched my shirt. My throat felt like sand paper.

Here's where being a doctor on the trail became a liability. I knew too much. Dehydration is a common cause of kidney failure because decreased blood volume causes injury to these vital organs. Ben dealt with this all the time. I was thinking about this too much already, when I realized that I had taken naproxen that morning which is a great medication for pain, but it further decreases blood flood to the kidneys: a one-two punch, we call it. So instead of enjoying the scenery and the weather, I pictured myself keeling over, rolling off a cliff and lost forever among Blue Ridges. How embarrassing would it be for a kidney specialist to have his wife die of kidney failure? I imagined Ben asking, "How many liters did you drink before you left the shelter? How often have you urinated?" What color was your urine?" *Oh, crap, I hadn't peed for at least two hours.*

I tried to think about something else. And I did. For about 30 seconds at a time before my kidney perseveration would rev back up. When patients come in saying their kidneys hurt, we doctorface them, because generally, you don't feel your kidneys unless you have an infection or a stone. But I was beginning to distinctly feel mine shrivel like raisins, their rough edges rubbing against my back with each stride like an unwelcome boot seam against my heel.

A huge commotion to the west jerked me back to the trail. I halted, feet and poles planted like a fearful deer facing an oncoming car. Suddenly my kidneys felt fine. Watching the trees, I traced some*thing's* course right toward me. Frasier fir and yellow birch shook and parted, then swayed back into place. I fixed on one tall elm, the top swinging back and forth, ticking down my life's remaining seconds. Left, *five*. Right, *four*. Left, *three*...Crash! Huge and powerful plowed forward. The mountains seemed frozen, waiting.

My mind flashed back to the mama bear and cub; I didn't want to surprise whatever barreled toward me. I banged my poles together, then held them up, trying to look big. Wait...was that for a mountain lion? Maybe I was supposed to be small, and not look a bear in the eye? My facts refused to assemble themselves for useful interpretation. Before I could decide, a huge buck burst from the brush. He balked facing me, splayed-legged, the shadow of his chandelier rack reaching across dirt. Our eyes met. We sized each other up. I worked to convince myself that he was the prey animal and should be afraid of me. He came to the same conclusion because he suddenly rammed into trailside brush on the other side. At first, I felt relieved. But then wondered, *What was chasing him?* I suddenly had to pee after all but hurried on another twenty minutes before stopping.

About two hours later, I pulled up short when I realized I'd stomped into the Tricorner Knob shelter-area. I nodded to Uncle Bob and Draggin' and headed right to the spring. Using iodine for water purification is useful because the iodine is light, and you don't need a pool to pump from, as you do with filters. But one disadvantage, and one that I felt keenly that afternoon, was the need to wait for twenty minutes before you drank. I sat in the shade to let the iodine work. My throat felt cemented closed. Uncle Bob handed me his water bottle.

"We can filter some more," he said, when I hesitated.

"You made my day," I sighed between swallows.

"I'm about to make it even more," he laughed. "Look what I have." He handed me my orange foam Ridgerest ground pad. "You left it at Icewater." What a generous thing to do, carry another hiker's gear for fifteen miles in the mountains.

On the fifth day, I walked out of the Smokies into Davenport Gap and stopped for a rest at Mountain Momma's Hostel. Uncle Bob and Draggin' were pushing on to Hot Springs. I felt disappointed, but I needed to rest. Uncle Bob and I kept in touch and walked briefly together on other sections. I couldn't know this then, but Bob and his brothers would help my family in a time of need.

Chapter Twelve

Holding the bulky white porcelain mug between my fingers, I savored my last cup of brewed coffee. Patches had been right about my filtered coffee system; I now carried instant, but it was more for simplicity than weight. I had zeroed and resupplied, now heavy with new food, and a new book (*Secret Life of Bees*). The screen door creaked and slammed behind me as I busted back to the woods.

A few miles in, I almost missed the couple at a road crossing leaning on their shiny sedan in the shade. They called out a greeting, so I paused to say hello back. The couple smelled so...*clean*. Shampoo, deodorant, scented soap. The man, in a light green polo shirt and plaid shorts offered me a bag of peanut M&M's. I considered refusing, but the woman said with a German accent, "Please, we insist... . It's trail magic."

Trail magic is a term describing kindnesses hikers experience. Guidebooks mention it. Hikers share stories. Had the couple, whether locals or visitors, read about the legendary Appalachian Trail and about the long dirty miles, hunger, fatigue, and loneliness? Had they hoped for a "thru hiker" sighting? In that case, despite my miles, I felt like an imposter, and hurried along with a wave. I aimed for Roaring Fork shelter, ten more miles north, and about two miles past a famous local summit.

"Max Patch," at almost 5,000 feet was originally forested, before it became a logging camp and homestead. Eventually the USFS acquired the land and keeps the summit clear and grassy with 360-degree views of Blue Ridge Mountains. As I climbed, I thought about my two attempts to traverse the Great Smokies. Like strained tendons, infections, and broken bones, emotions need time to recover. If a fractured femur took longer than I wanted to heal, I might be frustrated, but wouldn't assume it somehow reflected an inherent weakness. It takes as long as it takes. And like a re-knitted bone, my psyche wasn't quite as strong as pre-injury, patched together with scar instead of pristine, undisrupted tissue. I would probably be more susceptible to future injury. I returned focused back to the AT, imagining how exhilarated I would feel on Max Patch, feeling cocky, skipping rest breaks and snacks, eager for the top-of-the-world perspective.

Sunlight and bright green had already leaked through the dense trees when it struck. Suddenly, I felt...shaky. Uncertain. Unsure what I was doing out there, and unable to take a step in either direction. Not panicked, not afraid of a direct threat, like I had when the buck crashed through. It started with a keen awareness of my surroundings: wind through birch leaves, a chipmunk rustling next to the trail, swallows darting. Hair stood up on the back of my neck, and gooseflesh popped. Edgy. Nausea rolled over me. I forced myself forward, stamping, because the ground seemed to shift beneath my feet. I hustled to emerge from trees into sunshine, into meadow. I scoured my surroundings—trees left, trail, trees right, poison ivy, boulder—almost tripping over roots and stones, and even stopping to shake my head. Disoriented. Was this how a declining elder felt? Vulnerable? Unsure in an unfamiliar place? The downside of being a doctor, again, my self-diagnosis with early dementia.

I reached the bright summit at a dog trot and in danger of executing another "Superman." I forced myself to sit on a spruce log under sunshine, take deep breaths to manage the nausea, look around. Were there hidden eyes, jolting my consciousness? Nothing obvious skulked in the surrounding grass; the blades were actually friendly—*waving* in the wind. An Appalachian Azure butterfly flitted from blade to blade. Dandelions, buttercups, Indian paintbrushes, even tiny scarlet pimpernels dotted the grass. A child could hunt for Easter eggs here. But instead of enjoying the 360-degree vista, I focused on a dead and gnarled hardwood, its shadow reaching toward me with bony arms. I wiggled my toes in my boots and smacked my palms on the ground. *I just got through the Great Smoky Mountains!*

Amidst my unease, an embarrassing compulsion to multi-task nagged me. *As long as my pack is off, I should pee.* And it occurred to me to eat, too, so I wouldn't have to stop again. Times like this, I annoyed myself with my drive to be productive, unable to simply sit. But I indulged it, because it implied there was a place beyond this feeling, and that I would get there. Confidence gained from past struggles. And anyway, distractions were good. Since I didn't yet have the courage to stray off the trail, I started with the recently acquired peanut M&M's. I forced them, one at a time, between my teeth. It felt like chewing gravel, except for the red ones which seemed especially gross: like chewing bone marrow.

Calm washed over me within a minute. Chocolate: superfood. I wrinkled the yellow package between my fingers. Was this entirely new type of discomfort due to low blood sugar? I'd been in such a rush to get up to Max Patch, certain a substantial breakfast would carry me, that I hadn't maintained a constant stream of calories. I suspected I'd solved another mystery of backpacking alone.

Runners call this "hitting the wall." Cyclists call it "bonking." I also saw this in diabetic patients when they used too much insulin, or didn't eat at the correct intervals, after their blood sugars plummeted. Bewilderment was likely my interpretation of the sensation between exhausting glycogen stores in my muscles (carbohydrate) and switching to burn fat. If I dared, I should experiment with this theory, but the experience had been awful, and maybe dangerous to a person alone, so I wasn't sure I could muster the nerve.

I hoisted myself from the log. In a few steps, the panorama captured me. Forested mountain tops for miles. Peaks and hollows undulated, creating the illusion of movement. Occasional dirt roads wound through. Three red tail hawks drifted on a thermal, before one dove out of sight. I felt small, but part of it all, part of the web of life. So much to see, so much to do, so much ahead of me.

After the view from Max Patch, I knew I wanted to finish the Appalachian Trail. Hike all the way to Maine. To Mount Katahdin. I would get there. I ambled toward Roaring Fork shelter, reaching every few steps into my pocket to enjoy another mouthful of trail magic.

Part III: Trail Magic

Chapter Thirteen

I scowled at my feet. This was absolutely the last time I was wearing these socks; they were stiff and filthy already. Stale. Mud caked the fabric between my ankles where my boots brushed with each stride. Fatigue pulled me down onto a decaying log. *How could the feeling of 'slog' have hit me already?* I had at least a hundred miles left. I stared at the dirt track stretching north.

A few months before, the grainy blue socks had sparkled from the Recreational Equipment, Inc. (REI) rack. Cushy, thick, with an elastic arch support. Perfect for the Appalachian Trail. I would bounce in these socks! I tucked them into my titanium mug, stored with my lavender bandana, Whisperlite stove, and rest of my evolving gear. The AT had become an annual ritual—indispensable—yet filled with long, hard days. Any extra boost would help.

Ben and I had settled into our new community when I resumed my hike. Before this, since at least one of us had always been in training, our jobs had felt temporary. But now we were finished, and we'd cobbled together money to buy our first home in the hills between Sonoma and Napa Counties. After lugging the last box, we slumped down for cold drinks at our recently assembled Crate and Barrel table. My limbs hung limp, but I managed to pivot my gaze around the outdated kitchen, chipped brick and stained tile poking through stacks of cardboard, piles of books, assorted furniture. There seemed so much to wade through, not just detritus of our past lives, but new challenges. New positions. New city. In the past, I'd always been working toward something: final exam, project, degree. The path forward had been clear. Was there any "toward" now? Any forward? Or was this where we became stationary?

I reached over, wiped a smudge from Ben's face, and said, "I think we've finally grown up."

A tickle under my thigh reminded me that insects populated rotting wood. Ants, earwigs, centipedes. I shifted on the log, brushed my skin, resisted temptation to bolt up. It was all part of the trail: bugs, fatigue, soreness, sweat. And dirt. I looked down again at my socks and picked at embedded twigs and bits of leaves, keepsakes from the journey. Tokens for my soles?

This section I aimed for Dennis Cove, a little shy of the Virginia line, and past a few famous landmarks: Nolichucky Gorge, Roan Mountain, and the famous Overlook shelter fashioned out of an old barn, all welcome features to interrupt long days hiking. For me, the bugs, and my socks.

I would feel better after my overnight in Erwin, where these clothes would get washed, fumigated maybe. Black flies buzzed around my sticky skin as I scuffed from the trail onto the deserted road to town and plopped onto my pack, nursing a sore back. After fifteen minutes, I peered around for a shady place and contemplated whether to prop myself against a tree and open *The Time Traveler's Wife*, but insects buzzed inside the tree line. Finally, an engine thrummed, and I sprang up to see boxy white utility truck trundled into view. Before I'd even stuck out my thumb, the red-haired driver slowed and jerked his head toward the back. I swung my pack up and hopped on. Then I was cruising, legs dangling, watching the trail crossing vanish behind heat shimmering from the road.

I slid off near the Holiday Inn and almost jogged toward the door. I yanked it open but then stopped. The clean, air-conditioned lobby reminded me of my grime. I took a hesitant step and the clerk, a round-faced man with a chin that hung over his collar, waved me over. This motel catered to backpackers, and staff was used to us leading with sweat and smell, trailing moss and leaves. He pulled my supply box, labeled "Hold for AT Hiker," from behind the counter. Besides holding packages, they offered a free load of laundry. The man handed me a plastic cup of detergent, and stack of quarters. Then he held up a finger and ducked into an office, returning with a broad smile and a box holding several pints of Ben and Jerry's.

"Pick one!" he beamed. "For hikers." I sagged with gratitude, leaning over round tops: Cherry Garcia, Phish Food, S'mores, Chunky Monkey. I chose Half-baked, since it seemed to describe my day, resisting the urge to hug him, instead mouthing a thank you as hurried toward the elevator, supply box clutched to my chest, pint of ice cream balanced three inches from my nose. No stairs for me. All those trail miles had bought my legs a break.

In my room, I delayed collapsing. Instead, I opened my pack and tipped it, shaking loose clothes, jackets, pot, stove, food, book and then finally, my "town" clothes. I peeled off my soiled trail-wear, dropping everything, especially my socks, onto my placemat-sized, super-absorbent camp towel. I did it gingerly, as if being careful could prevent my muckiness from contaminating the room. I rolled it all up and headed to the washing machines to start the general scrub that always occurred in town.

A cleaner me rummaged through my new supplies. The box held the usual mix of home-assembled dehydrated meals: instant minestrone soup, fortified with dried beans, dehydrated onion and garlic, and freeze-dried vegetables; spiced lentil couscous with raisins, dried mango bits and mushrooms; white cheddar bunny-mac and cheese. Jammed in the corner I found my pre-packaged, freeze-dried meal. One per resupply: expensive, but priceless. No prep. Boil water, shake or stir. Afterwards, I could flatten and fold the pouch, and reuse it to soak whole-grain cereal overnight. Perfect end-of-long-day meal, especially if I got into camp exhausted, and tempted to dive right into sleeping bag without eating. This time, Mountain House Pasta Primavera.

Earlier that spring, the packaged Pasta Primavera had shimmered amidst a mound of instant rice and dried vegetables during my parents' visit to see our first home. I had left the AT supplies sprawled on the counter, probably hoping my parents would express interest instead of disdain. My dad stared. Of course, freeze-dried (instant!) Italian food would offend my Sicilian father. I leaned against the counter, gripping a cup of coffee with both hands, wondering why I hadn't thought to bury the obvious *gaffe* under couscous and peanut butter. He reached with his disabled left arm and turned the foil pouch, affecting patience, as if he wanted credit for trying.

"*Mama mia*, sweet Mother of Jesus! Italian food in a bag?" He held the bag toward me in his left hand, pointing with his right.

I felt like a teenager caught with cigarettes. And for a moment, was catapulted to my younger self: the same scene in a different kitchen, where I sat on a swivel stool watching him examine my high school report card. Why, exactly, had my Social Studies grade dropped from ninety-nine to ninety-seven? The dishwasher chose that moment to end its cycle, and I sat in silence under his familiar glare. I looked away, spinning my stool back and forth, generating *creak-squeak* noises, eventually spinning in circles. When he arrived at his "college-administrator expertise about getting into med school," I squeaked one last time and slid off to unload the traitorous dishwasher.

The warm mug in my hands grounded me in my California kitchen but the scene had generated a stomach knot. I felt pinned against the spinning stool again.

"It's great on the trail, Dad," I blurted, as if it would matter. "Easy when I'm tired." Why did I even care? I was a forty-year-old physician—*a professor*—feeling my face flush, my shoulders touch my ears, my stomach acid flare.

I see now that he didn't really feel critical of my freeze-dried food; he wanted to express pride in his Italian heritage in his usual roundabout way. And he wanted to advise me—be a parent and mentor to his daughter who lived a foreign life.

I wanted to hear from him, "Wow. Tell me how you do this. I'm proud of you."

He wanted to hear from me, "You know so much. I want your help. I'm not leaving you behind."

Chapter Fourteen

I spread dinners across the hotel desk. Food was the most complex part of preparation: planning, shopping, measuring, assembling...making sure meals were palatable and enough but not too much. Food you didn't eat was just extra weight and sometimes hard to dispose of. When Ben hiked with me, I put together more substantial food because single pots and plastic sporks didn't impact his expectations. No matter how many miles we hiked, dinner remained his most important meal.

I wondered about this sometimes, how easily, eagerly even, I took on meal prep for the two of us, a typically female domestic role. Of course, I loved to do things for Ben, but my socialization was stubborn, clinging like a burr as I tried to live my gender-independent life. And to be honest, control played a role. I had figured out some great meals: how much food, and the best, *lightest* ingredients. I secretly worried that if I left meals to Ben, we'd be living on sugared instant oatmeal packets, chocolate bars, and Gatorade, and carrying frozen chicken breasts and jars of mayonnaise. But probably the predominant factor was process. Preparation drew me more than end-goals. More than once, I've registered for official races, but never run them, happy to have engaged myself in the training. Before hiking, I loved thinking about meals, making lists, shopping, and finally tucking the final combinations into neat re-used meal baggies.

One meal—coconut prawns—required a trip across town to "Asia Mart," to pick up tiny, dried shrimp and powdered coconut milk. Assembling the meal in one pot over my Whisperlite was a project, requiring the vegetables to be rehydrated in a particular order and just enough water for the noodles, rehydrated coconut milk, and smudge of green curry paste. Fellow hikers hovered and sniffed, asking questions, and hinting for a sample. But Ben always ate all of it. Besides coconut prawns, preparing peanut curry, and Moroccan couscous were also big productions. But no one noticed when I tore open prepackaged foil pouches for dinner—Pasta Primavera or anything else—and tipped in boiling water.

A new book: *The Cider House Rules.* I shed extra pages to make it lighter. In the box's bottom, I found a single page, "Courage," from Ruth Gendler's *The Book of Qualities.* A hand-drawn beech curved up the page, sheltering the words. I had underlined some phrases: "When Courage walks it is clear that She has made the journey from loneliness to solitude...Courage has roots...She sleeps close to the ground." The words gave me chills. I slid the folded page into my hiking shorts pocket, then wedged food into my red stuff-sack. I'd only have to duck out for peanut M&M's—a recently designated staple.

I spread my arms and legs across the bed, ran my toes along clean bedding, pictured melting into the mattress, and reveled a stretch of uninterrupted sleep, a ritual I practiced at home. Even years after my residency, I luxuriated in my own bed every night, slipping under my own sheets and comforter, and feeling my husband's warm body. I still took call, meaning the pager would wake me when the residents admitted an ER patient or had questions, but I rarely had to rise and go into the hospital. I *never* had to sleep there. Still, shrieking pager calls startled me awake, so I learned to put the pager on vibrate and clip it to my pillow case, and it woke me in a gentler way.

Next day's walk was up Nolichucky Gorge, about 4500 feet, then a few miles of ridge-walking. Sixteen total miles to Cherry Gap shelter. The hot shower, as usual, had rinsed away fatigue and miles, leaving me eager to hike again, just as it did after the first steamy wash in Neel's Gap. Falling asleep, I felt at peace. When I opened my eyes, it would be morning—when the sun's rays glowed through bright green leaves, and I fell into a steady, energized pace. I would feel strong, and ready for distance. My goal each day, besides the next shelter, was to hold onto morning's mood until I dropped my pack for the night.

I'd been a morning person for as long as I could remember. As a child, I woke in the dark, knowing the clock radio on my dresser said 4:53. It always did. The white numbers sat on tiny black slats, which flipped to register each new minute, each new hour. With my eyes closed, I'd listen for the almost imperceptible click—and then six more—meaning the time had changed to 5:00. At that magic hour, I pressed the button on top to illuminate the numbers, but I knew the time, just like I knew I was alone, surrounded by my lavender wallpaper, lit by the street lamp on the corner of Harrison and Madison Avenues. I wasn't allowed to leave my room or wake my parents or brother until 6:30, so it was just me and my imagination. Until I invented my friend, Gordon.

Gordon and I sang "Puff the Magic Dragon" together and cried when *Puff that magic dragon, ceased his mighty roar*, vowing to always be friends. We played marbles and jacks, or Mousetrap. This worked well enough until one morning when Gordon knocked over my dresser, and my parents came clambering across the hall. I looked up at them from the floor, contents from my dresser strewn around me: Winnie-the-Pooh bank, jewelry box, assorted ribbons, jacks, marbles like little jewels in purple shag, and the clock radio—glaring 5:45.

"Gordon did it," I said, pointing. Gordon glared, too. *Tattler*. He was banished, like Puff the Magic Dragon, into his cave, and I was left to bide my time alone in the purple room until dawn.

Before I came to appreciate the solitude of mornings, I would have loved to morph into a night person, to become "nocturnal," as some people seem to be, snapping awake as the sun sets, alive like stars until the dawn chases them to bed. I tried to attend events with my college and med-school classmates, even movies. But my efforts to stay awake succumbed to my natural biorhythm, and I wound down around eight or nine, ready to doze by ten...by eleven, tormented by drooping lids. If I forced myself to stay up, no matter how late, the pre-dawn light—mere hint of sun—animated me against my will. I would open my eyes and find myself revving up for the day ahead.

Eventually, I came to love dawn, especially on the trail. Peace. Solitude. Opening my eyes to pink and yellow light—brightening as I watched and stretched, stirring with the world around me. My community rallied at dawn: unfettered, natural life, untainted by cement, road sounds, nine-to-five culture. Silhouettes of leaves emerged against the tent, and birds greeted me with complex layers of song. Smelling crisp, new air and basking in cool greens and blues of the forest, I felt sorry for "sleepers." This was when life emerged—yawning, reaching, unfolding into sun's warm glow.

Chapter Fifteen

I was buoyant starting up Nolichucky Gorge. My boot heels smacked dirt as I raced lilies and mountain laurel, chipmunks and butterflies, for first glimpses of the new day. Spider webs, dewy and new, stretched across the path, floating behind me like veils. Thanks to a friendly, snaggle-toothed oldster who had slowed his battered pickup as soon as I stepped out of the motel, I got an early start. I turned to wave goodbye and almost tripped over the Igloo cooler in front of me. Paper taped to the handle announced, "Trail Magic for Thru hikers," in thick blue marker. The anonymous good Samaritan had stuffed the cooler with ice, fresh orange juice, and sodas. If I hadn't just come from town, I would have likely plunked down and gulped a cold drink, as I'm sure subsequent hikers did.

I thought of trail magic like alms offered to pilgrims: grain doled out to trekkers on *Camino de Compostela*, or water poured for hajj caravans enroute to Mecca. On the AT, it was Tupperwares of homemade brownies at lean-tos, jugs of water placed at dry shelters, rides to town, an offer to fix boots or a broken pack-strap in a garage workshop. At Blue Mountain shelter, a local pot-bellied chef had lumbered in and roasted russets in the fire, making potato salad for tired hikers stumbling in. More than once, encountering these special gifts, I had reflected on my journey through medical school and residency, wondering if such kindnesses had been more common during long days and nights, would I have felt so battered? Would I still have fled to this remote and solitary pilgrimage among trees and boulders? And now, after my first year as a faculty member, often facing defensiveness and competitiveness from other doctors, I wondered how to bring trail magic back with me. Encountering acts of generosity at unpredictable times enchanted me— kindness more powerful than gifts themselves.

In the Nolichucky River, playful eddies jigged near shore. My pack bounced with my energy. Like Blood Mountain, my first big climb in Georgia, I left my emotional weight at the bottom, rising farther above it with each footstep, emerging pure and childlike the top. Even climbs that started tough transformed as I ascended. Like North Carolina's Roan Mountain. That day, I hoped to make Apple House shelter, a tough nineteen. Roan Mountain wasn't the only climb, but it was the biggest. Rain made walking slick and climbing harder. Even with poles, my boots lost purchase, causing me to lose ground, like a cartoon character spinning her legs. Finally, I plopped onto wet grass in a jumble of limbs and gear. The rain poured, dripping off my hood. I glanced at my Raggedy Ann wrist watch and my heart sank. Eight-thirty-five. So defeated...so early?

I recalculated. Instead of Apple House, I would shoot for Roan High Knob shelter at the summit; I would have all day to climb this one banana-peel mountain. When I hoisted myself with my poles, I found my braid had tangled with one of the baskets. I tugged, unwound, tugged again, but instead of freeing the pole, I had a soaked rat's nest and a sore scalp. I wrenched my pack around and rooted in pockets, finally finding my pen knife and unfolding tiny scissors. Half cutting and half sawing, I amputated my braid. I didn't bother to extricate the tangle from the pole, but started walking, driving the mass of hair into mud with each stride. Somewhere, the rat's nest stuck in the ground. What must the next hiker have thought when he came

94

across my braid? When the track entered trees, it became moist but walkable and I found my rhythm, my spirits lifting with each step. Hiking moods are fleeting—if I persisted, even the worst would pass. When I reached Roan High Knob shelter, smiling like the sun, I heard a cheery welcome.

"Hidey ho! How goes it?" Three retired men, volunteers working on the shelter, poked their heads out and gathered to chat. They offered me a rubber band for my hair and a peanut butter sandwich on wheat bread which tasted like a miracle. I made it to Apple House.

Over years and miles, I considered why climbs cleared my mind, initially crediting endorphins, hormones released by our central nervous systems during aerobic exercise that act on opiate receptors. Endorphins are responsible for feelings of wellbeing, for example the well-known "runner's high." Also, my synchronization of footfalls and breath resembled a Zen meditative practice called "kinhin," or counting meditation, performed while walking. Kinhin practitioners strike a wooden block called a "fish" to facilitate rhythm, and my poles' steady click served this purpose for me. While I'm certain both endorphins and Kinhin played a role in my climber's calm, it turns out that exertion in the forest contains its own unique boost.

Leafed and needled flora, trees in particular, release chemicals into the air and soil as part of a complex communication system. These chemicals have little do with humans, other than to alert neighboring shrub and sapling to our presence and intent, yet they do impact us. Terpenes, one chemical group, is actively under study. Inhaling these molecules activates the vagus nerve, our relaxation trigger, resulting in lowered blood pressure and heart rate. In addition, we experience mood elevation and calm. As I tromped upward, over Blood Mountain, Roan Mountain or through the Nolichucky Gorge, I elevated my cardio needs, breathing more often and more deeply, increasing my exposure to the air born molecules.

By noon in Nolichucky, I closed in on Mt. Unaka's summit, sun still claiming a brilliant blue sky. Flame azalea and mountain laurel crowded the path like party decorations. After Unaka the trail ran for a few ridge miles before Cherry Gap shelter at mile sixteen. I marched right through the occasional shallow puddle, slapping my boots, feeling vindicated as splashes assaulted my socks. Fatigue crept into my quadriceps, but I reveled in the physicality of long-distance hiking.

Not everyone enjoyed the long days, sore muscles, and aching joints, especially those who started with a romanticized version of backpacking. Of course, there were "The Indestructibles," which is what I called young men in their twenties on summer break or just after college, who viewed the trail as one big party. They charged through twenty-five-mile days in rubber-soled sandals, existing on Coca Cola, Donettes, and Pop Tarts. The Indestructibles stumbled into shelters after dark wearing headlamps, and eschewed bear lines. But youth aside, I found men, rather than women, more disgruntled by the long days and rough terrain. Earlier in this section I had encountered one brawny guy parked trailside on top of his pack. He watched me approach through hunched shoulders.

"Hot Feet," he offered, as introduction. I noticed his blistered bare foot. *Ahhh, first problem.* Then I noticed his ripped red t-shirt, which said "Hot Stuff." *Ahhh, real problem.* "This trail is idiotic!" he said, tossing his boot onto the ground. "It goes to the very—I mean *very*—top of every mountain, whether there is a view or not. And mileage? Totally off!" He waved his map. "I'm getting off at the forest service road." He pointed to a spot. "You should, too, especially a girl like you."

Later that day, scolding my own stubborn, pinky toe blister, I thought about what Hot Feet had said. Female hikers were scarce; I'd decided bears outnumbered women three to one. But I wondered if women who started the trail were more likely to finish than men. Since Springer Mountain, I'd seen many men approach the Appalachian Trail with a confidence that seemed out of proportion to the situation—taking for granted that the trek from Georgia to Maine was perfectly within their physical capabilities...a normal "guy" activity. Many started the trek with no training, and minimal preparation. On the other hand, it was a rare woman who set out. Some were elite athletes, but others were just willing to give it a shot for their own reasons, and only after a great deal of preparation and planning. And maybe a little extra Courage tucked away in their pockets.

Chapter Sixteen

Hephzibah was one of those women. As implied by her trail name, Hephzibah's journey was a spiritual retreat. In observance of her Seventh Day Adventist sabbath, she stayed put on Saturdays, contrary to typical hiker compulsion to use every day to get closer to Maine. She stood out in her dress, paired with substantial socks and clunky boots, but most impressive was her devotion to her bulky, hardback bible—bulkier than the one I left behind at Hawk Mountain shelter—which she toted every mile.

Hephzibah and I covered similar daily mileage, but she moved deliberately, so walked longer days. We frequently encountered each other trailside or at the same campsites. I referred to it as pulling taffy—the way we moved past each other—so I wasn't surprised when I caught her in the gorge. She moved more slowly than usual, placing her feet softly, leaning on her hiking poles. I called out to avoid startling her because on the tiredest days, any sound from behind could be interpreted as a hungry bear. Without turning, Hephzibah lifted a hand.

We were both headed for Cherry Gap. She had "stealth camped" the night before, on an unsanctioned spot off the beaten path after stumbling on a creek—a gift from God she'd said—where she could set up her tent. I flushed, aware of my own unwillingness to bushwhack for a spot. Bear-bait, I worried. At times, a sense of vulnerability clung to me like cat hair, even though my closest bear had been taking flight outside Nantahala.

I'd never met a threatening person either. In the Appalachian Trail's history, there had been only nine recorded violent deaths, a fact I read without emotion when I first set out from Springer still numb from my training. As I re-engaged with my life, I viewed the statistic with relief, and defensively quoted it to anyone questioning my choice to go it alone. Hiking the AT was safer than flying. Than driving. Than walking in downtown San Francisco. But since risk, however small, seemed to be related to other people, I avoided campsites and shelters near roads where local hooligans had drive-up access.

What Hephzibah was feeling was not vulnerability, but pain. Limping along, she told me about her shins. We looked together at her legs. Hephzibah had the worst case of "shin splints" that I had ever seen. The medical term for shin splints is tibialis tendonitis, or tibial stress syndrome, which are fancy words for "tendons attached to your shin bone are irritated and inflamed." This condition results from overuse, like jogging too much too soon, or say...walking several hundred miles with forty pounds on your back. Most people have pain with stepping, and maybe a little tenderness, but Hephzibah's shins were boggy. I wasn't sure what to do. Or more accurately, say. I was afraid to butt in. She was independent and capable. And I knew doctors could be arrogant, always looking for opportunities to establish superiority; she could misinterpret my concern. The last thing I wanted to do was act like I knew something Hephzibah didn't. If she wanted my advice, she would ask.

But I did know something she didn't, right? I faced this problem a lot. I had been in medicine long enough to lose perspective on what non-medical people knew. Whenever I spoke about health issues, I felt uncertain...trapped between talking "over" people by

99

using technical terms and concepts that I took for granted, and sounding condescending by over-explaining ideas that everyone understood. On top of that, each person had different knowledge and comprehension based on their own experiences.

"How long have you been walking with so much pain?" I asked. *Neutral.* "You don't have to answer. It's none of my business." I focused on picking a leaf fragment off my shirt.

"For a while. But worse this last week," she said. We took a few steps in silence.

"Tried anything?"

"I've been praying," she said.

"Has that worked?" I asked. *Oh, shit. Did she think I was ridiculing her?*

"I'm still walking," she said, staring straight ahead. *Defensive? Was she anti-medicine?* I thought for a split second: Seventh Day Adventist, not Christian Scientist. I peeked at her; she still looked intently at the trail.

"Ice?" That sounded safe.

"No. I have some Advil," Hephzibah said, "That'll help, right?"

"I meant in town. The ice. But you maybe could soak them in cold water. A stream," I babbled. "And yes, Advil might help. Do you know how to take that? I mean, with food, and plenty of water."

"I'll take a break in the next town. Rest there for a few days," she said, looking away.

"If you want something stronger, in camp, I have something... ." I kicked a stone, and it bounced ahead of us. "I won't bring it up again. You just ask me. To help you sleep, or whatever," I said it all too quickly. We were two porcupines, waddling next to each other on the Appalachian Trail.

"Thanks," Hephzibah said, red-faced. "I'll be okay." She glanced at me and then away, as if she was trying to be respectful by meeting my eyes, but the effort was hard on her.

100

"You're walking faster than I am," Hephzibah said suddenly. "I'm holding you up." She shoo-ed me forward with both hands.

Chapter Seventeen

At Beauty Spot gap I doubled down, focusing hard on forward. Bushed. Want in camp. In dry clothes. Out of these socks. Unlike other hikers, I hated walking late in the day. Tennessee was my third state, and by now I had discovered what I liked and didn't. I liked to be set up by midafternoon, to read, and maybe nap, even in beautiful weather. And these Tennessee afternoons weren't always so beautiful. The mountains beckoned thunderheads, and they crowded the sky—dense and black—putting me on edge, worse than usual tired and hungry. Appalachian clouds weren't like laid-back Californian ones, which merely hid the sun, teasing it and producing lighter, albeit lasting showers. West coast rains, buttressed by the long dry season, lacked bombast that accompanied storms here. Looking up, I felt small. Like an ant. I tightened the shoulder straps on my rubber tree plant.

Evenings, settled and cooking or cleaning up, I would watch other hikers wander in, leisurely and unconcerned, especially The Indestructibles, and wonder how they felt so confident walking as dusk approached, when the sun slanted low and air chilled. At this eerie time, I wanted to be hunkered down, by the campfire, or in my tent. I felt vulnerable, when I was naturally winding down, less alert and less engaged. A few times, I asked a later-comer about his day. Was there a secret or a trick that made evenings more welcoming? I tried to be round-about, not sounding critical, not wanting to imply I thought he should be walking on some other schedule. Like a doctor, I thought, obtain information in a nonjudgmental way.

"How was your day? Easy? Long?" I would look up from my stove, stirring lentil couscous, adding dried onion, scooching myself and my things over on the shelter's wooden floor. Not always enough space for an additional person, but a gesture: hiker etiquette that newcomers were welcome. Always space for one more.

"Great day," the recent arrival would answer, bearded and thin. In sandals. Indestructible. He would relax, stretch his legs, tip up his Nalgene to drink the last of his water. *Sheesh! He'd have to go get water now,* I would look at the setting sun. *And cook, too. How could he stand it?*

"Did you get held up?" *A twisted ankle...side trip to town for a gear malfunction?*

"Nope! Started up from the road about four," would be the reply, or "You know, hanging by the river." Or lazy day in town. Or left shelter late, waiting out rain. Or smoked pot with my friends at lunch, pigged out on Donettes, pork rinds and Snickers, and fell asleep. However he spent his days, he felt no compulsion to get to the shelter before evening.

"No reason to rush," he might say. "I mean what is there to do in camp?" *Lots. Read, putter, write. Nap. Read some more. Watch young guys like you, with your relaxed attitude toward wilderness, and toward life in general.*

"Water's over there. Privy's there." I'd offer some info about the site, which I had already scoped out.

"I'm a morning person. First light, up and out," I'd then say, somehow feeling like a strait-laced geek.

"Guess we won't see you, then," he'd say, stuffing his food sack in his sleeping bag.

Chapter Eighteen

I hit the ridge thinking about Hephzibah's determination, and how I whine about socks. I tried to ignore my aching feet and nagging left hip. Even with her limp, Hephzibah wasn't complaining. She had called out, "I'll get there. I have faith."

I practiced my kinhin, thought about dinner, repeated the mantra: mac and cheese (inhale), mac and cheese (exhale), mac and cheese (inhale). Clouds got blacker, sky bigger, air closer. Wind picked up. An ancient rock fence accompanied me to the east. I admired the craftsmanship. Settlers had lived here; this had been their property line. Now it belonged to wilderness, and quick gray squirrels, hopping the uneven top, disappearing between crumbled stones. And probably, I sniffed for cucumber, for copperheads.

I tried to avoid thinking about what else lived on the remote ridge. Wooded hillsides fell away on each side, and I felt exposed, even though trees above reached over me, reminding me of a moth-eaten umbrella. Headlines assembled themselves and taunted. *Appalachian Hiker Eaten by Yeti*. Absurd, of course: it was Sasquatch that lived in North America. An eastern fence lizard darted along the rock wall. Just beyond, a gust of wind shook trees and a branch fell with a crash. I froze. According to the map, Cherry Gap shelter was three miles past Mount Unaka. I was close.

Although I couldn't see the sun, I was pretty sure it was late afternoon, and I felt conflicted about taking a break. I was low on calories and knew my edginess could explode into hypoglycemic disorientation if I didn't eat...knotted stomach, sweat, quivering earth. I remembered peanut M&M's and Max Patch. Those tourists had no idea they were giving me more than calories. One big hill later, the yellow package I wrinkled between my fingers gave me insight and helped during one of my toughest days.

Mere recall of trail magic boosted me: rides to and from Erwin, Igloo-cooler orange juice; pancakes from the parents of a thru hiker, cooking outside their battered RV and waiting hopefully for their son at a road crossing; local school teachers who lived a half mile from Sassafras Gap shelter and hiked in on Thursday nights with pizzas and chocolate chip cookies; gallon jugs of water left at the "dry" shelters.

I sank down on a log, releasing my pack. My back felt cold and naked without thirty-five pounds of nylon snug against it. My pack was my best friend. *My pack has my back*, I always said to folks who asked me about backpacking alone. *How much does it weigh? Do you forage for food? Do you carry a gun?* Exhaling, relaxing my shoulders, I slowed down to eat. At these times, I wasn't exactly enjoying myself. I often compared hiking the Appalachian Trail to writing. It was about process—not always fun, agonizing at times, but there was something about the highs and lows, and working toward a goal, that kept me coming back.

I reached into my pocket and pulled out my "Courage." Maybe I should have left it with Hephzibah. But then Hephzibah wasn't walking alone; she had God by her side. I ran my fingers along the page's torn edge, paper grainy like sand. Cheap stuff I remembered drawing on with fat number two pencils in Mrs. Blasetti's first grade. Words beamed, unapologetic about their stage, as if the message were so true that it hardly needed a podium of processed, bleach-white paper. Courage does not need a marquee. I chewed a few almonds and raisins, drank a few swallows of water. Wind had picked up and scattered rain drops fell. They tapped gently on my bare neck. Like a finger: *tap, tap, time to get to it!* I rocked up to my feet.

My hips ground with my first steps, almost audible, like steel wheels of a locomotive. Age strikes at any time, I'd always quipped at my friends. And so did illness. The older you got, the more likely it was to swoop out of nowhere and disrupt your plans. I remembered a pristinely healthy state park ranger who was diagnosed with pancreatic cancer. This tall slim man had walked state park trails for forty years at home, vital and serene. Eyes green as springtime, dreadlocks swinging with his strides, he advocated tirelessly for open space. He turned yellow one day—painless jaundice we call it—and a CT scan showed the mass on his pancreas. Over the next few months, he wasted away and was gone. Mother Earth called him home, I thought, or Mother Nature...and on her own schedule.

It was one of the hardest things about being a doctor, watching unpredictability of health and wellness. Choices—exercise, clean diet, cholesterol and blood pressure medications—increase odds for a healthy, longer life, but they don't guarantee. Doctors want control, and so do patients, so they act, and take pills, and hope. But I've experienced control as an American myth: a twenty-five-year-old woman with multiple sclerosis, a thirty-year-old with rheumatoid arthritis. Cancer especially doesn't understand statistics and doesn't read text books. An eighteen-year-old with leukemia. A fifty-year-old state park ranger with pancreatic cancer. A thirty-nine-year-old Sicilian-American father with osteosarcoma. *Well, he beat it*, I thought, *against those damn odds.*

It goes to show that I should enjoy this day. I smelled damp earth, and hovering rain, massaging my knuckles into my hips, waggling my poles in circles behind me. According to the map, I would pass through Low Gap, then over a small peak…maybe a mile more.

I stopped dead, smelling wood smoke. Hard to mistake. The shelter couldn't be that near, and it was unwise to underestimate distance, or I would end up frustrated. On long days, the miles seemed to stretch as the day progressed. The scent came and went, and I could almost convince myself that I imagined it, but soon it was clear and steady. I instinctively twitched my nostrils east. Too faint to pinpoint; some special instinct had tugged at my nose. No voices, just wind, rain on leaves, and my own footsteps. Occasional thunder rolled. I lengthened my stride. Suddenly I was stalking the shelter.

I had rediscovered my ancient olfactory skills, smelling "campsite" from almost a mile away. It had provoked a surge of emotion. Of all the senses, smell is the most intimately connected with emotion and memory. This relationship is anatomic. Smells are processed by the olfactory bulb, directly adjacent to the amygdala, or the seat of emotion, and the hippocampus, a memory center. That's why for example the scent of strawberry conjures affection and then grief as we recall drinking a milkshake with a grandparent, and why smoke kindled memories of camping with friends and family, in particular my Aunt Bonnie and Uncle Don, and a sense of contentment and security that spurred me forward.

How many other abilities had humans buried under concrete and fluorescent lights, behind computers, deadened by smog? After hundreds of miles alone in the woods I had rediscovered more than one: a sixth sense that distinguished human activity from other animals, and a seventh, an ability to recognize locations in the forest and along the trail, even having been there just once.

When I saw the trail ahead bending out of sight that I knew I would turn the corner and it would be there. I craned my neck, needing to see the sign a split-second sooner. There it was: Cherry Gap Shelter, 0.1 miles, marked with a bright blue-blaze instead of a white one, as are all offshoots from the AT. I turned east at the weathered beacon and barged forward, a little too fast for the terrain, no longer noticing wood smoke.

Chapter Nineteen

Fire crackled from the rock ring, its heat reducing raindrops to hisses on stone. Five round male figures crouched around the blaze. In unison, they turned, revealing graying facial hair. Next to The Indestructibles, I encountered retired men most on the trail, remarkable for their activity in wee hours. My first year hiking the Trail, I had been amazed by the rustling, clunking, and stumbling as men got up to empty their bladders. But I preferred the night time excursions to one guy who, reticent to venture out into darkness, simply relieved himself into his modern-day version of chamber pot, a two-liter plastic soda bottle next to his sleeping bag.

I guessed these were local buddies in the woods for a week. I waved, glad for company, but gladder that I had my own sleeping quarters. I tossed my pack in the shelter amidst Wild Turkey, chewing tobacco, beef jerky and canned beef stew. A round-faced man, who introduced himself as Walrus, came over to make room. I eyed his mustache and thought it was an appropriate trail name. I'd be tenting, I said, but told them about Hephzibah, in case she might want the roof in the storm.

Hephzibah...I paused, staring at the shelter's worn wooden floorboards, then busying myself with camp preparations. First task: fetch water. Second task: set up tent before rain really starts coming down. Water bag in hand, I turned to my campmates. Walrus pointed, and I groaned. The blue blazed sign pictured a water drop and read, "Spring 0.4 miles." Downhill from the looks of it...*And then back up*, I thought, lugging the awkward, sloshing water bag. Another mile before I could even set up and cook dinner.

"The water's back in Erwin?" I asked, hands on my hips. Walrus nodded.

"Mebbe pick up a pizza when you're down there," a man called Bearbelly said. My laugh was cut short by lightning, followed by an intimidating roll of thunder.

I glanced up at dark, roiling clouds, and changed my mind about fetching water. I pulled on my rain jacket and rain pants and headed back toward the Appalachian Trail. Without weight, I zipped along, hoping I looked confident to the guys, whom I could feel watching my back. Out of earshot, I sang. First, "Good Day, Sunshine...dah, dah, dah," and then "Raindrops Keep Fallin' on My Head." After about a half mile south, I had resorted to "Puff the Magic Dragon."

I had no idea if I would see Hephzibah. Maybe she had stealth camped again. I should have grabbed my watch and set a time to turn around. I cut short one chorus of "...And frolicked in the autumn mist in a land called..." when one foot slipped forward, and I landed on my behind and somehow rolled downhill. I took a few breaths where I landed, watching rain drops sprinkle into a puddle next to my face. I clambered up, claimed naming rights for this new type of tumble. *The Banana Peel. The Black Ice. The Charlie Brown.* A dried oak leaf pelted my forehead.

I was struggling with how much farther I should walk when I saw Hephzibah's dress, flapping with gusts. She saw me, near tears but determined...Courage jumping off the page. I waved and trotted over.

"I had to get away from that boy's club! Belching, farting, the whole deal," I blurted out.

"Hey," Hephzibah said. She kept up her trudge.

"Booze," I shrugged and shook my head. "I hope you're staying at Cherry Gap. Girl time would be good."

Hephzibah glanced at me. My face burned red. I pulled out peanut M&Ms, grabbed hastily as I left. They clattered like pebbles as I poured half out for her.

"Violet," Hephzibah said, looking down and then looking at me.

I stopped chewing to look at her, worried she felt patronized.

"They most certainly do melt in your hands," she said, holding up her colorful palm. Conversation came easy as we walked the last half mile in, raindrops stinging our cheeks.

Chapter Twenty

The guys bellowed as loud as the thunder when we arrived, and I realized that they had been watching for me. I stood by the fire, warming my palms and fingertips, affecting nonchalance, stalling to avoid the 0.4-mile trek to fetch water. When I finally went to my gear, my water bag was gone. I looked under, around, in my pack, upset rising, knowing wind had blown it away. A leaf blew in and stuck to my leg. I slapped at it, burning with frustration, forcing back tears. If I filled my two water bottles, that would be two liters. Enough for dinner, at least. No way I would borrow water; everyone here had made the trek.

Hephzibah touched my arm, pointed to a wooden peg on the wall. My water bag hung, tense and full. Condensation collected at its bottom and dripped, creating a puddle on floorboards. I watched each drop ripple in widening circles, expanding the edge. I called a thank you to the men...ignored. I lifted the water bag off the hook, and poured some into my pan, asking if anyone would like cocoa, but they shook their heads, staring into the flames.

I pulled out the instant Pasta Primavera. My dad would have been relieved to see me here safe and eating warm food, even if I simply added water and stirred. When he scoffed at the foil package, I wished I had taken the opportunity to connect with him. I wished I'd swiveled the squeaking stool and scooched closer to the table. Wished I'd said, "You can help me make this better right? Pasta would be a great backpacking meal." We could have scouted a local Italian shop and spoken about his childhood meal times. He would have said, "Remember, you only want extra, *extra* virgin olive oil. The other stuff is for the pigs." He knew nothing about backpacking, but that wouldn't have mattered, he would have loved being a resource. It would have brought us one step closer. I promised myself I'd work on breaking our old patterns. I was grateful he had survived his cancer bout in his thirties. I could know him now when I was an adult. We had time.

I peeled off my disgusting socks and left them outside my tent on my boots under the rain fly. I opened *The Cider House Rules*. Other hikers seemed surprised that I carried books. They were luxury items, unnecessary weight. But I couldn't imagine being without one, cautiously rationing daily pages. The words blurred with my thoughts. Book on my chest and close to the ground, I drifted off into an easy, deep sleep, aided by fatigue, and steady beating of rain.

I woke to the appalling smell of my socks. Acrid. Through the tent's close ceiling I sensed rather than saw clear sky. I pondered the vicissitude of both weather and my moods in the mountains. I would have enjoyed relaxing and daydreaming a little, but, frankly, the smell was too much. Shimmying out of my bag, I pulled on my shorts and damp t-shirt—cold on my back. I fished into my pack's bottom and pulled out my pink socks from the gallon zip lock bag that protected my town clothes, reminding myself to ask Ben to include a pair of socks if he sent a care package...some fun color. "New socks in a box," I sang. It was morning; I felt good. Conjured words assembled themselves in a familiar cadence:

Red ones, blue ones,
green, orange, chartreuse.
With so many colors,
which one will you choose?

I imagined Dr. Seuss benevolently reciting my poem from beyond, or wherever. Maybe I'd think about that on today's miles: where did people go, park rangers, Theodore Geisel or anyone else, after they were done here? I tiptoed breaking camp, hoping not to wake campmates. Then tossed my old socks into surviving embers—a sacrifice for protection from the storm. No amount of trail magic was going to resurrect those. The socks hissed and steamed, sour scent repelling me back a step.

Heading toward the Appalachian Trail, I paused, raising my hand to Hephzibah, who was bent over her camp stove. She looked up, and waved, signaling that she'd be fine. Then she looked up again.

"I tried to thank God last night for sending you," Hephzibah said, stirring. Then she added, "But He said I should thank you instead."

My heart rose into my throat, and I suddenly felt warm. My tongue thickened and stuck to my front teeth. I looked away, then nodded again at Hephzibah, hitched up my pack, and hurried along the blue blazed trail to restart my journey north. Dennis Cove, I would get there; I had faith. The bright green birch leaves shook cheerfully in the breeze, while sunlight pushed its way onto the trail in front of my feet.

Part IV: When It Rains

Chapter Twenty-one

Rain tapped the roof at Dennis Cove's Kincora Hostel as I stuffed the last of my gear into my pack: sleeping bag, thermals, long sleeve Polypro, bear-line, travel-sized toothpaste, folded toilet paper stash. I topped off my fuel from the community Coleman tin and deposited a dollar in the honor-jar to cover a handwritten price of 10 cents per ounce, then wedged the red fuel bottle into my cooking pot next to my Whisperlite stove.

The sky hung dense and gray over the Tennessee mountains. Steady drops sprinkled my palms as I gauged my potential to get drenched. Today would be wet. I re-tightened three sets of drawstrings: Hefty bag extra-liner, pack's nylon top, separate pack cover. I was determined to protect my portable possessions. T-shirt, underclothes, shorts, and socks could be soaked as I splashed into camp, my exertion keeping my body temperature up, but I would need dry clothes and dry bedding when I settled in.

For this section of the AT, I aimed for Virginia's Catawba Gap, 285 miles north, and would be alone for more than a week until Trimpi shelter where I hoped to meet Smoky Mountains-buddy, Uncle Bob, where our sections overlapped for a few days, and then Ben for the last fifty miles into Catawba. Today would be a short ten to Watauga Lake shelter. Despite the weather, I almost darted for the trail, eager to un-schedule myself, to sink into hiking rhythm, to clear my head and order my thoughts, which seemed to swirl like eastern seaboard hurricanes that had pushed this rain inland.

This year, my schedule had elbowed my annual hike into August. Work and family events jostled me for months, forcing me to tightly stack each day, leaving me sinking onto the sofa each night to unwind in front of news for a few minutes before sleep tugged at my eyes. I'd been to see my parents several times for my dad's doctor appointments and surgery. When he could, Ben joined me. Then, at work, we welcomed new interns, requiring intense faculty engagement. Finally, as summer wound down, I was able to get away.

My legs settled and reached forward almost without effort. I passed Laurel Fork shelter in under an hour and dipped for water at Waycaster Spring. I hurried on, as if I might stay drier by moving. The day's only climb beckoned, 3700 feet to Pond Flats, offering a chance to quiet my monkey brain.

As the trail sloped upward, relaxation descended like the rain before I gained my first foot of altitude. My boots and poles synchronized, and my shoulders dropped. The woods stood silent except for the gentle patter on leaves and the occasional wood pecker's rap. My chest opened, deepening my inspirations. I imagined I could smell the terpenes, like the "sweet air" my childhood dentist had used as an anesthetic. They mingled with fresh fern and wet earth. I didn't yet understand the complicated interconnection—physical, psychological, biochemical—that contributed to my affinity for these mountains, but it emerged as soon as the green tunnel reached overhead, and the tangled brush closed behind.

Re-wilding started early, as sweat and rain dampened my skin. Dirt rimmed my finger nails from kneeling at the spring. *Getting dirty* has a variety of meanings, from raucous intimacy to intense engagement in a task. Out here, besides describing my usual state of hygiene, it meant experiencing another aspect of biophilia. Most of us accept that gardening enhances wellbeing, but benefits extend beyond harvesting beans and tomatoes, and communing with hollyhocks. Gardening is a stress reducer and is associated with a lower risk for dementia.

Terpenes claim a role, with studies suggesting they decrease nerve inflammation, but there's more. Soil germinates more than flowers. A bacteria, *M. vaccae*, also grows there, a microorganism that when touched or inhaled, increases serotonin, a neurochemical associated with positive mood. *M. vaccae* is just one bacteria in a teeming soil. Neuroendocrinologists describe the *old friends* hypothesis, suggesting that humans co-evolved with various microorganisms in our environment, and we formed invisible biological partnerships. When we moved away from hunting and gathering, and direct agriculture, we *lost touch* with our old friends which has led to changes in our bodies we are just beginning to understand. Contact with certain bacteria inhibits overactive nerve white blood cells, for example, which is one cause of conditions like dementia and Parkinson's disease. The chemicals also inhibit cells that cause allergies, asthma, and autoimmune conditions like rheumatoid arthritis. We disrupted a subtle and vital symbiosis when we abandoned our unkempt existence for anti-bacterial soaps and antiseptic lives.

I made steady time over Pond Flats, my boots slapping through shallow puddles, keeping me company. Giant fern painted slashes on my rain paints. Beech and maple stretched overhead and shielded me from most of the rain. Branches intertwined but somehow remained distinct amidst tangles, maintaining fidelity to trunks from which they sprang.

How did they manage to sort themselves out, I wondered, as I catalogued tangles in my own life? Teaching, marriage, patients, family. And it had all just become more complicated.

The autumn before, my father had felt nagging left arm pain, and after describing it to his orthopedist golf buddy Bill, had been whisked away to Bill's office for an x-ray. There he received news that hit harder than his Big Bertha driver—films revealed a lesion on his damaged humerus, the one that had survived his previous osteosarcoma. It appeared a new tumor grew right where the old one had been.

"Can they come back after twenty-five years?" my dad had asked over the phone, tremor apparent in his voice.

"Not usually, Dad," I said, feeling the blow in my own body, like a gut punch. My thoughts swarmed like paper wasps on aphid nectar. I struggled to align them, think logically, speak with precision. I toggled between doctor voice and daughter voice, unsure where to land, a conflict I would face for the next year and half. "You had a lot of radiation in that arm, it might be a new tumor altogether." My father didn't deserve this; he'd already beaten osteosarcoma. But of course, illness, especially cancer, doesn't play fair. Cancer cheats like a cowbird, invading and consuming what doesn't belong to it.

Over the phone, doctorface doesn't help; I struggled to claim my doctorvoice when I said, "You know, it might be a bone cyst, an x-ray artifact, or an infection. Did Bill refer you for any studies?" I deliberately avoided the word *biopsy*, which screamed cancer. Apparently, Bill had mentioned the same possibilities and did refer him. *Coward*, I thought about the orthopedist, rationalizing my own vagueness as appropriate because I was the daughter. The doctor should have been franker. It was a *goddamn tumor*. My dad and I agreed not to worry until we got more definitive information. But of course, we both did.

Chapter Twenty-two

The AT skirted a deserted Watauga Lake, running along boundary of trees and shore. Barren sand and somber sky unsettled me. I tugged my rain hat tighter and zipped my jacket to my neck. On the lake's far side, I passed an older man fishing from a low lawn chair, hunched against the rain, pole held out like a two-handed sword. As I scuttled past, he looked up from under his khaki booney, gray hair and sunken cheeks jolting me, dragging forward thoughts of my father like a hooked fish.

The last months had aged my dad, dulling his full head of black hair, allowing white to streak more than his sideburns. Illness and worry paled his face. His eyes sank into their sockets. His limbs thinned and his belly rounded. He had morphed from robust to an apparition. Living with his cancer recurrence had been trial enough without relentless physical assaults. Within days of the x-rays, he'd broken his arm while pulling on pants, a devastating event because the fracture released cancer cells into his blood stream and throughout his body. I don't know how much of this he understood, but, when we heard, Ben and I sank into chairs in unison. Then, finally, after he had kept his left arm for twenty-five years, surgeons took it. I visited just after surgery. My dad was skilled at navigating his life with one functional arm...still, amputation took more than his limb.

One afternoon, I changed the surgical dressing, assaulted by the exposed muscle, yellow granulation tissue, seeping serous fluid. I reeled, woozy and unnerved, unable to see the wound as a clinical case, but rather as what it was: lacerated flesh. My own rotator cuff ached in empathy. I stopped my fingertip from tracing the heart-shaped wound where his arm had once been and struggled to come to terms with my dismembered dad. We moved to his kitchen table, and I grabbed his favorite snack, Planter's peanuts. Our eyes met when I twisted and broke the vacuum seal. I asked him if he wanted a cold Utica Club. Neither of us cared that he shouldn't be drinking.

As I recapped the peanut bottle, he mumbled, "Love peenits," like he always did, and instead of my usual annoyance at his quirky upstate New York speech, my heart broke.

"I can beat this again, right?" he asked, staring across the patio, eyes never leaving the manmade canal that ran behind his property. I thought again about tracing the wound's raw edges, offering some comfort, some intimacy that had been absent from our relationship.

He would ask me the same question over and over in the next months—*Can I beat this?*—and I would feel so helpless and frustrated that sometimes I would snap at him. This time, the time I choose to remember most often, I could live with my answers.

"I don't know odds, Dad," I said, watching his face, "Especially with how stubborn you and your Sicilian genes are." *Sure, I did...with that fracture? Slim to none.* "Why don't we take this one day at a time?" He looked where his arm used to be. "Have you been to mass?" I asked. His faith would help him.

"Saturday nights. Like always," he said.

"This might be a good one to bring God in on," I said. "God's going to be way more effective than doctors." *There, I said it.*

My dad looked at me, then noticed Ben passing through the patio gate from his run and start stretching. A grackle hopped from fence to tiny patch of lawn. A small party boat drifted by, snatches of country music on the breeze.

"You two docs do okay," he said.

Chapter Twenty-three

I reached Watauga Lake shelter late afternoon and scouted for a tent site. The shelter perched on slanted ground slicked with shale fragments. Not a flat inch. I pictured me, my sleeping bag, and my tent sliding—or worse, tumbling—down toward the stream. And passing hikers belly laughing at a squawking tent, flopping in six inches of water.

I'd gotten used to having my own sleeping quarters, a retreat at day's end, where I could relax the vigilance that came from being unsheltered in wilderness. Or avoid conversation, escaping colorful language, locker room talk, and general bluster. An unexpected benefit: my tent muffled the inevitable snorer who left shelter mates tossing and turning or staring in frustration at the roof. On the bright side, at least I wouldn't be packing and carrying a wet tent in the morning, since the drizzle showed no sign of easing. I unrolled my sleeping mat along the wall and wondered if I would have the shelter to myself. It had never happened in the almost 500 miles I had walked from Springer, but I could hope.

I scouted for a suitable bear line branch which I always did right away. For lots of reasons: day light, and claiming the nearest manageable branch were two. But mostly it was because the later it got, the less motivated I got, and thoughts of rousting myself after dinner, and searching, lobbing, lobbing again, filled me with dread.

I found a nearby maple sprouting branches high and sturdy enough to hold my food bag. I knotted a rock to the end, making it easier to aim and throw, planning to jackknife my line for later when I would only have to hook and hoist. Most thru-hikers hung their food from cords dangling from shelter rafters. Bottom-up tuna cans were fastened partway to hinder mice who tended to climb down and help their squeaky little selves to trail mix, ramen, and peanut butter stashed in the sacks. I'll admit that I had taken this short cut myself after long days, when shelters were populated, rationalizing that the multitude of bodies would ward off any snack-sniffing wildlife. But today, under this gray sky and alone, the last thing I wanted was a food bag swaying over my head, wafting peanut M&M's, mac n cheese, and power bars.

I lobbed the stone-weighted line and watched with satisfaction as it arched neatly over the intended branch. Unfortunately, my boot heel rested on the rope's edge which jerked the stone to an abrupt halt. Instead of falling to the ground, the rock wrapped the line several times around the branch, then swung back and forth. Like it was taunting me. *Naner-naner-naner.* I had no idea what to do. My line was caught, at least fifteen feet in the air. Unusable. No amount of rope tossing and wiggling freed it. I looked around for rocks or logs to stack so I could climb up. Things aren't supposed to go this way. Disarray was following me from home onto the trail. I searched for an abandoned rope for another bear line. No luck. I looked at the mouse-proofed shelter hangers. My only option? Surely someone else would come in who could either help me get my rope down or contribute to the human-scent talisman to ward off boogie-bears.

Dusk fell with me stretched out, reading by headlamp. My food bag sat next to me. I glanced at it every page or so. The way it sagged resembled a frown, like it was judging me. Like my mother's expression as I told her I was hiking this summer. She had stared at me over her scotch-filled coffee mug, then nodded in my father's direction. Message received. I was doing the wrong thing, taking off on my own. Resentment and guilt rose like steam, scalding.

My sixth-grade self appeared, stunned and staggering, without tools to navigate a diagnosis of osteosarcoma in my too-young, devout-Catholic, star-college quarterback recruited by the Buffalo Bills superhero father. How could he have cancer? Cancer was for old people: aunts, uncles, grandparents. After the diagnosis, my dad and mom regularly drove to New York City's Sloan-Kettering for surgeries, treatments, follow ups. Hush governed our house after they returned, especially after chemotherapy when my father sat with a vomit-basin for a day, wracked violently at unpredictable intervals.

"How are you doing?" my dad would ask from his partially reclined rust-colored, velour easy chair, good hand resting on my shoulder, in a voice too soft, too pleading for me to reconcile with his usual growling, controlling self.

"Fine!" I'd announce, standing tall, looking him in the eye, unable to mirror his vulnerability, to face how afraid he must have been. I reached for anything, a book, school project, hair brush, dog's leash, to show my life was unperturbed.

"I'm walking Brandy," I said one night, clipping the lead to our miniature poodle's collar, eager to escape this now unfamiliar house, filled with un-parent people. Quiet, rural roads lined with oak and maple called. Trees whose branches stretched open like arms and whose whispering leaves comforted. Ancient trees that had been there since my memories had formed, unchanged except to become taller, richer versions of what they had always been.

"The hell you are," my mother spit at me from behind her coffee mug. "You stay with your father." Even an eleven-year-old could hear the slur in "stay," could feel guilt fired like darts, pinning me *in*, keeping me from *out*, and from my silent and soothing, leafed companions.

Now, like then, I needed a safe place to recover among the welcoming trees. My mom had always pushed a lot onto me, the oldest. As she vanished farther into the bottle, I filled the gaps. Laundry, meals, eventually driving my brother around. Monday mornings loomed since she was always "sick," leaving me scrambling to assemble school lunches, collect belongings, usher my brother out the door. She never owned any of it, defensively ramping up her criticism; every mistake, every conflict, every miscommunication, was my fault, every attempt to advocate for myself or my needs—to be a *kid*—labeled selfish. Resentment brewed in both of us, but for different reasons.

Finally, I slid out of my sleeping bag into evening cool, calmer than I should have been, given my dad's impossible cancer recurrence and the intrusive thoughts of my mother. Neither of them understood how the forest called to me. And how my journey through the Appalachian wilderness would result in extraordinary, unexpected support for my father.

My remaining thoughts scattered into bracken. I brushed my teeth, stuffed my toothpaste and toothbrush into the food sack, filled a small Tupperware with water and quinoa to soak overnight and settled it amidst my snacks and toiletries. I slung it all under an inverted Chicken-of-the-Sea can and scanned one last time: moon-glow glistening on wet shale, indistinct forest shapes, and silent trees silhouetted against dimming light, circling my camp spot like wagons.

I checked in with my muscles and joints. Toes okay, no blisters. Feet good. Knees ached less bent over a rolled jacket. Thighs, stinging with fatigue already. Hips...My mind floated again, into a scramble of thoughts that refused to be corralled. Did something hurt? My hips: they were sore. I shifted and listened for owls, for footsteps, hearing only raindrops and burbling stream. Indestructibles still might crash in, headlamps like locomotives, bearing down through darkness. Nothing disturbed this quiet clearing now. My first night on the AT seemed like a metaphor for the rest of my life as I wondered, drifting off, what would happen next.

Chapter Twenty-four

Morning's silver light brushed my cheeks, and I woke slowly, pivoting my head. Still alone. Rain still fell. Above me, my food dangled like a solo earring. I hoisted myself up and stared at my bear line in the maple tree, then stomped over, pulled the line tight and cut the rope like it was my braid, salvaging as much as I could. The rock swung in response. The remaining line would be a prize for whoever got it down.

Morning flew by like a diving kestrel. Pebbles and puddles shimmered, highlighting the way. I splashed north, my goal Iron Mountain shelter. Thick trunks bounded me on both sides. I wanted distance, perspective, time away from a work fraught with unexpected challenges. When I accepted the faculty position, having been directed to this exact position by mentors, having heard again and again that this is the only way to teach, I hoped I would love it. And I did love it, seeing my own patients but spending most of my time overseeing residents' patient care in the hospital and clinic. They took histories, performed exams, and formulated possible diagnoses and plans, then ran it by me. A resident's independence varied based on their year of training, confidence, and skill. But it didn't matter whether the resident formulated a complex differential diagnosis and plan by themselves, or I joined them in the room for more questions and an exam we performed together, the days engaged me, and

I learned as well as taught. At times, the responsibilities felt heavy, but like the trail, where it wasn't the physical difficulty of walking with a thirty-five-pound pack that posed the biggest challenges, at the office it wasn't nuts and bolts of being faculty—not hours, teaching, patient care—but psychological and emotional aspects that made the job hard. Before this job, I hadn't understood what workplace politics meant.

I chugged forward, planning to lunch half way at Vandeventer shelter. Guidebooks mentioned an escaped emu that lived around there. An odd wildlife specimen for Appalachia but this was a trail where hikers flouted idiosyncrasies. I'd seen one guy hiking with a skeleton strapped to his pack, another with a rainbow wig, and read about a cat carried in a rigged-up pack-top bed. The emu held a sacred place in trail lore and hikers cherished it as part of the diverse, individualistic community whether they caught a glimpse or not.

A work conversation bubbled up as I recalled varied trail-personalities.

"Well, he definitely has his own way of doing things," the chief administrator said, straightening a stack of papers, and setting them to the side. She laced her fingers together and set them on her desk, looking at me as if she had concluded the conversation.

"That's your response to the fact that Evan doesn't show up on Mondays?" I asked, wide eyed. I had made an appointment to discuss my curriculum time, important hours free from patient care and teaching, designated for curriculum development and reviewing educational documentation. "Last week, he had four residents to supervise; I got pulled from my time *again*, to cover," I said. My coworker Evan routinely failed to show up. An improbable number of his Sunday night flights got canceled. Or he swore he had arranged for the day off. Or he had been swimming and lost track of time. Or his alarm failed. Or no excuse at all.

"We'll start keeping track, and act if this is a habit," she said, writing something on a pad. I was furious. This had been proposed before; they *knew* this was a habit.

"Daniel doesn't show up on Mondays, either," I said. "If he calls at all it's to say he forgot about some other commitment at the high school clinic, or wherever."

"He's very involved in the community," she said, smiling tightly. "It's an important value here. Is there anyone else you have a problem with?"

"Not fair!" I tried hard not to, but I knew I sounded edgy. "I never get my Monday curriculum time because one or both guys doesn't show up." I stared, willing her to look at me. She offered an impatient look, as if I was an overtired, cranky child. An animal emerged in my stomach and started pecking. Maybe an emu.

"Maybe you have too much on your plate..." she started to say.

"I've kept track," I said, pulling sheets from a folder, unsure why I was blushing. "For the last thirteen consecutive Mondays I have been pulled off curriculum to cover for either Evan or Daniel, or both." I tried to return my voice to a low-pitched, even tone.

"Oh, please, that's an exaggeration. *Thirteen* weeks?" she answered. She looked like I had claimed that a sasquatch lived in the conference room closet.

"I brought the schedules," I said, offering them across her desk. "And documented what happened each Monday." But she looked down, refusing to take them.

"Daniel was here last Monday," she said, in her unflappable tone. *How did she do that?* "I saw him."

"He showed up," I said, "And after about thirty minutes, he hurried over to me, hands waving," I waved my hands, imitating him. "And said he forgot his pager. Would I cover for him until he could get it? Then he never came back."

"All I'm asking," I said, feeling the pressure behind the bridge of my nose. "Since you won't address this behavior, is to be scheduled to teach on Mondays anyway and have my curriculum hours on another day. So, it impacts me less."

"We have enough teachers on Mondays."

It felt like the seat of my chair dropped out from under me.

"So...these guys have no accountability," I said, stuffing schedules into my folder. "It's a consistent issue with Evan," I said, no longer careful with my words or voice. "It's not just Mondays." And now I had strayed off the Monday-subject, which I had promised myself I wouldn't do. "He doesn't show up on time even on days he *does* show up; he was an hour late on Tuesday. He blows off his call." I had gotten into the unhealthy habit of allowing residents to call me in the middle of the night when Evan wasn't responding.

"I told you. We'll watch him," she said. "As for Dr. Hernandez," she continued, frowning. "He's the only Latino faculty member we have. It doesn't matter how often he doesn't show up, he's not getting fired."

My thoughts muddled. Had she really said that? I hadn't suggested anyone get fired... . And how did ethnicity come into it? Shame and guilt overwhelmed me as I collected my folders and retreated to my desk.

Chapter Twenty-five

I reached Vandeventer shelter around noon. Soaked. I paused at the spring to fill my pot with water for tea. My favorite tea on the trail, especially when I felt chilled, was *lapsang souchong,* a Chinese black tea smoked over pine, which I mixed with powdered creamer and sugar to make rich stuff that I called soup-tea. I couldn't wait to wrap my hands around my mug and let warm thick liquid spread through my core, and then my arms and legs. With my focus on the heady tea, and between rain, running water, and rustling gear, I failed to notice another hiker's brisk steps approaching from the north.

"Glad to see you!" he called, almost on top of me.

I startled so violently I fell backwards. I stood and brushed off my behind. "What's up?" I asked, thinking the emu might have caught him by surprise.

"I just saw a mama bear and a cub on the trail! They crashed through," he said, pointing behind him. "Scared the shit out of me." He looked around, then at me. "What's it like south of here? Haven't seen another soul all day."

"They're gone, right?" I asked, looking and listening for rustling brush. Or growling. Or roaring. "The bears, I mean. And I haven't seen anyone since Dennis Cove."

"Weird," he said, "Usually folks out walking."

I settled my pot on blue flame, enjoying human contact. Or any mammal. The trail felt desolate. "Hey, I've got hot water going. Want to slow down and enjoy some tea or soup or cocoa?" Suddenly, I wanted conversation over lunch. The gloomy sky dampened my mood, and I wanted to avoid being alone with my thoughts which felt just as cheerless. I looked ahead at downpour breaking through green tunnel, listened to drops hammer the shelter roof. Almost in sympathy, I began to shiver. I tried unsuccessfully to keep my teeth from chattering.

"Gotta keep on," he said, adjusting his dark blue jacket and wiping drizzle off his face. "You be careful, though." He started south, then stopped and turned. "You should put on something dry and stay here for the night." Then looking me in the eye, he said, "And you probably shouldn't be out here alone."

He stamped south, water dripping off his pack, mud spattering his calves.

I peeled off my t-shirt and slapped it to the slatted floor. I stared at it. *Toddler*, my trail name should have been. Then I tugged a long-sleeved polypropylene over my head, feeling better as soft, dry material moved against my skin, and donned my two-ply beanie. When the water boiled, I poured it over two tea bags and let it steep while I mixed instant hummus in a baggie with water and olive oil. As I kneaded, a little too aggressively, iodine made the chickpea paste slightly blue. I added a few crackers and leaned back against the shelter wall to spork lunch from the bag.

So it's in Tennessee, too. In North Carolina, Hot Feet had commented on me "being a girl out here." Other hikers looked at me with surprise when I walked into view. Older hikers, often far less than fit, thought they should hang around. A little piece of my workplace, right here on the Appalachian Trail. I sipped too soon, burned my tongue, and growled at my tea. I was getting crabby. I scanned trees, hoping to see a big bird. They say animals, especially prey animals, can sense moods,

133

read body language, and know when to keep their distance. No way that oversized chicken was going to approach Vandeventer with my pique radiating out on the gusts.

Tea-steam warmed my cheeks. The liquid went down warm, thick, and sweet. It spread outward like rays. Rain slowed. Low clouds softened and diffused the forest light as mountains rippled around my small three-sided shelter on a rise. I stilled and became small. Yet vast. Not a conqueror, or even explorer, but simply a member of this wild community that existed without walls and clocks. Existed from one moment to the next. Perspective wrapped around me with the green light, and I felt the calm that comes with empathy and connection to other living things. I wondered if this was the tea, my dry clothes, calories, the lovely green light, terpenes, or the combined melody soothing my savage beast.

That lasted about a minute and a half before I got riled again. But not quite as badly, and with new understanding. So many of my emotional reactions stemmed from expectations. I *expected* to be treated like a competent fellow hiker, even if I had initially enjoyed surprise on male faces when I emerged alone from the trees. I expected to be spoken with, consulted, and included in discussions about terrain, distance, and gear. Not protected, patronized, and warned off.

I had the right to walk and to be confident in my ability, and in a perfect world, other hikers wouldn't bring preconceived notions onto the AT. But they did. And I did. And it shouldn't matter. At first, I thought I should prove them wrong, be successful, demonstrate what I could do. But that was a reaction to their perceptions, as well. My walk—my experience—should be independent from how other hikers responded to me whether they expressed admiration or disparagement. I wanted to observe them and their behaviors, as I observed trees, or boulders, or emus wandering brook and bramble, my momentum unperturbable. I looked

134

south, and took stock of the trail, almost as if I could see Springer Mountain, 500 miles ago. I did that, hiked that. Over mountains and rocks, through rain and heat, past bears and rattlesnakes, despite fatigue and thirst. I can do this as well as anyone. Other hikers and their attitudes couldn't keep me from my goals; the only barrier to *forward* was me.

Work was exactly the same, only the opposite. I *expected* to be treated with equality, even as youngest faculty member and only full-time woman. I worked hard to be good at my job: punctual, reliable, interested in improving resident experience and training to produce excellent doctors. But at times my efforts felt inconsequential, swallowed by a complex job fraught with complex interactions. I faced unexpected consequences, like resentment from peers when I put in extra effort, whether it was curriculum work—cataloguing knowledge and skills landmarks by years—or bringing meals to residents on holiday call. My colleagues didn't *see* me, assuming my hard work was competitive, instead of what it was: my own personal ambition to put 100% into everything I did.... It was just me trying too hard.

Like the Appalachian Trail, could I unentangle myself from the perceptions and behaviors of my colleagues? Just *observe* my supervisor's statement that I never got left in charge because he "didn't want curtains on the windows when he came back"? There were so many examples of what I should ignore. The director's comment that I "socialize" at professional meetings while my male colleagues "network." The day he interrupted me during grand rounds to ask if I had considered being a hand model. The morning the hospital CEO called me "Kiddo." Donning Teflon would be difficult: I lived in a stereotype—interrupted in meetings, patronized, ignored until my thoughts were endorsed by a male colleague, described as pushy or competitive when I exceled. Some days I checked the year like I checked my watch...yep, still the twenty-first century.

But unlike the Appalachian Trail, my co-workers could affect my *forward*. Even if I avoided reacting, maintained my motivation, I still missed out on growth and skills development when supervisors shot down my ideas, or denied me responsibilities. And my performance was directly impacted by Evan and Daniel's behavior. I tried to imagine a woman regularly AWOL on Mondays, and a man repeatedly asked to step up and cover. *That* scenario seemed unlikely. I felt disrespected and undervalued...my work experience sacrificed to enable these two guys to underperform.

I had a part in all this; I could hold myself back. So far, I hadn't been successful in simply observing. I got too pissed off in meetings, scowling and crossing my arms and legs, leaving too abruptly. I complained about my colleagues, and too much in general. Once I packed up my desk and threatened to leave. I had allowed the administrator to force my retreat by warping my self-advocacy into an attempt to get the only Latino faculty member fired. I fell for it. Shame had descended like a net, and I couldn't escape fast enough. If standing up for myself was a skill, I never learned it. Clearly, I had my issues, and my own work to do.

...And miles to go before I sleep, I thought, packing up my food and stove. I couldn't stomach the idea of a cold, soggy t-shirt against my skin, so I strapped it to my pack and pulled my rain jacket over the dry poly pro. As I started north, I glanced back at the shelter and dripping trees, relinquishing the roof to a rogue bird haunting the hillside.

Chapter Twenty-six

Six miles to Iron Mountain shelter should have gone quickly over gradual terrain, but my pace seemed sluggish, as if stones, mud, and roots conspired to resist my progress. I waded as much as walked and stumbled too often. Chill rode my shoulders, and I second guessed my choice to wear my dry shirt between camps. Rain and overcast sky and creepy-silent forest surrounded me...or was it life's recent turmoil that stalked me onto the Appalachian Trail? Maybe I was wading through work and family stress, along with miles.

But I didn't own everything, something I still had to work on. Sometimes things didn't go right, and it was outside my control. At work, or with family. The key was how I responded. I reminded myself to take fearless inventories, carefully assigning the appropriate pile for life's foibles: my-responsibility, not-my-responsibility. A recent situation with my dad for example: I knew he missed his garden, living on a small Arizona lot, where summer temperatures reached 120 degrees. Last spring I'd sent him a hydroponic tomato-growing system for his birthday. Hydroponic systems grow tomato-plants upside down, using a nutrient-solution instead of soil. He could set it up next to the prickly pear on his patio.

He wouldn't have the benefits that come from sinking his hands in the dirt, but he might inhale some terpenes, and he could harvest homegrown tomatoes to make his tomato salads or his special pasta sauce. When he called, as I was getting home from work, I knew he had received it.

"Hi, Dad, how was your birthday?"

"Good. After golf, grilled some fillets," he answered.

"Did you have a cake?"

"Ah…no. That would have required your mother to cook, and she was already…" he started.

Almost as a reflex, I squawked at one of the dogs to get his paws off the counter. Both dogs were sprawled on the couch, but I wanted to head off my dad's complaints about my mom.

"Just get home from work?" he asked.

"Yeah," I dropped my bag, scraped a chair over and collapsed onto it, resting my elbow on the counter, and my forehead against my palm.

"I don't miss work, I'll tell ya," my dad replied.

"They don't take me seriously," I said, thinking I should redirect back to his day. He played golf with one arm; I should tell him I'm in awe.

"I felt the same. What happened?" he asked.

"My supervisor is going out of town and he appointed one of the guys—*again*—to act as director when he's gone," I said. "It's always Dave or Evan."

I heard my dad sigh.

"I think it's because I'm a woman. A double whammy: I'm the youngest, and…"

"Mary-Mother-of-God, you're not starting with that feminist-Lesbo crap, are you? I had to deal with this all the time—for *years*—at SUNY. Everything is set up to support women now; they have such an advantage over men. Those guys, they probably have seniority?"

Inhale. Exhale. "No, Dad, we started at the same time, and we're all pod directors," I answered. I didn't bring up Evan's unreliability. "He just only asks the guys." I closed my eyes. Conflict again.

"Maybe he just sees them more often, and just asks the first guy he sees," my dad insisted. "You know, like in the men's room."

138

Right. This is why I get so frustrated. Rationalizations like this. I'd said it to friends: *None of them thinks they're sexist, but being the only woman makes for a permissive atmosphere for good old boys. Meetings are like sitting in a room full of 'my fathers'.*

To my father, I checked myself. I wasn't going to get sucked in. I didn't say anything about the lack of men's room, or the rest of it. My dad didn't want to hear any of that...*What was he really trying to say? What did he need?*

"Jeez, Dad, you were in admin for how long? Thirty years? How do you think I should sort this out? I'm at least as qualified. One of them barely shows up, especially on Mondays." I felt manipulative, mentioning the Monday thing, but I was trying to ally us and avoid the fight.

Silence. *Tick-tock.*

"First, make an appointment to see him, so he has time to talk. Then I would say—like this, see: 'I noticed that when you leave, you make either Evan or Dave acting director, but not me. Is there some reason you think I wouldn't do a good job?' He won't have a reason, right? He'll be stuck." *Oh, he had one, Dad, he had a reason. Curtains.* I pictured myself standing next to a urinal with my supervisor, staring at pink curtains on the wall in front of us.

"It'll have to be in two weeks or so, after he gets back," I answered, regressing, and letting him be the adult.

"Be patient. And don't mention the other guy not showing up on Mondays—boy, what an asshole—But making him look bad won't make you look good," he said. *That was great advice; I wish I'd taken that more often.*

When we hung up, I stood for a moment, hand resting on the receiver. The phone rang again, right away.

"Hi, Dad." I knew what he was going to say.

"I forgot," he said. "I called before to say thank you for the fancy tomato-grower. I can't wait to try it."

"I know, Dad. I know why you called." I heard him exhale. "Happy Birthday." He swallowed; he probably had a cold Utica Club. "And thanks for the advice."

Sun nudged through, lighting up yellow leaves among scattered trunks, warming my back and lifting my mood. I wasn't really in a Twilight Zone where the long green tunnel stretches and stretches, never leading anywhere, dooming me to walking in late afternoon, physical and mental energy dwindling, amidst rapid cycling memories, never reaching camp. A stream cut the trail south of the shelter, and, when I finally saw the creek, I trotted forward and filled Nalgene bottles, water bag, and pot. I staggered up under the load, determined to have enough water for dinner and breakfast, sparing myself the trip back.

Iron Mountain shelter was empty. I turned slowly in a circle, searching large flat spaces among trees for tucked away tents. No tents, no people, no squirrels, no birds. The ground bare, shelter absent of even usual hiker detritus. One Sterno can and a ketchup bottle. Probably some desperate hiker's version of tomato soup. I checked the log. Lighthearted comments filled the pages. Most entries described plans to *zero* in Damascus, Virginia, referred to as "the friendliest town on the AT." I was headed there for my first break. For an Indestructible, Damascus would be one long day's walk from Iron Mountain. "Going for it," BadBoy wrote in snarled blue letters. "Hoping for ice cream but up for anything but ramen."

Fog rolled in as I set up my one-person Quarter Dome. I rebelled against encroaching stillness, warded off isolation by stomping around, clicking poles, and rubbing nylon. I longed to lie down, close my eyes, and reach for morning and the reset I knew would come with it. But dinner first; I wouldn't allow myself to skip meals, no matter how much I wanted to escape this day. Earlier in the afternoon, dinner had nudged its way into my consciousness. First, fleetingly, like a sparrow darting between branches. Then images, even smells, took root, and over several steps I imagined navigating my overloaded spork from pot to mouth and subsequent warm mouthfuls. I suddenly felt more successful. I had been hungry, and I had begun to think about trail things more than un-trail things.

Chapter Twenty-seven

Sunrise woke me. I stared up at my rain fly and wondered what was missing. Light silhouetted mud spatters and leaves. Eventually, a mourning dove cooed, and wind rustled through brush. Ah, no rain. I tilted my head back to look through my screen at the shelter, about fifty feet away. Even upside down, I could see it was empty.

With my movement, Iron Mountain seemed to wake. Chipmunks scampered, scouting for handouts. Birds darted among leafed branches. A black rat snake slid under the shelter. Mice scurried across rafters. The company brightened my mood. The solitude I had craved at my first steps from Dennis Cove now seemed burdensome. I loved walking alone all day, savoring hours with my undisrupted thoughts, like some people felt settling into an airplane seat: *you can't reach me here*. Sometimes I daydreamed about possible and impossible ideas (I mean, I couldn't ever *really* be a mermaid, right?), sometimes miles flew by, unaccounted for. But even after marathon solo days, when I'd walked from 7 AM to 6 PM with only ground squirrels, birds, and mosquitoes as company, someone always appeared at night. I'd never realized that, even if my shelter-mate and I never spoke a word, which was common if I was sequestered among trees with my tent, another body still comforted, endorsed the location. I suddenly wondered if the local Appalachian Mountain

Club had issued a warning, hustling hikers off the trail. Threatening weather? An escaped murderer? One of the werewolves that I was now certain lived in Appalachia? It occurred to me that I had done it again: imposed expectations on my experience. This time my hike was victim. I had carried with my clothes, food, stove, and tent, the expectation I would see other travelers.

I skated my spork on the surface of my favorite breakfast, making sure to get ten grain, peanut butter, and at least one raisin with every bite. When I thought about it, it made sense, the empty woods. Indestructibles were further north with the thru hiker bolus, and weather had likely discouraged others. It didn't matter anymore, in context of my expectation insights. I liked exploring wild spaces alone, plus it was therapeutic, with or without human companions. I would be like one of Snow White's dwarves, skipping through woods to work every morning, pick-axe in hand, with forest creatures swooping and darting in company.

Sun-warmed air, dense broadleaves, and rows of vibrant ferns helped me reclaim my feeling of community with the mountains. My adjusted outlook transformed the weight on my shoulders into simply my pack, and the knots in my stomach into warm ten grain and fresh ground nut butter radiating energy through my chest and limbs. I knew my trek between Iron Mountain and Abingdon shelter would shimmer, be what I called a perfect day. The rare day during which miles darted under my boots, and I arrived in camp mid-afternoon, taxed, but not assaulted by an interminable march and cloud of black flies that made me wonder why I do this. The type of day that folks who romanticize long distance imagined described every day. I started to hum, and then to sing. "Hi-ho! Hi-ho! It's off to work I go..."

Trees and brush ushered me into wild space. I drifted among trunks and boulders and morning rays bursting through canopy. I reached for times like this, when rigid ideas associated with a professional life—a scheduled one—evaporated away with the clouds. It was like the elusive runner's high; I didn't find it every time but often enough to motivate my regular jogs. With each step toward Abingdon, a broader perspective took hold, a sense of peace, and I found myself thinking of my dad's life in a dispassionate way. I remembered the first childhood realizations he was sick, the first sense that he was mortal. His illness had bucked me from carefree days, and I had intermittently dissociated, wandering to and from school over cracked, moss-covered sidewalks, sliding in and out of prefab desks, moving half-heartedly through playground kickball games, sitting rigidly at home in my bean bag chair, waiting for opportunities to escape outside, to greet the giant maple in our front yard and then ramble along the quiet lanes lined with benevolent oaks.

Trees on the Appalachian Trail—oak, maple, chestnut, beech—were younger than my childhood companions, emerging after the last twentieth century clear cuts, and now protected by the National Park Service's management plan. Trunks grew straight, reaching for light, and gently directing hikers. I never wandered off track in forested sections where such stalwart guardians made the path clear, unlike grassy balds, where capricious blades misdirected me, or along roads where blazes never seemed frequent enough to keep me headed the right way with so many streets forging left and right. The trees accompanied me now, clearing the way north, and offering refuge as I allowed thoughts to visit and assemble themselves in a way I could manage.

Cancer had blind-sided all of us again, as it does to so many. Walking after hours into his friend's orthopedic office, my dad had been thinking how lucky he was, to have such a convenient "in," to getting an x-ray. Osteosarcoma didn't even enter his mind. Hearing my dad's shaky voice on the phone, I fought becoming that little girl again, despite my bewilderment, despite my years of experience, my stethoscope, my lab coat. Despite all the things I'd seen. My father's illness became a series of unlikely assaults, things we weren't ready for, that weren't normal events in medicine. My father's fracture, within twenty-four hours of the re-diagnosis, as if merely knowing the tumor was there made his arm more fragile. Later, when he complained of shortness of breath, I knew the cancer cells had broken free, swarmed through his body and started to grow in the lungs which is a typical course for osteosarcoma. But my father's lung CT showed no tumors, making my head spin and sending me back to textbooks. Next, he received an echocardiogram to see if his heart might be causing his breathing issues, since the chemotherapy he had undergone in his thirties had been heart toxic. In the cardiologist's office, my dad and I sat under stark fluorescent lights, listening to the heart specialist bicker with the radiologist over the phone.

"What are you taking about, Jack?" the cardiologist said. "That just doesn't happen."

We heard the radiologist's murmurs.

"Looked at the echo myself... . Never seen that in my forty-year career. You're off your rocker," the cardiologist said.

More indistinguishable words.

"You're wasting this gentleman's time," the cardiologist said as he slammed the phone into the cradle. He turned to us. "We're ordering a cardiac MRI."

I stopped hearing the words because I immediately pictured my father with his eyes closed, prone and desperate to be still while he rolled into the humming cave, amidst circling clicks and whirls cataloguing his insides. Then I was shocked back into the conversation.

"The radiologist *claims* there's a metastasis in the right atrium, intermittently blocking the tricuspid valve," he said, shrugging.

The tricuspid valve connects the right atrium and right ventricle. But a metastasis there wasn't possible.

145

Metastases get caught in the very smallest capillaries, where blood vessels have narrowed to tubes allowing single cells to slide through. That's where a single cell can snag and grow. They don't implant in high velocity, high flow areas like the chambers of the heart. And certainly not a *single, first* metastasis. I explained to my dad it was like an acorn in a river, unable to land and grow where water rushed and roiled, but more likely getting stuck in a trickle far down the line. He listened, then stared at the floor. Jiggled his knee, checked his watch. His breath looked shallow, but I couldn't tell if it was upset or shortness of breath.

"No answer today," I said, "About the shortness of breath." The cardiologist shook his head. My dad sighed loudly and looked up at the ceiling.

Like the single osteosarcoma cell that had taken hold in my dad's heart chamber, uncertainty took hold in me. The ground seemed in perpetual motion, and despite my experience, nothing seemed predictable. My family continued to look to me for answers, but I didn't have any. We played different waiting games then, my parents and brother waiting to hear that the heart tumor had been solitary; Ben and I waiting for news that metastases had spread all over my father's body.

Life is under no obligation to give us what we expect, according to Margaret Mitchell. And the implied corollary is that we're better off eliminating expectations. And maybe she learned that lesson, but it continued to elude me. For me, expectations emerged from experience. Whether it was a restaurant's food, climate in Hawaii, or illness progression, I recognized patterns, applied them, generated a picture of how things should go. It was comforting, having rules that governed events, alleviating uncertainty and anxiety.

And made me feel, erroneously, that I had some control.

The trail ran along a leaf-covered berm to the east. I turned my face to catch sunbeams filtering through leaves, wallowing in the clear sky and brightness, and in gratitude for time to allow my mind to stretch and rotate, seeking both dark and light places. The journey to Abingdon shelter felt like a leisurely stroll.

Suddenly, a loud commotion from over the berm interrupted my musings. I stopped short and listened, poles poised in midair. Something crashed through brush and leaves, heading toward the trail. It sounded monstrous. I recalled the Smoky Mountain buck plowing across my path; this was probably a deer. I inched forward. *I mean, what could it be? The boogie man?* I forced speculation out of my mind, trying to estimate how heavy the thing might be, by volume of crashes and estimation of leaf mass. Pattern of foot falls—definitely not two-legged. So many legs. Too many legs. A giant spider. *Stop it!* The ruckus moved at a diagonal, on a collision course with, well....me. I resorted to frazzled speculation again: mama bear and cubs, mountain lion, pack of wolves, T-rex. *Shit.*

Sweat ran down my temples.

Surely whatever the creature, it was more afraid of me than I was of it. I smacked my poles together and called out, "Hey, bear," like my Uncle Don had taught me on our Adirondack trip. He banged two pans together, one cast-iron. My flimsy aluminum pot sat stuffed in the bottom of my pack. I stomped and hopped, clanging the mug fastened to the outside of my pack. It surprised me how suddenly and easy words burst out as I began to sing. I felt better, and my voice partially drowned out the approaching crowd of zombies. I tried for rock n roll, but only Gloria Gaynor's

"I Will Survive" came out. Eventually, all I could muster was "I've Been Working on the Railroad."

As I belted out, *Dinah won't you blow your hoohoohoorn!* the trees and wind grew quiet, and I worried I sounded like a wounded animal. The fracas neared. A growl rumbled over the rise. I started to shake. It was all I could do to not collapse. I slowed my gait even more, to a shuffle, telling myself and Dinah, that there was really nothing to be afraid of on this sunny, lovely afternoon in Appalachia.

When humans feel fear, our nervous system unloads chemicals like epinephrine and norepinephrine into our blood stream, generating an excited response, preparing us for "fight or flight." This response to danger evolved when we regularly faced predators. Scientists postulate that modern-day increases in anxiety and panic partially result from a disconnect between our bodies' evolution and our sedentary, contemporary lives. Intense activity depletes our stores of activating chemicals, and this is why regular aerobic exercise helps.

Clearly, daily exertion through these hills wasn't helping me. Light shot through the canopy and seemed to focus on the exact spot havoc and I would collide. I sucked in my breath and planted my feet. Fight it was since there was no fleeing with thirty-five pounds on my back. I thought of my life in California, of grape vines and live oak and the den of fox pups in the back yard. Of Ben and how we hadn't experienced nearly enough together. Of my dad...and I wondered if he lived with this fear daily, paralyzed, waiting for his own monster to rear up. I waited with him, anticipated the assault, the bad news of his metastases, unseen yet crashing over the rise.

Dust came first, like a cloud lofting from the horizon, then leaves, lifting and swirling into view. I closed my eyes, then opened them, raising my hiking poles and pointing the tips forward. Ready. Ready for the... ?

Two thirteen-inch beagles, snouts flaring, ears flopping, and (here was the height of indignity) tails wagging, who crested, and paused, *posed*, really, displaying their regal selves. I collapsed to my knees, relief flooding my body. I looked up at their proud, yet disappointed brown eyes, faced with, well, a lady, instead of the big game they had been stalking, been snuffling after, had hoped for. They looked at each other and bounded out of sight, while I hauled myself up, shook my arms and legs, and put one foot in front of the other. Only thoughts of the "friendliest town on the AT," kept me focused, as I strode on, poles clicking, and cup clanging.

Chapter Twenty-eight

The AT ran silently, unperturbed along the ridge, among birch and maple. By the time I hit US Rte. 421, about four miles short of Abingdon shelter, I felt better but I still gripped my poles too tightly and hunched my shoulders, feeling the ache from the pack's weight on clenched muscles. I sought out the white blaze on the other side of the road. Four more miles, and yet it might as well be Katahdin. What a setback.

My perfect day had turned into a battle against myself. Clouds intermittently blocked the sun, casting a shadow and spitting rain. I summoned courage and energy for the last few miles, imagined climbing into my tent, reading, closing my eyes knowing it would be morning when I opened them. I thought, too, about meeting Ben close to the section's take-out point, and Uncle Bob sooner, in just a couple days. Motivation to keep moving. Ben, I could reach, but not Uncle Bob and I couldn't leave him waiting at Trimpi shelter.

As if Uncle Bob hadn't done enough for me. First, providing company as I faced the Great Smoky Mountains, then becoming my first section-hiker buddy, keeping in touch as we swapped stories, making our separate ways north. But now there was more. Earlier that summer, Uncle Bob and I had been emailing about Virginia's 500 AT-miles, figuring out where our sections might overlap when he asked about my dad.

"He's really taking the amputation hard," I wrote, thinking that Bob would understand, given his family's business. "He's getting a prosthetic, right up your alley. A fancy mechanical arm, with all the ropes and pullies."

"Awesome," Uncle Bob wrote back right away. "Easy to get the hang of, and not too noticeable, either."

"There's newer technology," I wrote. "A more realistic arm that works with electrodes and wires. Almost robotic." I thought Uncle Bob would have heard of this. "Elbow joint, hands, and fingers controlled by micro-contractions of shoulder muscles. It's called the Utah Arm." I paused for a few seconds to think more about engineering. "But, bummer, the ortho-doc said it's not available. Only a couple guys in the country know how to make them." I hit send.

I answered a few other emails, waiting to see if Uncle Bob would answer, then stood to feed the dogs. My cell phone rang.

"Jo...Violet," Uncle Bob said. "Can you talk?"

"You wanna plan Virginia?" I asked. "Better to see overlap by talking over maps." I pulled out my AT guides from the shoebox.

"No, listen," he said, "My brother Ron." There was a pause, and I knew he was thinking how to ask about a medical problem Ron was having. I sat down at the desk.

"What's up with Ron?" I asked, happy to do something for Uncle Bob.

"He knows how to do it," Bob said. My thoughts shuffled and assembled, unsure. Uncle Bob continued, "He knows how to make a Utah Arm."

Complex tasks often seemed undoable until they were done. Residency, marathons, packing to move.

When I wrote scientific papers, the blank white page daunted me. But I got started by getting one section down, then another: results, interpretation, conclusion, introduction. Always the same system, start with doable chunks.

About two thousand steps in a mile. That means eight thousand to Abingdon. Just start, one hundred steps at a time, then another hundred, and soon the blank page fills. I waited for the impulse to lift one foot, finally setting my right foot onto the pavement's edge.

A car pulled up, and two young men got out. I paused, straddling dirt and pavement. As they pulled packs from the trunk, a black dog leapt from the back seat, ears perked, tail swishing. He scampered through puddles and nipped at insects. Occasionally, he slowed to nose roadside fescue. He looked right at me, but he was the only one. The guys slipped on their packs, waved to the driver, and started north. The shaggy dog jumped and circled, dispersing joy that fell around me like fairy dust.

I crossed Rte. 421 so that the trio would be in my sight longer. Probably a single overnighter for them, into Damascus, this section of AT practically their backyard. Suddenly, I could do this. The guys walked toward the tree line, through bluestem and oatgrass that ungulated gently, talking and waving poles with hand gestures. I pulled my waistband tighter and stood on tip toe, squinted, lifted my chin, swept my gaze left and right, scanning for the dog like a beacon. Had he bounded after a rabbit? Fallen into a hole? His companions kept strolling, didn't seem to notice, and vanished from sight. Dog-gone, I felt deflated...Until a furry black head with a white snout popped up from behind a blackberry tangle in front of me. He panted, tongue lolling, tilted his head, barked once, and hopped in a circle. I laughed out loud. We took our next steps north together, oat and timothy blades tickling my shins.

Dogs have always made life better. And not just mine. Studies show that people with dogs live longer and that animals in general can make us healthier. If I wanted to be technical about it, "interaction with animals" was its own biophilia category. Hippotherapy, for example, is physical therapy that uses riding horses to improve balance, core strength, and confidence in children with musculoskeletal disabilities. Simply grooming and interacting with horses promotes verbal and emotional progress in children with neurocognitive conditions, and some utter "horse" as their first word. Swimming with dolphins improves depression. Owning any type of pet helps kids develop more confidence, better coping mechanisms, and a sense of responsibility. But the most impressive studies involve canines. Why else would hospitals allow therapy dogs to roam halls and comfort inpatients? Dogs relieve stress; petting a dog can lower heart rate and blood pressure. Heart attack patients with dogs are more likely to be alive a year after the event. Dementia patients with dogs have improved cognitive function and less agitation. And apparently Appalachian Trail hikers can continue through loneliness, grief, and fear in the wake of a wagging tail.

I never knew what to call this dog, but "Mars" popped into my head after my thoughts of Uncle Bob. He once had a black Labrador he named Mars after a shade of black paint. "I miss that dog so much," Uncle Bob had said as we traversed the Smokies, "Don't think my heart could stand another one." I liked thinking that here was Mars, yet another of Uncle Bob's good deeds, sent to lift my spirits and carry me forward.

Mars and his unfettered glee helped me achieve my rhythm, but I knew I would face challenging times farther north. Each time I made it through a rough patch, whether it was through grit, trail magic, or a little help from my friends, I gained experience and confidence, more tools to help me with whatever lay ahead. True, too, with family, work, and most things.

Mars raced forward, then fell back, circled me, and trotted alongside. He stopped and raised his twitching nose. He darted after a rabbit, or squirrel, or butterfly, or maybe he was looking for Uncle Bob, a few days north. Whatever kept him energized and bounding ahead, tail visible above the swaying blades, he was leading the way to Abingdon shelter, and the Tennessee-Virginia line.

Part V: What to Bring

Chapter Twenty-nine

By the time I made it to Virginia, I knew how to plot mileage, plan food, choose airports, find shuttles, and I had whittled my gear to the absolute necessities. Planning the journey had developed into a familiar spring routine, right down to the hours leading up to the flight. So I felt confident when I took a leave of absence from work to hike the remaining 1500 miles from Catawba Gap, Virginia to Mount Katahdin, Maine. The Appalachian Trail called, and I longed for the green light that held beauty and solitude, for the sense of accomplishment that came from making it through tough stretches. For perspective.

My dad had died. Cancer claimed him suddenly and cruelly with a blood clot that launched from his right leg to his lungs after his oncologist admitted him for palliative chemotherapy, to improve quality of life after his cancer had spread. None of us was there when the clot flew. The nurse said he was watching a *MASH* rerun when he bolted upright, eyes wide and sucking a sharp breath. He jerked his legs and grabbed his chest. His team used everything they could to make him comfortable which included oxygen delivery and intravenous morphine, until we could all get there.

Blood clots are common in people with a high tumor burden, and metastases had crowded his lungs and spotted bones. Still, the clot surprised us, because he had continued to be active, even after open heart surgery months earlier to remove the single tumor in his right atrium. He walked, worked out gently at the gym, played golf, socialized with friends. And he had chosen to conceal the new bone pains, and the swelling in his right leg.

Though my days hung heavy with grief, I hadn't yet considered taking time away from work to finish the AT, even when the trail began its siren call early. In February, I finally gave in and pulled the red and blue Saucony shoebox off my bookshelf, where it was wedged between *Medical Spanish* and *The Little Handbook of Acid-Base Disorders,* and underneath Ben's neon yellow running shoes, which I absently noticed seemed to be gone more than usual lately. I shuffled into the kitchen and claimed the table's corner for my preparations. I reached into the box, between maps, hostel and restaurant fliers, and other trail info for my pencil and a home-made calendar page with blank boxes. After I tallied available days, I jotted dates in each box. I liked to travel with spring in the mountains, when daylight seemed to lengthen with each step, temperatures stayed cool, when my wound-tight-self unfurled in sympathy with trillium and fiddlehead ferns. In southern Appalachia, that meant late May into June. From the moment my pencil hit the page, numbers flowed instinctively, as if Mother Nature herself was guiding my hand. And, like a seed, excitement took hold in my chest. Almost unconsciously, I kept it in shadow, limiting its growth so anticipation didn't interfere with an increasingly taxing work.

I spread the maps on the table and used mileage books—*The Data Book* and *The Thru-Hiker's Handbook*—for distance between campsites and shelters, water sources, and road crossings. I plotted one day at a time: a starting point and destination, and food needs. I aimed for thirteen to seventeen miles a day, sometimes wiggling to land at a camp spot or road. Even this far north, I second guessed my physical abilities. *Could I make sixteen miles up and over Main Top Mountain? What's my back up plan if I stall out after nine or ten?*

What I couldn't see from the maps was the character of the terrain. Aside from bits of trail gossip, I could never know whether I would be picking my way through rocks, climbing over boulders, or striding along at 4.0 miles/hour over hard-packed ground. Pennsylvania, for example, was a pretty flat state, so just looking at the maps I might think I could breeze through. Not so, over the pointy, cobblestone-like footing. Luckily, trail lore had reached as far south as Georgia and prepared me for the excruciating pace. Then there was this hiker joke, heard at an equally excruciating frequency: *Why does Pennsylvania have such a low unemployment rate? Because they're all out sharpening the rocks on the AT.* Rain and mud also affected daily mileage. And Ben...on the short stretches he walked with me, we shortened our days, enjoying relaxed dinners and lingering to enjoy sunrise coffee or spectacular views. My vacation and accumulated comp days totaled three weeks, I decided to try for Harper's Ferry, West Virginia.

On a rainy Saturday in early February, I rummaged for my backpack and other gear. I had made a few upgrades since Georgia which usually meant lighter or smaller (and more expensive). My *Femme Nikita* backpack, for example, which transformed my hike with its better fit. Early on, I swapped anything wool or cotton for lighter, synthetic material, less likely to get soaked and heavy. I purchased a compressible sleeping bag and a titanium mug, relegating my blue-enameled cup to car-camping. When I approached Pennsylvania, I sprung for a freestanding tent, afraid the ground would be so rocky that I wouldn't be able to secure my old standby with stakes.

I needed so little on the AT and felt liberated by this, viewing my American daily life as wasteful. Trash after a five-day section fit into a sealed quart-sized plastic bag, which I emptied in town and reused (true for all my plastic until it disintegrates). Food, clothing, shelter, everything...all portable. A sandwich baggie held a small tube of toothpaste, toothbrush, three-ounce bottle of saline, contact lens case, eyeglasses. A two-ounce bottle of biodegradable soap replaced all the daily specialized soaps our lives compel us to use: facial soap, deodorant soap, hand soap, shampoo, laundry detergent, dish soap, dishwasher soap.

I donned the same clothes every day, right down to my socks, and put on the same warm layers every night in camp. During rain, mornings could be vexatious, as I shimmied into the same wet t-shirt, dreading the chill on my back. I learned to sleep with my underwear and shirt between liner and sleeping bag, so my body heat would leave them warmer and drier. Of course, this system occasionally generated frantic searches for undergarments at dawn as I pawed among belongings in my tent. One morning in Tennessee, after a twisting, contorting search for a liner sock, I emerged to grins and chuckles, not quite sure about the joke. Finally, as I joined the shelter inhabitants for coffee, Antelope commented through the crumbs in his beard, "Wrassling a grizzly in your tent? Wondered if we needed to rescue you."

"I wasn't worried," chimed in Boot Straps, over his cocoa. "I just called dibs on your gear when it was all over."

"Don't bring what you won't use," one seasoned hiker warned. But there were two things I carried every year and was happy to ignore: rain gear and first aid kit, both stowed within easy reach, but largely and thankfully forgotten for most of the journey.

Every hiker had discretionary items, more about comfort than necessity, and a highly personal choice. For me, those were a camp pillow and a book. At Gentian Pond shelter one, Indestructible had blurted, "Wow! Book's a lot of extra weight," while offering a swig from the 1.5 liter Jack Daniels jug he had hauled in. Some folks carried musical instruments. One older hiker, Tortoise, trudged into camp with an empty two-liter soda bottle strapped to the outside of his pack for use as a nighttime urinal.

My last non-essential item I called my "paper-bag," even though it was a plastic gallon Ziplock, battered from the miles, cloudy like a cataract-ridden lens. It made all the trips, from Georgia to Maine, although the contents varied slightly over time. Constants were a few pieces of stationery and stamped envelopes, addressed cards for events that would occur while I was hiking (like my mom's or brother's birthday), paper for notes, and a violet-inked ballpoint pen for signing the shelter logs, one end wound with a thick strip of duct tape for inevitable gear repairs. The year before I had added a single "quote" card given to me by a friend, with Virginia Woolf's words:

> "For now, she need not think about anybody. She could be herself, by herself. And that was what she now often felt the need of—to think: well, not even to think. To be silent; to be alone."

And another quote, handwritten on spiral notebook paper, that had mysteriously arrived the year before at the Pearisburg post office. As I turned to leave with the expected supply box, the postal worker had called out "Wait! One more thing!" and placed the plain envelope on top. No return address.

> "Above all, be not the victim, but the heroine of your own life." Nora Ephron.

Again. Film maker, writer, journalist. I had quoted her years before, in my residency application essay, from her *What Five Things Are You?* commencement speech at Wellesley. I didn't remember what five things I had called myself at the time but had described how I wanted to evolve into five other things I also couldn't remember, except *humanist* and *doctor*. And now?

Was I heroine of my own life?

Chapter Thirty

"Can't make lunch today," Ben and I said in unison, both grabbing bags and keys, and hurrying toward the door. On Thursdays, we carved out time to share the midday meal.

"Financial meeting," I said, around the apple wedged in my mouth. The hospital had been threatening to close the residency unless faculty came up with cost-savings.

"Is that why you were tossing and turning?" Ben asked, through his grapefruit section.

"What doesn't keep me up lately?" I asked, sliding in to my car. I closed my eyes. Grief still strangled me, but I fought it on this day. "You must have been awake, too. What's up?"

"Transplant team meeting," Ben said, jaw tight. "Shit show." The senior transplant surgeon had retired, and the restructured team, led by a younger surgeon, was struggling. It was unusual for a small city like ours to have a kidney transplant program but invaluable for patients and families, who wouldn't have to drive hours for surgery and follow-up care. Given the increase in kidney failure, mostly due to diabetes, this program should be growing, not fighting to survive. "Then I'm running at the state park." His khakis sagged as he piled into his car. He dropped his gym bag onto the seat, neon yellow running shoes dangling by the laces.

"Running lots lately," I called through my window.

"The woods," he said, reversing his hand-me-down Volvo. "Are only thing keeping me sane." He air kissed. "And you." He wheeled around and crunched up the gravel drive.

I shifted and followed, my chest lurching a little as his car vanished from sight. Ahead: morning faculty meeting, then supervising residents in clinic, then early afternoon financial brainstorm session. I punched the radio volume higher for distraction and threw the half-eaten apple onto the passenger side floor.

"So it's the *commune-with-Bambi* curriculum?" a colleague asked, with a slanted smile, looking around the table at the rest of the faculty.

"It's called Medical Ecology, how human health is related to the larger environment," I said to my papers, only occasionally risking a glance for reactions. "And it's not just the obvious: extreme heat or cold, or floods or tornadoes, although those things are important."

"Like what else, pollution and asthma? Like that?" asked the director.

"We don't need a curriculum for that," said a colleague. "And anyway, what would we instruct residents on? 'Tell patients don't breathe'?"

I doctorfaced them. "It's both subtler and more complex *than pollution is bad*," I said. "I gave hospital Grand Rounds last week," I said. "And Kaiser Grand Rounds the week before that." I wondered if any of them had attended. "There are five main areas: emerging infectious disease, like Lyme or Hanta viruses; pesticides and toxins, especially hormone analogues called endocrine disruptors; large scale environmental change, increases in temperature, drought, or storm intensity; biodiversity, balance in food and other interaction webs, and where we learn from other plants and animals; and last, biophilia which is benefits to being in nature, including interaction with plants and animals." I had their attention.

"There are data now about physiologic effects from inhaling chemicals released by trees and other plants," I said. "Some organizations have started writing 'nature prescriptions', to get patients walking in parks."

"Wow, this training program is *really* out there," the chief administrator said.

After that, supervising clinic felt like an over-stuffed armchair. I supervised four bustling residents, white coats trailing, as they darted from room to room. Each was a third year, close to graduation and we would discuss every visit, but they could see patients independently. Occasionally, they would have questions. *Can I prescribe penicillin with oral contraceptives? Is it methimazole that needs a blood count if the patient shows up with flu symptoms? How often do patients on hydroxychloroquine need eye exams?*

I dropped Jack H's thick Volume II chart on my desk. Mr. H was scheduled as Dr. Keith Manning's last patient. Jack H had a history of injection drug use, incarceration, and came in monthly for a long-acting morphine refill for his chronic back pain. Dr. Manning walked an agonizing tight rope with this patient between trying to address non-addiction and addiction needs. Jack H was demanding at times, but respectful. But still, I had to tamp down the "irked" feeling, a deep gnawing I felt with chronic substance users—what was it that riled me? It was just out of reach, like the name associated with that face you recognize. Clearly, I brought my personal baggage into these interactions, so I compensated by studying the cases closely.

I flipped open the manilla chart to the "Labs" section, looking and re-looking.

An hour later Keith sat down to review the visit. He presented Jack H as here for opiate refill, asking for an increase in dose.

I asked, "Are you checking studies on him?" He looked up. "I mean to rule out evolving issues. Or just refilling his meds?"

"He hasn't been imaged in a while, not since jail," he shrugged, then slid the progress note onto his clipboard. "He just wants meds, more meds, nothing else."

"Pain changing? Fevers? Looks like you've gotten a few blood counts," I said, and handed him the open chart. The most recent white blood cell level (sign of possible infection) was elevated.

"Probably a stress response," he said. "Jones-ing for his meds. I'll repeat that. It'll be normal."

"That's possible. But what's the differential diagnosis? Given the possibility of IV drug use..."

He sighed and cut me off.

"I really don't have time for this. He's a scammer. He wants his drugs." He stood to leave.

"Sit down," I said, a little too harshly. "He doesn't need a 'repeat' blood count. His whites have been elevated for six months."

Keith looked startled. His face reddened as he turned pages. "Could be anything," he said, "Skin, some other cause. It's not an epidural abscess, if that's what you're thinking." An epidural abscess is a walled-off infection between back bones and the membrane lining the spine. Injecting drugs is a risk for this.

"Could be, or something else," I said. "An MRI or CT to rule out..."

165

"Fine. Imaging. I'll send him to the ER," he said, standing again.

"Let's talk to him together. I'd like to...," I started, but Keith dropped the chart on my desk and stalked out. I called after him, my own reaction flashing in starbursts around me.

Late afternoon, after the financial meeting I sat at my desk, my uneaten salad still in the small cooler Ben had bought me for Christmas. I peeked at it and ate the chocolate bar, instead. I finished reviewing and documenting in resident charts, except for Jack H, who had been admitted with an epidural abscess. I was thinking about how I should have kept my cool better, when our nurse practitioner breezed in.

"I'm so glad I caught you! Are you okay?" she asked, wheeling over a stool.

"I could have handled it better, too," I said. "I'll circle back to him." She had obviously heard about Jack H. and Dr. Manning. "They get defensive. I'm sure he's already figured out that the patient's health trumps his ego."

"No...the financial-thing. Your plan to consolidate specialty clinic staffing to reduce overhead. Obvious now that you bring it up," she said.

"Sometimes it seems the same people have done things the same way here for so long, they need fresh eyes to..." I started to respond.

"They just moved on. No 'thank you,' or 'good job,'" she said, searching my face.

"It didn't register," I said, turning to look at her, wondering when I had gotten so used to being dismissed. "I guess I barge in with how things should be done differently and sound critical."

"Don't take their stuff on," she said.

166

"I have that problem, too. But we're definitely stuck," I said. "I can do this; I just need to break out of the smarty-pants-arrogant-upstart role." A pang spread through me and throbbed a few beats; I pushed it away. The sensation emerged again, and I absently acknowledged the nagging quality, finally brushing it away like a fly. I would have to manage the situation because I loved teaching, and needed this faculty job to continue.

Chapter Thirty-One

Surrounded by scents of pine and soil, I climbed through acros. Rogers' dense, faerie-like forest. Air settled, wooly and damp, buffering sound except for my shoulders brushing against wet needles and the sprinkle of condensation dropping from branch to pillowed moss. I almost floated over the smooth track, unfatigable, despite the summit's almost 6000 feet. If not for night's inevitable fall, I could walk to West Virginia today, or farther, a million steps, all the way to...

The dog door. It slammed open then pendulumed in and out. A barking, jubilant Chase, our brindle greyhound, had crashed through, pursuing a trespassing gray squirrel. And then Tommie, our red fawn greyhound, bounded out right after him. Both now howled at the sheltering live oak.

I barely heard my name, still half way between Mt. Rogers and my back yard. "JoDean!" Ben called again as he slid over in his socks, carrying his muddy running shoes.

I turned, disappointed at being pulled from my daydream. Superlative moments routinely drifted into my days. Looking down at Burke's Garden (also called God's Thumbprint) from Chestnut Ridge; sharing my lunch in Knot Maul Shelter with a dangling bat; wild ponies in high grass in Grayson Highlands. The forest no longer felt like an escape, it felt like returning home. "How was your run?"

"That place is a gem," he said, about our local state park. "Where were you?" The late afternoon sun reached through the window and lit up his moist skin. He glowed.

"The Appalachian Trail," I said, wrapping my arms around his middle and squeezing.

"I'm sweaty and gross," he said.

"And you smell, too," I said, holding tight.

On a February Sunday, I loaded my pack with clothes and gear, added several cans of soup and a ten-pound dumbbell. I grunted, hoisting it to my shoulder.

"Don't forget this!" Ben said as he lobbed a fat can of peaches. I caught it with two hands, laughing. On Ben's first backpacking trip, before we met, he had toted the heavy fruit. After he finally ate the contents and swallowed the last of the cloying liquid, he was still stuck toting the bulky, sharp-edged can until he got back to his car. "You hiking today?"

"Up and over Sugarloaf Ridge," I said.

"I'll join you," he said, filling his water bottle.

"If you can keep up." I watched him work his jaw, his eyes fixed on the faucet's flow.

"So...things at my practice...," Ben said, through deep breaths as we scaled the peak, rust-colored scrabble sliding out from under our boots.

"Another Don-bomb?" I asked, stabbing poles in the loose ground, trying for purchase on the slope. One of Ben's partners, Don, shirked hospital and clinic responsibilities. He faced two malpractice cases and had been terminated by an affiliated clinic which had horrified Ben, and increased everyone else's load.

"Don is sabotaging the new transplant team—the new surgeon—claiming poor quality of care. He went to the hospital administration behind our backs." He offered me his water bottle.

I stopped climbing. "*Don* is criticizing someone else's patient care?"

"He's crashing it," Ben said, shaking his head. "It's so 'old boy.' They've all been here for decades, and they stick together."

"Transplants are so important," I said, wiping sweat from my forehead. Dialysis patients were tethered to a machine several hours a day, several days of the week to stay alive; a transplanted kidney would allow them to return to a more normal life.

"The program adds extra call, extra work, and he's always looking to do less," Ben said. We started again along exposed trail, bordered by scrub. Scree clattered downhill behind us. Ben took a breath. "And he is truly change-averse...stick in the mud."

A familiar tenseness settled on my shoulders. I breathed in but got mostly dust, glancing around at tangled red manzanita trunks and low brambles. Clouds rolled east like a blanket, covering the sun. Terpenes reach their highest concentration in summer, when a canopy traps the volatile substances near the ground. This open, winter space wasn't as helpful as the lush AT.

"There's such a disconnect," Ben said, "Between how the older partners want to wind down and how the younger ones want to update, do things differently." We reached the ridge and turned to survey rolling green hills, eucalyptus stands, vineyards.

"Same," I said, thinking about the Medical Ecology curriculum. "I assumed you were having an easier time of it," I continued. "You're better at work politics than I am. I get all amped about new ideas, get thoughtless, bust into everyone's space." A whitetail cut across a grassy spot below us, vanishing into live oak.

170

"Get pissed off when they don't immediately get on board." We leaned into each other, bumping hips and shoulders. Ben's skin felt warm against mine.

"I have awful news," he said, turning to me. I mocked fear, widening my eyes. "Don pulled out of transplant on-call, and we don't have coverage...If a kidney becomes available and we're called to transplant, it'll be another nail in the coffin if we have to refuse it because of no nephrologist." I thought about telling a patient that the kidney they had waited for—sometimes for years—had to be declined because we didn't have a kidney doctor available.

I stopped because suddenly I knew. Wind picked up and chilled my bare arms. Leaves and debris zinged like darts across the rutted track. Clouds parted and closed, sunrays pulsing like caution lights.

"No..." I said and held up my hand.

"Your dad's memorial service," he blurted. "Everyone has refused to cover..." The ridge fell silent, and I started walking, needing to get warm. And to get away.

"I'll meet you at the car," I said, adrenaline propelling me along the ridge like the road runner. With a forty-pound coyote on its back.

I yanked open the car door, dropping sideways onto the passenger seat and reaching for my thermos. I uncapped it and let mint soup-tea steam hit my face. The smooth taste and calories soothed me. I hated what Ben was going through, his challenges to providing quality patient care. The affronts to his values. His frustration hummed daily, spiking periodically with events like this. I remembered too many wee-hours shattered by unexpected pager blitzes because Don had told operators to contact Ben. Too many times Ben had scrambled to address emergency lab values and patient calls because Don had ignored them or left early. Ben still felt junior and struggled to stand up for himself.

Now, here was another Don-boondoggle. Lose-lose. I could insist Ben attend the memorial, that my loss—our life—trumped work, but that would amplify the conflict and risk his long-term resentment. Or mine if he refused. Plus, there was the greater good: preserving local transplant-access. But why was that Ben's responsibility? Wasn't Don the saboteur?

I heaved my pack into the trunk and loosened the drawstring. My hand found the huge peach can. I lifted it, shook it. The bottom line: too much guilt asserting my needs. I was a fledgling, tiny beak gaping just above the nest's rim. If I insisted, a deep burn would kindle in my gut, and I'd shrivel around it, wake at night with vague panic, reach for Ben in the dark, as if he might have imploded under my neediness-abyss. I didn't know how to stand up for myself, either. I was starting to have insight into where that came from.

Gravel crunched on the other side of the trunk. I punched the lid with my tooled jackknife, leaving metal triangles around the rim. Ben perched on the bumper. I pried the lid, offered the can to Ben. He shook his head.

"I miss your dad," he said. "This is hard on me, too."

I tilted the can, poured syrup into my mouth.

"I've been thinking about how to feel better about work, less out of control," he said. "If I had something outside the practice to focus on, so I wouldn't get so enmeshed." He loosened his boots. "Where it was only me, working toward a goal, without complications."

I cut more wedges in the peach lid and folded back the top, leaving a circle of shark teeth.

"I've been training, timing myself. and I want to qualify for the Boston Marathon," Ben said. That year, he would need to run three and a quarter hours to qualify. But Ben was athletic and successful at setting goals; he could do this.

And he needed to. Ben had a deep sense of dedication: to his patients, to update and to improve, but his medical practice stifled him. Ben was one of *those* guys: white, tall, blond-haired, and blue eyed. He expected success whenever he applied himself, whether it be a grant, a job, or a kidney transplant program, aware only philosophically that his experience was sociocultural, not universal. For the first time—maybe in his life—impediments became literal and hindered his progress. The trembler in his worldview ripped a fault-line; it was wrenching to watch. But I briefly toggled between a smug *how-does-it-feel* and empathy. It wasn't that I begrudged Ben success, but rather that I thought we all deserved to journey without obstacles based on our phenotype.

"Sounds like a plan," I said, offering the can. He reached between sharp points with two fingers, pulling out a half peach, dripping syrup.

"As long as we're setting goals," I said, "I have an idea, too."

Chapter Thirty-two

"You're going to miss me," Ben said, as I surveyed my gear with an eye for 1500, rather than 300 miles. *Twenty-two-ounce fuel bottle. Spork. Lighter. Spare lighter. Inflatable ground pad. Maybe another athletic bra?* The pile distracted me. I looked from boots to tent to rain hat.

"You think you can go the whole summer without me?" he asked, picking up the *Appalachian Trail Companion*, and flipping through the pages.

"I'm *sure* I'll miss you," I answered, stuffing my pack cover into a pocket, attempting to stuff my apprehension with it. We had been married fifteen years and rarely spent more than a few days apart—my annual time on the AT being our longest separations.

"Just pointing out," Ben said. He picked up my Whisperlite stove and pretended to study it, unfolding, refolding. "You don't like to be away from me."

"I'll call from resupply stops." I looked up from my pack and over my glasses. "And maybe I'll have service on peaks."

"McAfee Knob, Tinker Cliffs. Imagine those views. Without me. And the Shenandoah National Park. Places to share."

I kept my mileage plan for the first few weeks but figured the longer I walked, the more fluid the schedule. I mean, the trail happens: good days, bad days, need for rest, meeting friends. I had never had a snafus with my supplies, or been sick or injured, but mishaps seemed likely. One year, norovirus spread up and down the trail, causing lots of hiker lay-ups with fatigue, vomiting, and diarrhea. Another year, I ran into an older hiker who had fallen onto her knee, necessitating helicopter rescue. I encountered the most serious sidetrack in Virginia, finding a woman flat on her back at a shelter, sweating, complaining of right-sided lower abdominal pain. I mentioned ectopic pregnancy or appendicitis as possibilities. Her boyfriend and I split her gear and helped her to the next road for emergency transport. Delays weren't all catastrophic. Gear malfunctioned. Legs needed rest. And once I encountered a man who had lost his supplies to an energetic young bear who shook a tree until his food sack ripped. Resupply cost two days in town.

Working out details calmed my jitters. Obsessive and compulsive behaviors are the psyche's way of soothing anxiety. Over-preparing certainly helped with mine, whether it was for a lecture, grand rounds, or hiking the AT. It also distracted me from what I should have been thinking about, like how I would feel disconnected from Ben, and if it was a good time to be apart, with the tumult in both our lives.

For the next few weeks, I packed and Ben ran, vanishing into Sonoma County's bucolic corners. As he climbed up and over Fountaingrove Parkway, I would plot mileage...*Could I manage sixteen miles up and over Mount Stratton? How fast could I move through Maryland's flat forty miles?* When he traversed the well-trodden paths in Annadel State Park, I contemplated logistics... *Iodine, or UV light pen? Pump and filter?* As he set out down the mountain to Napa, I experimented with food...*What else for lunch besides dehydrated hummus? Where had I seen freeze-dried berries?* Eventually, Ben would come through the front door, flushed and sweaty, carrying his muddy shoes, and we returned to our daily routines.

On a stormy Saturday in early March, Ben ran a local practice marathon splashing over the finish at exactly the pace his training manual dictated. We piled into the car, sitting on towels, smiling through the drips, confident he would qualify in his May race. We chattered the whole way home about the following April's Boston trip, and my spectator spot on Heartbreak Hill.

The next day, I organized, rolled, and wedged my gear into my *Femme Nikita* backpack. Loaded, it weighed thirty-three pounds.

Chapter Thirty-three

Ben's yellow shoes heralded his approach as he rounded the bend ten minutes ahead of qualifying time. I launched from my lawn chair positioned at mile sixteen under towering redwoods, ready with sports drink and energy gel, screaming my support. He blew by. I grabbed my blanket and chair and scurried to the finish.

When the clock hit 3:05, I stood and craned my neck, eager for my first glimpse of Ben on the bridge. 3:06, 3:07...3:10, he'd burst into my field of vision anytime now. I felt confused, then worried when the qualifying time of 3:15:59 ticked past. Was he injured? Had a car hit him? Had I missed him? In shock, I scanned the crowd at the finish, first the faces, then the shoes.

We've all read stories about long distance runners dropping dead. The most famous case being marathoner Jim Fixx, who authored *The Complete Book of Running* before collapsing on his daily run. About 1 in 100,000 runners die of cardiac arrest each year, the risk highest among middle aged men in the last four miles of a marathons. Thoughts of it swirled around me like the crowd. The theory is that sustained high output spurs the heart into a disorganized rhythm called ventricular fibrillation. The cardiac muscle wriggles like a bag of worms and can no longer pump blood. The runner topples. Suddenly, I no longer heard the announcer, the cheers, the thrum of conversation as a vision of Ben gasping, halting, and dropping to the ground flashed. His eyes remained open, his face gray while runners moved around him. Blood rushed from my head, and I almost dropped myself. I knew this was unlikely, but I couldn't shake the worst-case scenario.

When Ben finally came into view, I sank back against the guard rail, feeling only relief, unaware that the image of Ben in cardiac arrest under towering conifers would return to haunt me several years and twelve hundred miles in the future.

He loped across the finish, shoulders hunched, eyes straight ahead.

"How bad was it?" he asked. I watched his pink cheeks and his regular, strong pulse, visible just above his clavicle and thought how I didn't give a shit about his time.

"Crossed at 3:29, smokin' fast...."

"I blew it." He bent over, hands resting on his knees, catching his breath. I searched his body for scrapes, bruises, swelling...any clue.

"Fabulous achievement. Qualifying for Boston is an arbitrary standard," I said.

"I went out too fast," Ben sighed, "Bonked in the last six miles." He watched the Eel River below us. It seemed dull, thin, weak, as rivers go. "The books say that. For every minute you push under pace early, you lose five at the end."

"So you got cocky," I said, waiting for our easy camaraderie. "Run another one this summer, you'll qualify." We had a plan.

Ben mixed a cup of sports drink with a cup of water, downed it, crumpled the cup, and pitched it in the bin. He turned and was gone.

"How about if I drive home?" I called after him, clutching my things and hurrying to catch up. I watched his back, shiny with sweat as he stalked toward the car.

Chapter Thirty-four

The next day I sat crumpled in the passenger seat while Ben drove me to the airport. I had assumed we would be chatting and laughing, reliving triumphant mile by mile marathon details, but, instead, I was keenly aware of his pall. Running a race slower than planned might seem trivial, but Ben had really needed to feel in control of *something*. I recalled the long-legged ultra hiker from my first day on Springer Mountain, and how he had sparked my newly-liberated brain to speculate about his reaction to barriers. Here was Ben's reaction to his stymied career, turned inward rather than outward, bewildered. I had to have faith he could adjust and recalculate his trail north.

Green hills and vineyards flew past as I clutched my paper-bag with boarding pass and ID. I smoothed the distressed plastic, then rocked it like a snow globe wishing I could crawl in and hide from the last several months. The violet pen shifted from one side to the other, offering no comfort. At the terminal Ben hopped out and hauled my pack out of the trunk. He slid it onto my back.

"You expect me to carry this thing the whole way?" I asked.

"You're a rock star," he said, trying to hide his tears. "You'll be in Maryland by the end of the week." He hugged me too long while cars crowded and honked, then he jogged to the driver's side, blew a kiss, and slid in. My stomach knotted as the old Volvo disappeared into the mass of cars.

I hustled into fog-shrouded woods and climbed steadily for a few miles, disconnected and disoriented until I found Catawba Mountain shelter. The buffered quiet seemed so different from my cyclone life. The register held the usual sign ins: who and when; a few hand-drawn cartoons, one of Superman carrying a backpack with super stench emanating from his armpits; the requisite bathroom humor related to trail food; depiction of a diabolical shelter mouse who emerged at sunset. I listened for its rustle as I fished out my purple pen. "Violet was here. Katahdin."

The mist shifted and swirled, veiling the trees, sequestering me. From what? Was it trapping or protecting? Was it fair to assign such motivation? Fog and trees and spotted salamanders existed independent from me. I tented on a slant, levelling my ground pad with leaves underneath, thinking I hadn't seen fog this thick since my first days at Springer...how many years before? Here I was again, fleeing my life for quiet and simplicity. The difference was that now, despite my best efforts, I had expectations—an opinion about what it *should* be like. The tugs of my hectic life should be falling away. I should be drifting into calm, my mind stilling, my stomach unclenching. I moved slowly, unpacking, arranging gear, spreading my sleeping bag, fluffing my pillow. Breathe in. Out. In. Out.

I stretched in my bag, pictured myself melting into pine needles and moss. I stared at the tent's ceiling, inhaling mild mildew. I hadn't been able to air out my tent properly because it had rained twenty-seven out of the thirty days in April. I tossed. My neck cramped. My teeth ached from clenching.

Ordinarily, I love my tent. A cocoon, snug and safe at day's end—from bears, werewolves, and sinister thirteen-inch beagles—but I couldn't get comfortable. I turned. Laid on my back. Propped my knees. Wadded my jacket under my head. Tried to read, but I had brought *Geek Love*: dark. Finally, I took a Benadryl to drug myself to sleep.

Morning found me sequestered by fog and a Benadryl hangover, uncertain about the time. I gathered my gear, leaving *Geek Love* in the shelter but scoring *Peace Like a River* from a far corner. Things were looking up.

Without the oversized peach can, my pack felt featherlight, and I stepped without effort, yet somehow weighed down, wading through the thick air. Low lying clouds robbed me of the view trekking over McAfee Knob, referred to as the best view on the AT. Views—in particular those from height, that include groups of trees and water have been identified as the most calming, generating a sense of awe which is perceived as a type of euphoria. I hadn't realized how much I was counting on this until the opaque mountain cloaked the landscape. On the way down, I encountered a father and son at Campbell shelter.

"How was McAfee? We're heading south and looking forward to it."

"Socked in," I shrugged, plopping onto the shelter floor.

"Dang it. Tinker Cliffs was crappy yesterday, too," the father said, slanting his closed lips to one side. "Katahdin?" He tilted his chin toward my pack. I nodded.

"Been out a long time?" he asked. "Daleville's close." He studied my face. "You look tired."

Geez, I'm five miles in, not five hundred, I thought.

The boy was around twelve, and pouting. He scuffed at loose rocks. Annoyed, I called over, "You're lucky to have a dad who does this stuff with you. Don't take it for granted." He looked up, furrowed his brow, and kicked the fireplace. He didn't yet appreciate it, but natural spaces are great for kids, increasing concentration, creativity, and ability to interact with peers. Time away from cities has been shown to decrease chronic illness, including asthma. In 2005, the American Medical Association released a recommendation that children should participate in unstructured outdoor time daily. I wondered if this father had read Richard Louv's *Last Child in the Woods*, in which he coined the term "nature deficit disorder" to describe contemporary childhood. Or if this dad understood intuitively, even if his son didn't. I waved goodbye and headed out, hoping the sun would burn a path to Tinker Cliffs before I got there.

It didn't. And the miles ahead loomed. I convinced myself I was just tired (and apparently looked it) from my outside life and three time zones. Surely the smazy day had contributed to my apathy, a new sentiment for me in Appalachia. In planning for the lengthy summer, I had been concerned about more intense emotions, the episodes of irrational fear, for example. I wanted to maximize my chances for success, so asked advice from our residency's behavioral medicine specialist.

"I can't think myself out of it," I told her. It happened rarely, most often when off-trail stress piggybacked my trip, combined with isolation, low blood sugar and fatigue; and it could cripple me.

"Irrational?" she asked.

"Definitely not grounded in anything I can identify," I said.

You can't intellectualize your way past irrational, silly." She looked me straight in the eye. "Here's what you do."

I was riveted. Why hadn't I asked her sooner? A behavioralist focuses on how behavior is related to health and illness, both how behavior causes illness and how behavior can mitigate illness. This is especially helpful for people who are not "thinkers," and for conditions that will respond to actions. I was a thinker—an overthinker, really—and that wasn't working.

"When you feel it coming, measure your breathing. In, out, in, out. Don't disrupt your pattern." She paused.

"What if it escalates past that?" I asked. "Because it does."

"Have you tried the four-seven-eight breathing?"

Four-seven-eight breathing is when a person inhales to a count of four, holds the breath for a count of seven, and then exhales to count of eight. This irregular pattern forces a person to continue breathing, and concentrate on the counts, rather than the escalating agitation. I had used this before but found it difficult during physical exertion.

"Then, try this," she said. "Massage the web between your thumb and forefinger."

I tried it in front of her, picturing myself stumbling along, rubbing my thumbs while managing my hiking poles. I thanked her and headed to my desk.

"One more thing," she called after me. I turned. "Xanax. Pack some Xanax." Xanax is the trade name for alprazolam, a short-acting benzodiazepine (like Valium). We use it sparingly for difficult-to-control anxiety and panic but only as a last resort and only in people for whom cognition and behavior (and other medications) don't work. I viewed it as a crutch; it was for people without coping skills. People who had *problems.*

"I'm not taking Xanax," I said, hand on hip.

"I didn't say take it. I said carry it. If you have it, you'll never need it."

The bottle weighed less than an ounce and sat tucked into my first aid kit between the antibiotics and pain medicine. Because it was new, I imagined I could feel its weight, that I could hear tiny orange pills rattling with each step. Apparently, the Xanax worked, because fear was nowhere to be found on this leg, despite the gloomy woods. Instead, I was nagged by ambivalence and concern about home. I trudged, my thoughts returning to Ben like a tongue to a sore tooth.

I descended Catawba Mountain, waiting for the wild to claim me, for the rest of it to fall away...work, worry, grief. The wide green landscape would help me settle, sink into where I was. I inhaled deeply, knowing terpenes would be in high concentration here: under the canopy, in moist air. I opened my lips, expanded my chest, waited...Instead I tripped on a rock and almost executed a perfect Superman.

Usually during the first few days, I fall apart, and I don't mean in a scary way. I mean leaving my life's complexity and varied roles trailing behind me like bits of litter—my stethoscope sticking out of a gopher hole, my petty punctuality hanging like kudzu on an ancient oak, my worries scattered like pebbles in the moss. There for someone else to find...or no one, as they evaporated into the mountain air. Facing each day with none of the "things" that propped up my identity, white coat, clothes, job, house, car, even friends—none of it to hold up the mirror for me—forced me to be a purer person, more authentic, defined only by what fit into the pack on my back, and my own thoughts. Seeking this place, I had hoped to heal and grow that summer.

In other words, I was waiting, face to sky and arms wide open, for biophilia to shine on me like sun cutting through fog.

Chapter Thirty-five

I tented at Lambert Meadow campsite, hoping limited miles, a nap, and a good night's sleep would help me hit the reset button. I was right. I woke to the sun, and absolute clarity.

Heroine of my own life.

Striding, singing "Rockin' robin, tweet-tweet-tweet, rockin' robin...," I marched for the next nine miles over Ruckers Knob, past Hay Rock, over Tinker Creek, and right to US Rte. 220. In a Daleville truck stop, I got a motel room, and called Ben.

"I'm coming home."

Silence.

I worried. Worried that he was disappointed. Worried that he was glad I was away. Worried that he was worried.

"You were right. I miss you too much," I added, picking at the loose threads on the bedspread.

Static.

"I can't be out here," I said, talking faster, "Leaving you alone with this stuff going on." I stood, paced between the queen beds, as far as the cord would allow.

"I'll just be around, working in the garden, recovering. It'll be okay." He was disappointed in me, embarrassed. I had made such a big deal about having the summer to hike, told colleagues, told friends, told family. *Set a goal.* But for once, achieving the goal didn't matter. What anyone else thought didn't matter. I cared what Ben needed, what I needed. I fell back onto one of the beds. I smelled stale cigarette smoke, stared at faded curtains, noticed a stain on the ceiling.

Ben inhaled.

"I'm so happy," he breathed out, shuddering, unable to speak a whole sentence. "This summer...sucked without you...Thinking about it..." He swallowed. "How far did you get?"

"Twenty miles."

"Twenty miles closer to Katahdin," I could hear his smile.

A million miles closer to you.

Ben and I hiked together in June, during vacation time he insisted on after having to miss my father's memorial. We pushed through the rest of Virginia, crossing the state line into Harpers Ferry—the original section I had planned. Hikers call Harpers Ferry the psychological half way point, a transition between north and south. And it felt that way, as if suddenly I was no longer stepping through Dixie. The actual, geographic halfway point is at mile 1090, in Pennsylvania near Pine Grove Furnace State Park.

Objectively, I knew my carefully packed *Femme Nikita* weighed thirty-plus pounds, yet I felt both empty and weighted down as I trekked through Virginia. Grief emerged and retreated. I was relieved to have Ben, to split my roiling pain like we split our gear. Sometimes I brooded, stalking north in silence, allowing my feelings to surround me like mist at Catawba Gap. Other times, I chattered, words falling and spinning like leaves on a windy autumn day. Ben hiked quietly near me. In front, behind, and on wide tracks, next to me.

I carried guilt about conflicts with my dad, replaying confrontations, minimizing successful ones. Walking in Tennessee, insight had struck like lightning in the mountains. About how our "first order" interactions—my dad's concrete words and actions— swept me up, rather than nudging me to step back and focus on the "second order," or his actual, unstated needs. Since I had the insight, I should have disrupted the conflict cycle, especially during our stalemates about my mother's escalating alcoholism: daily drinking, public scenes, blackouts. Cancer cheated us and underscored the Buddhist adage: the trouble is, you think you have time.

Words and regret spilled out. At times, I paused only to take a breath before restarting my jabber. "...So, she tries to get in the car with her half full wine glass in one hand and an open wine bottle in the other..." I was rehashing an explosive episode. My mom had blown up because we wouldn't let her bring wine into the car on the way to dinner, shutting herself in her bedroom. My dad had desperately needed to vent, and I had shut them both out, leaving the next day.

"I've read about addict-behavior, but this is the first time I've really seen it," Ben said, between sips of his water. "Denial, refusal to take responsibility, or acknowledge her impact on you guys." He glanced at me to make sure I wasn't getting defensive. I wasn't, I saw all this, too. "She's textbook."

"It's as much about my dad," I said, crushed by my guilt. "He really needed help, but I couldn't be the sounding board." My father seemed to unconsciously recognize that he shouldn't be complaining to his kids, because he would often couch his complaints with "concern" about my mother, creating the first and second order split that I found so frustrating. *Here are my keys. Your mother's* already *drunk, make sure you drive if you go anywhere.* We weren't going anywhere, and the word "already" was loaded. My father meant, *I am so angry at your mother's out of control drinking.*

I want you to be my ally. I can't handle this pain. I never responded, amped up by his first order approach, remaining distant. He saw rejection.

Was this part of why nature comforted me? Because wild things don't dichotomize between first and second order, simply acting what they mean? Trees crane toward the light and bore into soil for water and nutrients. Bears steal food bags and root in rotten logs, rattlesnakes rattle against threats, squirrels scamper up trees, otters splash in the shallows, whippoorwills trill. Hunger, fear, joy. And bruised and exhausted doctors flee into wild, green spaces to order turbulent thoughts.

My dad needed support, Al-Anon, for example, a program for loved ones of addicts. I never used my authority, my knowledge to recommend therapy to him, caught up in my own second order fear, that he would hurl my words like a spear at my mother. "Your daughter, *the doctor*, says I need to go to Al-Anon because of your problems with alcohol." At that time, I was only starting to understand how her addiction impacted my own emotions and reactions.

"She didn't used to be a caricature," I said. "She always drank, but she was more functional." I sucked water out of my camelback, thinking how little Ben and I drank alcohol. We worked, jogged, read, cared for our animal family, neither wanted to be sidetracked, by intoxication or hangover. "They retired, that was one step in her decline, then Dad was gone." Ben and I had never said these exact words before. "Bang!" I punch forward with my right fist. "No more checks on her behavior; she sank."

One afternoon, two miles shy of Fish Hatchery Road, I bubbled over. We aimed for the Dutchhaus, a hiker B&B, for a shower and rest. Plus, it advertised the south's best peanut butter pie. Despite the pleasant, sunny day, I traveled with my own storm cloud, emotional debris circling. We paused at Seeley-Woodworth shelter, and I suddenly threw my pack on the ground, plopped onto the picnic table, and melted down. Grief flooded, through tears and irregular breath. I hiccoughed. I shook. Ben peeled a foil wrapper and offered me chocolate as light rain started.

Ben grabbed our gear and bolted for the shelter, but I was looking for a fight and interpreted the scattered drops as a taunt. I faced off with the sky, screamed and warned it to stop. The clouds gathered, darkening, as if sucking in elbows and raising fists. They obliterated the sun, then opened and threw a drenching rain. I refused to move from the picnic table, instead standing on it, unflinching under flaring lightning, threatening thunder, and raindrops that jabbed at my face. I tried to yell but what erupted was a roar, as grief and guilt and anger launched from my body. The air in front of me stilled. And for once, just this once, I held the sky at bay. Thunder ceased and low dipping clouds collected my rage and retreated, leaving me empty.... A small woman on a picnic table with her house on her back, cradled by the vast woods of the Appalachian Mountains.

Part VI: Far Enough

Chapter Thirty-six

Rumor of dawn woke me, the sky shifting from indigo to silver and lighting the treetops. I rummaged for my pants, leaving the legs zipped on. My hips were tight from yesterday's hustle, and warmer would be better. Later, I'd graduate to shorts if the sun stayed out. It was Memorial Day weekend at Dahlgren Backpack campsite, seventeen miles north of Harper's Ferry.

I stuffed my pillow and sleeping bag, then unscrewed my ground pad's valve, air whooshing as I rolled. Brisk spring air leaked into the tent. I headed to the bathhouse and warm showers, an unusual feature on the AT, and testimony to how remote the Maryland Appalachians were *not*. I hoped warm water would loosen me up...actually, warm anything: warm water, warm air, warm coffee. Warm thoughts. I had turned forty in April, an arbitrary number, but I worried age would affect my subsequent miles.

This section between Harper's Ferry and Boiling Springs, Pennsylvania, was a short hundred miles wedged into a week. Ben was attending an east coast conference and would join me at Pine Grove Furnace State Park for my last overnight. I suspected the miles would be fast going, but it was hard to know, especially given Pennsylvania's notorious rocks. I pictured myself, twenty miles out from Boiling Springs, hobbling atop relentlessly jagged earth, cursing a swollen, sprained ankle, desperate to meet the airport shuttle. The

Appalachian Trail wasn't forgiving in the face of poor planning, waning energy, or injury.

It was Sunday, and I'd been scrambling non-stop for a week. Long work days, trail prep, then rushing to SFO for the red eye to Dulles, landing early Saturday and heading straight to the curb for a Trail-shuttle Ben had set up. Finding rides to the AT was the hardest part of planning, and the Dulles to Harper's Ferry route had proved almost impossible. It was a word-of-mouth business, and I had called hostels, hikers, and shuttle drivers from previous years. One guy had retired; the other had a disconnected number. A third was already booked for the holiday weekend. When Ben, witnessing my frustration, had said he'd arrange it, I exhaled in relief.

Until I staggered on swollen ankles to the curb outside Dulles baggage claim, pack slung over my shoulder, exhausted and greasy from the overnight flight and saw a driver leaning against his car holding a sign, *Welcome Violet.* When he saw me, he straightened, tossed the sign onto the front seat, then adjusted his tie with one hand and opened the shiny rear door with the other. My shuttle to the Appalachian Trail was a limousine.

My phone buzzed as I settled onto the polished leather, grimy and self-conscious. I flipped it open and read, *Happy 40th, Beautiful. You're going in style.*

Chapter Thirty-seven

The limo pulled up to the Appalachian Trail Conservancy Headquarters in Harper's Ferry, and I noted with relief a single Indestructible lounging against his pack. He stared but didn't speak. However, when the oversized sedan rolled away, it revealed three more Indestructibles perched on the front stoop, surrounded by the requisite breakfast of Pop Tarts, bear claws, and Dr. Pepper, their eyes huge above gaunt faces and bushy beards. All three chewed between slanted grins, as if I sported a tiara rather than a canvas hiking booney. I hated feeling this way, privileged. My family had average resources, and I had worked hard to get through schooling and work, facing plenty of barriers as a woman but still aware of my advantages. My face burned as my boots found the Appalachian Trail.

I couldn't be too annoyed with Ben since he had propelled the whole AT section that year. I had committed my time to other things: supporting my newly widowed mother, a fortieth birthday dude ranch trip, and an upcoming celebration for my Aunt Bonnie and Uncle Don's fiftieth wedding anniversary. When I realized that using both weekends and the holiday, I'd have only eight days to travel and hike, I considered skipping the trip altogether. All that prep for what, a hundred miles?

Ben said my perceptions had gotten skewed.

"You've lost perspective," he said, over Indian food at our favorite place. He sipped his Taj Majal lager, then scooped chicken tikka masala with naan.

"That hundred miles can't be hard," I said, grabbing his beer. "It's the four-state-challenge section: the Indestructibles sleep a few feet north of Keys Gap, Virginia, then hammer the whole segment to Pen Mar Park in one day: Virginia, West-Virginia, Maryland, Pennsylvania."

"You think anything you can do," he said, snatching his beer. I knew what was coming. Bollywood music twanged into the pause. "Must be easy. It's not."

"It's too little compared to other years," I said. "I should be building, not shrinking." I bit my naan and continued with food in my mouth. "I guess I made that rule up." I frowned.

Ben shook his head. "Okay, this: we can get to the half way point." He paused, nodding. "The *real* half-way point."

"What?" I froze my chews.

"You know, not the Harper's Ferry "psychological-out-of-the-south-thing", the *real* geographic half-of-2200-miles." He watched me over his beer. "Isn't that some state park in Pennsylvania?"

"No, no," I said, putting down my naan, faking a scowl. "What do you mean, *We*?"

Ben had come and gone from the AT based on his available time, and his interest in the geography. I had walked all of Georgia, North Carolina, and Tennessee alone, but Ben had joined me for part of Virginia, and he had already announced that I could navigate the Pennsylvania rocks without him. I re-walked a few noteworthy sections, either scenically or emotionally, like the Great Smoky Mountains, so we could share.

From the first night alone in the fog, I had felt drawn to walking solo. Sometimes, I retreated to the woods like an animal to a den, licking wounds and waiting for strength to return. Other times, I sought solitude among trees and vistas, the rhythm of hiking, simply for restoration. When Ben was there, I felt like a host, focused on his needs, which interfered with my self-care. We both leaned into this dynamic, reminding me that gender role socialization ran deep for us both, independent of education or vocation, and required dedicated effort to disrupt. I carried the Virginia Woolf quote about focusing on my own needs because the Appalachian Trail was a room of my own.

After my recovery from medical school and residency, I continued my solitary sections because of the beauty and because my forest walks offered me perspective on work and family. The summer before, in Virginia, it had become clear that the ritual of annual planning, and wilderness escape were more important than reaching Mount Katahdin. The trail itself called.

The AT crossed into Maryland just outside Harper's Ferry and offered a gorgeous stroll along the Potomac River. Climbing South Mountain, old memories rose, slid into focus, then slid away like the ornamented steeds on Ocean City's boardwalk carousel, a familiar childhood sight during our weeks on Maryland's Assateague Island. Like the forest did now, warm surf, soft sand, and wild Chincoteague ponies consumed my days. Marguerite Henry's *Misty of Chincoteague,* and *Stormy, Misty's Foal,* bought for me by my mother, had been cherished books, copies smudged with sand and suntan oil, hauled from tent to beach, where I waited for the shaggy herd to plod through dunes, so I could search for the famous duo, manes and tails waving with the grass.

An aged photo from that place and time, stood framed on a shelf at home. Ben often paused to study it, and me, as a five-year-old. "I love the polka-dotted bikini," he would say. "Toes dug in, bracing against surf like a little warrior."

I would nod, prompted to float on the same waves of memory that visited me now, claimed again by sun-filled days and thoughts of stretching out in shallow surf, sinking to usher sand from my suit-bottom, crabbing with chicken wings tied to twine, how I turned "brown as a berry," according to my grandmother, who greeted us when we got home.

Then abruptly, among trunks and leaves, gooseflesh rose. My memories shifted to frame two seemingly healthy parents on beach chairs nearby. Ache pulsed in my belly for that girl, capering through carefree summers, unaware that feelings of safety and protection would soon evaporate like the ocean's spray. The forest around me seemed to still as sorrow swelled through my body until it was almost unbearable. My instinct was to curl around the pain, but, instead, I stayed tall, letting my chest expand with emotion, releasing it like pollen into birch and oak lining the path. I offered silent gratitude to a million shimmering leaves, each trapping a grain, sharing the burden. I stepped lighter as I looked up and around, and it seemed we exhaled together.

Chapter Thirty-eight

The trail offered gentle undulations in Maryland, remaining under 2000 feet. Niplets, I called them after Tennessee and Virginia, and I took advantage of the forgiving terrain to sightsee among crowds of secondary hardwoods, so different than the conifers that lined the trails at higher elevations: several oaks, sugar and red maple, hickory, ash, and birch. Trees like the ones that lined streets and covered hillsides in upstate New York. Steady neighbors, who, with me, slowed and endured long winters, burst unfettered into spring, flourished under summer's expansive sunlight. During autumn's brisk days, they ignited, claiming a fierce, unapologetic position on the earth, radiating energy that belied their stationary lives. When I tried to explain to my California friends the luscious colors—canopies of lemon-yellow, cotton candy-pink, pomegranate-red—they would smile and nod, indulging my perceived hyperbole. The fortunate ones saw it in person.

Along South Mountain, I studied the tangle of spring leaves, noticing colors and shapes. Trunks grew equally distinct in hue and texture. Weathered stumps offered convenient rest stops, yellowed wood etched with curls from tunneling insects and shined smooth in places from bottoms that had sat before mine. While trees felled on the AT had most likely toppled from storms or old age, or been cut due to disease like chestnut blight or emerald ash borer, the stumps still engendered a deep loss, similar to the emotion evoked by Shel Silverstein's *The Giving Tree*. While described as a metaphor for women, or the planet, the book nonetheless leaves me grieving for the single tree that had sacrificed without hesitation or bitterness.

Trees can live hundreds, thousands of years. The oldest tree is a 5000-year-old bristle cone pine named Methuselah that lives in California's White Mountains, alive when Hammurabi walked the earth, when small bands of Ohlone and Pomo moved through California, when buffalo and grizzly bear roamed.

Leaves whisper, trunks groan, pines sigh, and I can't interpret, as much as I want to. But they understand each other. Leafed and needled plants release chemicals (like terpenes), to spread warnings about distress, danger, predators. Types of threats, from which direction and which defenses to use. In response, other trees release other volatile messages, lean and move, and click their roots in an action inaudible to us.

Tree-huggers were designated a deplorable bunch around my childhood dinner table, which is why I glanced left and right before I wrapped my arms around our front yard's ancient maple. I would wedge my fingers into her trunk's wrinkles, pull myself against the rough bark, exhale every molecule of air, just to inch my fingers one groove farther. It was a way of sizing myself up, measuring my growth the way classmates jockeyed around marks on our classroom wall, comparing their statures. The height ladder never interested me after the first day when the teacher backed us up and ran a pencil across our heads. But Maple did. I imagined her looking down, nodding at my growth as I moved through childhood and into adolescence.

My stomach growled for lunch and my thoughts about trees retreated; I stored them away. My sense of community with forest or grove, or solitary timber isolated me since no one seemed to yearn as I did. I hadn't explored those thoughts, but now I leaned straight into them. Unexpected nostalgia—sorrow—had emerged already in this Maryland section. I scooped an oblong acorn and rubbed its smooth surface, tucked it into my pocket and hiked on.

The AT stretched through Pen Mar County Park, on the Maryland-Pennsylvania state line. Under bordering trees, I skirted Memorial Day gatherings, American flags, baseball caps, and apple pie. Grilled hotdogs and hamburgers taunted my underfed stomach. I filled my camelback with tap water, before stretching out under a sprawling maple to doze, grass tickling my bare calves, listening to heavy branches creak.

I woke when a scrap of bark pelted my cheek, and scanned the leaves. I blinked. Squinted. Blinked again. A pigtailed girl straddled a branch about fifteen feet above. She watched me, swinging scabbed knees and unlaced Keds. A woman called *Suzeeee! Suuzzeeee Eleeeese,* the s-sound, more like a sh-sound. The girl put her finger to her lips. I nodded a tiny nod, small as a leaf's flutter.

And I tumbled back in time into a memory so vivid I almost trembled.

"Where the hell have you been?" yelled my father across the yard. "Where are the trash bags?" I sucked at my lower lip, tasting a mixture of tears and blood oozing from the split.

I was seven, and we had been clearing fallen leaves from the vegetable garden. My dad sent me to buy trash bags at the corner store before it closed, doling out exact change. I hopped on my green and white banana-seat bike with flowered basket, money clutched tightly in my right fist, and peddled as fast as I could.

Our sidewalk's aged squares had sunken and heaved, and when my front tire hit a raised edge, it blew out, causing my bike to lurch and slam down sideways. Money scattered like pebbles. From my position on the ground, left cheek pressed against cement, I watched the dollar bill flutter and coins clink and roll. Time slowed as a quarter spun like a top, then teetered, and lay still. A bee moved from one purple clover to the next in the bordering grass. Behind me, the neighbor's collie barked. An ant explored one of the shiny pennies.

I pushed myself up and scrambled on hands and knees grasping at coins. I counted. Counted again. One nickel short. I felt around with abraded palms, ran my quivering fingers along sidewalk cracks, pushing down fears about breaking my mother's back, pried up moss, patted grass. Finally, I lifted my crippled bike, and wheeled it back to our yard. My father's head jerked up when I hobbled through the gate. That's when he yelled.

"I fell," I had answered in a tattered voice, already fleeing toward the back door. "I lost a nickel."

"Wipe out!" my younger brother called, then shut up when my father rifled his glare toward him.

"Are you sure you didn't buy candy instead?" my father asked, pointing the end of his rake at me, pivoting as I arced past. "I'll go myself." He threw the rake and headed for his green Pontiac.

I beelined for my mom, screen door slamming behind me, but she was already through at least one mug of red wine from the box on the refrigerator's top shelf. She stood in front of the TV, switching through her bawdy talk shows, drink in her left hand, right hand up with her cigarette poised between her first two fingers, commenting and gesturing toward the screen.

"What happened?" she spit out, tearing her eyes away from the TV when advertisements broke the script.

A few syllables spilled between hiccoughs and sobs, amidst blood and mucous mixed bubbles, only "Dad" and "trash bags" intelligible. She looked me up and down. A drop of blood launched from my bottom lip onto the gold shag carpet. My mom shook her head, sank onto the couch and told me to get cleaned up, before returning to the TV's escalating banter.

I was a pinball, bouncing off one parent, then the next, slanting toward the dark pit at the table's bottom. I broke through the house and out the front door where Maple's lowest bough scooped like an extended hand. I swung myself up and climbed toward a shaft of light from the lowering sun.

We lived on the corner of Harrison and Madison Avenues in a neighborhood that fanned into undeveloped land, and despite the flock of kids playing hopscotch, pick up ball games, and hunting for pollywogs in the creeks, the ancient maple on the front lawn was my most trusted pal, standing like a sentry at our yard's boundary with two intersecting streets.

That evening, I sat snugged in the trunk's second fork, knees pulled to my chest. I surveyed the lawn, our front door, and the length of Harrison Avenue, cloaked among the riot of leaves, sheltered with soft green light. Maple breathed with me as my turbulent emotions slowed, until I released my fists and my involuntary shudders stilled.

The neighborhood changed with the years, families moved in and out, somebody's cousin came to stay, corner shops opened and closed, the motor boat store burned. But my tree was always there, protecting me from my father's friend Bill, shielding me from my fifth-grade teacher's stinging words, hiding me from cruelties children wrought upon each other. In third grade, when my friend Lauren was killed by a car, I sat stunned on my lavender pillow moving only when Maple brushed my window, and I lifted my palm to press against a single leaf through the glass.

There came a time I worried that lowest branch would no longer support my weight. But I still ran my hands along her bark in greeting whenever I passed, waited for her to bud in the spring. I'd come home from college and sit alone on my bed watching her leaves flutter and branches sway, thinking of the times she had offered me a sanctuary from the tumult all children felt and the tumult unique to my life.

Almost ten years after my encounter with Suzy Elise on the Appalachian Trail, I would return home for my thirtieth high school reunion, and after a few days of procrastination drive by my old house on the corner of Harrison and Madison. I would worry about the flood of emotion, seeing where I grew up, re-experiencing the events, noticing the inevitable modernization of the chipped cornflower blue paint, the creaky carved rail front porch, the brick chimneys. But as I approached, I viewed the new fence, beige synthetic siding, closed in patio with ambivalence. It wasn't until I saw the uninterrupted grass on the corner, no trace of Maple, that the past would erupt, and my body react. The tremor started deep, roiling to the surface as shaking and tears, leaving an emptiness I had never felt before. I dropped to the grass scanning for discolored blades, then feeling for a bare patch, fragment of a trunk, any trace that my ancient companion had lived there. Had lived.

It was as if I had put off reaching out to a dear friend—too busy, too self-absorbed—then finally stopped by, only to learn she had died of breast cancer. Except a sick friend could have called. Except I didn't get to know what happened to Maple. Had she sickened? Been struck by a car? Or lightning? Fallen prey to shallow human aesthetics? Or simply died of old age? I had thought of Maple as I thought of most trees, made wise by their long and anchored lives, at peace with the mobility of other organisms, even those who truly *saw* them, paused in symbiosis, yet eventually moved on. But as her time drew near, had she tried to call? When Maple's memory, resurrected by Suzy Elise hiding among branches, when Maple's vivid presence emerged in my thoughts on the Appalachian Trail, her branches holding me that one last time, was she sending a message, beckoning in her final days, through a thousand mountain-miles of clicking roots and tangled, quivering leaves?

Chapter Thirty-nine

My nose alerted me to Pine Grove Furnace State Park. First woodsmoke, then grilled camp food reeled me forward like a hooked fish. Kids shrieked and laughed. Horseshoes clanged. After a visit to the concession, I scurried to my site, arms loaded with snacks, and plopped down to wallow in the long, restful afternoon. I tugged off my boots, peeled free my socks, and set it all to air on the picnic table bench. My feet looked like underwater feet, pale and wrinkled. Gear erupted to fill the site. I drank a Diet Coke and crunched an apple and waited for Ben.

"This site looks like a shelter after the Indestructibles have blown in," he said, from behind me. "We're missing Pop Tarts and Twinkies."

I stood for my bear hug.

"Hungry? We're at another one of those Indestructible-challenge-places, like the four-state-challenge," I said.

Ben dropped his pack, raised his eyebrows.

"You're auditioning for the half-gallon-club," I said. "You get a half gallon of ice cream from the general store and eat it in one sitting. It's because we're at the half-way point." I paused, letting myself react to *half way*. Half way done. Half way to go. All that I did to get here, that much more to do. I felt excited and defeated at the same time, typical for the AT's constitutional roller coaster. Eager in the morning, vexed in the

205

afternoon. Fatigued just before lunch, restored just after. Days I can't wait to get off, then can't wait to get back on. The thrill, no matter what time of day, to see four-legged, two-winged, and slithering community members. This section, with its abbreviated summits, and parks, fields, and roads didn't engender the same amplitude of reaction. But fleeting, that was. Up north would be the ruggedest segments, remote and rough going, a real test of my endurance and relationship to wilderness. I acknowledged another reason I came to the AT alone: I had something to prove. When I started, I'm sure it had something to do with what people thought of me. Now it was about having confidence in myself. If I could sojourn through Vermont, New Hampshire, and Maine, what couldn't I do?

"Any flavor I want?" Ben raised his eyebrows, a twelve-year-old version of himself, a person I knew only from photos. We only had about twenty miles into Boiling Springs, and could probably get there tomorrow, but I wanted the two forested nights with him. Just us. No phones, emails, TV.

"Nope, only what's made it out here," I said, as we sat shoulder to shoulder, backs against a log.

We magpied an abandoned Presto-log from an adjacent site and lit a campfire, sharing a ground pad. Stars brightened overhead. Our shoulders touched. Smoke rose in a lacy column. Ben had yogi-ed s'mores ingredients and held a long, arched stick over the fire, trying for the perfect toasted marshmallow. He fumbled blindly with his left hand, unwrapping a Hershey's chocolate almond bar, then using his thumb to snap it in half.

"Excellent s'mores making skills," I said, checking a box on an imaginary clip board. "You pass the junior camper test. Those ones are harder to break for s'mores than plain Hershey's—they're missing grooves."

"*Those ones*," Ben said. "You can take the girl out of upstate New York, but you can't take upstate New York..." I socked his arm.

"Those ones. Tuesdee. Youse guys," I said. Then, "Peenits," and thought of my dad.

"Are you glad you did this section?" Ben asked. He blew on the thin flame hugging his marshmallow. "Even if it's only a hundred miles?"

"It's good to be farther north," I said. "But this section definitely feels...unique." I looked up at the stars and purpled woods. "Definitely easier." I missed the exertion of long days and big climbs. "There's something therapeutic about hard work, digging in to scale mountains.

"But I've been thinking about different things, and in different ways," I continued. "Maybe because I'm not conserving energy as much and because we're surrounded by maple and oak and ash—the woods look like where I grew up...I've been thinking about being a kid more." I told him how Suzy Elise had sparked thoughts of Maple.

"I've never really looked to trees that way," Ben said. And why would he? His life had been so different from mine, growing up with mild-mannered, healthy parents. Growing up white, male, tall, blond. Ben seemed to always take for granted he would be respected, that the universe would offer him whatever he strived for. I saw this when we walked together onto a hospital floor, when the nurses and other physicians would greet him by name and fail to notice me, walking right next to him. Once, a nurse hopped up and introduced us to a new employee as "Dr. Fritz and his wife." I bit my tongue to avoid saying, *That's Doctor-His-Wife*. And I believe Ben deserves these things, but we all do, and it felt cliché to acknowledge that the world isn't as hospitable to those who don't look like him. And on another level, don't look like me. When, exactly, would it stop being cliché, and start being passé? I knew the answer already: when we all dug in for the long miles and big climbs.

"You probably weren't searching the way I was, when you were growing up," I said. "You were surrounded by your family and your achievements, hopping from one success to the next, like stones crossing a stream. I wasn't engaged with celebration and people; I don't remember feeling safe unless I was alone. Or at least alone from other humans. My heart was open to other things, to nature, to the land."

"So, you made friends with trees?" he asked. He was smiling as he trapped his marshmallow between graham crackers and chocolate and slid the stick out.

"Eat your s'more." I squared my shoulders to the fire. I had forged north in my consciousness as much as the trail; I had never soused out these thoughts before.

"Sorry," he said, then swept around us with his stick. "A million trees. Is this a party?"

"Trees are like people. You're hanging in their city crowd, walking down their sidewalk. You vibe with some, not with others," I said, remembering the drive to my grandmother's house, and my eagerness to duck under the immense weeping willow in her front yard, to escape into unseen. And the massive sequoia that I detoured to greet each visit to a certain university campus. "Maybe not all trees are accessible, either. Maybe some trees have spirits, and some don't." Other cultures have names for tree spirits. *Kodama* in Japanese. *Yakshini* in Hindi. *Dryad* in Greek. A tree inhabited by a spirit is protected. If you injure it, you're cursed; I liked that.

"Some dogs mean more than others, some horses. And you never vibe if you're not available, if you're stuck chasing status, surrounded by cheap conversation, ear buds, phones, screens. If you can't slow and open your heart to things that whisper instead of flash and blare." I was the worst example of this, caught up in social media, running with ear buds, even on trails.

We watched the fire, listened to pops and crackles. It seemed the trees leaned silently, warming themselves in the dwindling glow. I breathed in, wondering if I could store calm. Ben bumped his knee against mine. "I'm glad we both hate people-cities," he said.

Chapter Forty

The next morning, we passed *the* sign. One arrow pointed south: *Springer Mtn 1090.5 miles.* Beneath it, another pointed north *Mtn Katahdin 1090.5 miles.*

Ben was right, what I had done seemed somehow less than what I had left to do.

"Alec Kennedy shelter?" Ben asked. "Or bust-it into Boiling Springs?"

I caught myself thinking, *we really should* push twenty miles into Boiling Springs, so we had at least one difficult day. Because that's the kind of hiker I was—the kind who walks twenty-mile days. I noticed my attachment to an intangible thing, an identity, not pausing to re-evaluate what would work for this person I am today, right now. And to struggle, a product of my upbringing, a family idiosyncrasy. Guilt was inversely proportional to toil. If something came easy, I viewed it with suspicion, didn't deserve it. And I never wanted to appear fortunate, explaining away successes with long hours and sweat, otherwise I courted a sledgehammer response from the universe. One of the last conversations I'd had with my dad bonked me like an acorn.

"Just before," he said about his cancer recurrence, while sitting in his recliner, tapping the remote control on his thigh. "I told your mother how great our life was." He looked around his Arizona home, coordinated furniture, pool, well-coiffed patio. "I spend the days however I want." He pursed his lips, stared straight ahead. "It's like I said it out loud and caused all this."

I don't remember how I answered my dad, but I felt as if he had poked a buried bruise aggravating my identical assumptions about the universe and how we influence what happens to us. I viewed worry as a talisman, protecting me from tragedy that untamped joy might summon. I watched Ben striding, unapologetically content, and I wondered what factors combine to produce a person so at ease with success and happiness. Upbringing? Experience? Wiring? Chance? Clean, unburdened hikers crossed our path, from the campground or one of the many road crossings, and I balked at my almost subconscious assessment that their relaxed hikes didn't really count.

"Alec Kennedy tonight," I said, thinking how a leisurely day with Ben would be...pleasant. A bland term—pleasant—something I needed more of. "Not many nights out here this year, so I'll enjoy this last one." I took in blue sky, sunlight, trees. Inhaled the fresh, untainted air. "Plus, then we'll have easy miles to town tomorrow. To shower, comfy bed, and clean room." I silently thanked the universe for the chance to clean up at Pine Grove Furnace. Boiling Springs didn't offer hiker accommodations, and the upscale B&B's didn't cater to AT traffic. Making the reservations, I had said only that we were doctors.

Ben nodded. He had no trouble with *easy*, celebrating success, accepting life's gifts—earned or not—gliding through achievements with grace. I imagined accepting and acknowledging good fortune the way I accepted adversity, like an unexpected opportunity to clean up at a state park. I would practice inviting blessings.

"Anything new with your mom?" Ben asked.

My gaze sling-shotted from a stand of ash to my husband, causing me to trip on a Pennsylvania rock, lurch and stagger several steps. I stopped and stared.

"What?" he said.

I sighed. "She finally called back, if that's what you mean," I said. My mother hadn't returned a call or email for more than six months. I visited regularly after my dad died, but then her communications had spaced out by increasing intervals until she eventually stopped responding altogether. I called at different hours, sent emails, even left messages asking what I had done and if I could apologize. In contrast, the trees suddenly seemed verbose.

"Well?" Ben asked.

"She refused to acknowledge ignoring me. Just chattered away about mundane things," I said. "Then she drops that my cousin is helping drive the rest of her stuff over to her new place in Florida."

"She bought a place in Florida?" Ben asked. She had house-hunted and bought a condo, without a word to me. I shrugged.

"You weren't in the loop?"

"Nope," I said. "I would have helped her look, helped her choose, helped her pack, helped her drive, helped with all of it, but I guess she didn't want me involved."

"Did she give any explanation?"

"When I asked, she said, 'See! You're upset. I knew you would be. That's why I didn't tell you.'" I *was* upset, but not about her moving to Florida. My reactions tossed, unmoored, pitching in my head, looking for a place to land.

"Maybe because we invited her to live with us? She didn't want to say she had decided to move near your brother and grandkids instead?"

"I definitely heard guilt in her voice," I said, "And defensiveness." I sat down on a boulder somewhere on Trents Hill. Ben squeezed next to me. "Maybe I should have been more excited for her." But I stopped, recognizing the old-wound-familiar hurt, like poking an ancient log, revealing a colony of termites that pulps your viscera. She had conditioned me that my authentic responses were wrong; I had no emotional rights. She had no accountability.

"When I got upset, it gave her ammo to blame me. To bend my response into a way to absolve herself," I said, with a sense of liberation; I was rising above this, with the thermal-surfing raptors. "I've been able to sort out that I didn't do anything wrong. She excluded me, and it's normal for me to feel hurt."

Ben looked surprised that I had to evolve into this realization. "Addict thing," he said. "Zero ability to introspect. Nothing is her fault. No responsibility." He tried to hug me around my backpack. "I've said it before: she's text book."

"She's not moving near grandkids," I said, watching straight ahead. "She's moving near enablers; addicts find situations where they can use. My brother and my cousin buy her Dewar's, let her get dysfunctional-drunk, clean up her messes." I picked at leaves and twigs on my socks. "We wouldn't tolerate it."

"Is that why she called? To tell you about Florida?" Ben asked.

"No! She let the Florida thing slip. That's another hurt, she didn't even mean to tell me." I looked up as if the answers grew among foliage.

"Was she going to let you show up in Arizona and find someone else living in the house?" Ben asked. Now my laidback, unflappable husband was worked up. I warmed, watching him rile in my defense.

"She called to ask if I was going to Aunt Bonnie and Uncle Don's fiftieth anniversary party," I said. "Maybe she was going to tell me in person." I took Ben's hand and studied the dirt under his nails. "She asked me if we could room together," I said. "Maybe she's trying to make up for it, be closer."

Skepticism flashed across Ben's face. He didn't understand how despite her chronic illness—her addiction—I still loved her. But her primary relationship was with alcohol, and she sank in and out, like a lover who came and went. When she had distance, she was witty and creative, crafting with paper and dried flowers, woodworking, taking dance classes. That was the woman from years ago, whom I still occasionally glimpsed—the one I yearned for.

A ground squirrel hopped through brush, and distant camp fire scent wafted. My palms rested on cool stone, my feet on earth. I took in the forest in every direction, sheltering under the canopy, encircled by a web of branches and leaves.

Chapter Forty-one

The sign for Alec Kennedy shelter appeared disappointingly soon. Ben would be happy to be home with his newspapers, medical journals, and cold beer, but I missed the feral feeling that sets in after a week, the wilding: shedding of hours and minutes as measures of time; absence of cues dictating sleep and meals; sharpened attention to surroundings. The feeling that would have set in by now but didn't since I was preparing to leave the trail almost as soon as I got on. Still, despite its brevity and proximity to development, this section had offered me escape and resurrected remote memories and thoughts. And I had been able to release a few old wounds to the mountain air.

Wild space was claiming more and more of my life—homes, vacations, time outside work—but I hadn't been sinking in. Not like here. At home, I noticed the leaves outside my windows, and absence of road sounds, and considered the environment a constant contributor to my quality of life, but I rarely quieted to consciously enjoy my surroundings during routine activities. Instead, I dashed forward, associating consequential time in nature with hiking or running. This trip, the strolls through Maryland, relaxed rest stops, long afternoons in camp, had convinced me that slowing down had value, too.

I fell asleep early, a Sookie Stackhouse novel on my chest, listening to small creatures rustle through brush, and trees breathe with the night. I heard the light patter of rain as a cloud drifted past. I woke in no rush to break camp, letting light crawl across the tent. I made coffee and slipped back into my sleeping bag until Ben stirred, noticed me still there, and asked if I was sick. But Boiling Springs was only a short morning's hike away, down into the Cumberland Valley, through roads and yards, and finally over Yellow Beeches Creek. No rush.

"Maybe I can slow down," I said, "In my life."

"You have two speeds," Ben said. "Fast and forward."

"You make me sound like a vector." Arrows and graphs from junior high math class popped into my head. I shrugged. "We picked such an awesome, remote home." I paused, leaned on my poles. "How often do we sit on the deck? Enjoy the view and huge trees on the property?"

"I try," Ben said.

"You're better at it," I admitted. "I'm going set a goal to relax outside for at least twenty minutes a day."

"A goal to not set goals?"

I smacked his pack with my pole.

"I get it. It's not your normal tendency," he said, "So you have to do it with purpose...Bask is what you want."

"Bask is a good word. But I was thinking of bathe," I said, finishing our last climb. "I remembered last night. It's called Forest Bathing."

"Sounds cold," Ben said. "I'm holding out for a Boiling Springs hot shower." He rubbed the back of his neck then looked at his palm as if assessing how much dirt had collected. "Do you think there are hot springs? We can bathe in those."

I was irritated, which sometimes happened when Ben harped on peripheral details. I felt dismissed, like what I was saying wasn't important and wasn't sure if he was avoiding intimate conversation or being obtuse. I sped up to put some distance between us, knowing I would be okay in a few minutes, feel like I overreacted. When people close to me discount my experience, it burns me out of proportion to the situation. My childhood likely engendered this reaction, parents with priorities that eclipsed me: ignored when I burst home after scoring in soccer, told to skip the drama when I described a dinner guest's tongue in my ear, called a baby when I complained about bullying. Maybe while I was enjoying our deck, I could work some of that out.

"Okay, what's Forest Bathing?" Ben asked when he caught me.

"It's a technique to experience biophilia." I looked up and around. "It really sunk in yesterday when we talked about my mother. And this shorter section; less time, short distances, but I still feel like I elevated my physical and emotional health. Just being out, experiencing the woods helped me feel better. It syncs you with the natural world. It's better known in Japan. *Shinrin Yoku*, they call it.

"You slow and experience nature with all your senses: see, smell, listen, touch, taste. You sit, even for fifteen minutes, but it still works. You can move but not purposefully, stay completely engaged. Obviously, this is something I am going to suck at," I said.

"So, you're letting nature occupy your senses?" Ben asked.

"Yep. Reclaiming your place before cement and artificial light and nine-to-five," I said. I held an oak leaf next to my nose to inhale, then touched my tongue to the veined side. I said, "Taste and smell are so connected. They're almost the same."

"So what's the deal?" Ben asked, "Besides getting away from screens, and stress, headaches, eye strain, blah blah." He was a real data guy, and so were lots of physicians. Just feeling more relaxed wasn't enough, they wanted info in their own language.

"It's stuff you've heard before, lowered pulse and blood pressure, better mood, improved concentration and memory." I looked over to gauge his interest. "Now there are data from small studies showing improved sleep in forest bathers." We both noticed longer, deeper slumbers out here.

Some children can ditch their ADHD stimulants if they spend enough time outside, whether forest bathing or not: any space, any activity. They slow down, so rapid-fire tech images and seven-minute sound bites aren't their only stimuli. Nature also enhances creativity, which I accepted without reservation because I always got my best ideas on my trail runs among the live oak, manzanita, and eucalyptus.

We paused at the same time to collapse and tuck our poles to hold hands. Vehicle and lawn mower sounds reached us among the trees, but even after we stepped out into the bright sun and houses, we stayed focused on the greenery. Hedges, yards, gardens. We stood over Yellow Beeches Creek and listened to moving water, watched the slow current, bugs skating next to edge. My overscheduled days, still out of sight, invaded my thoughts, not like the traffic sounds reaching through trees, but more like a grizzly barreling through thick brush.

"It was worth it," I called out, from behind a huge maple, where I'd ducked to change into my town shirt. I ran my hands over the maple's trunk, glanced up at the webbed branches and leaves. "But I prefer the wilder, dirtier, harder sections."

We knocked at the bed and breakfast and a stocky, balding man in a collared, short-sleeve shirt answered, smiling. He looked us up and down, frowned and stepped forward, resting one hand on the door, his belly barring entrance. "We're full, you can sleep over that way under the pavilion roof." He gestured with his free hand.

I gave him our names. He looked us up and down again.

"You said you were doctors."

"We are."

He rolled his eyes. "Fine! Go around back and wash off at the hose. Then get those boots off, leave them and your socks on the back porch."

We turned to skirt around the house.

"And leave those packs out there, too," he said. When I turned, I could see his cheeks had reddened. He worked his jaw, and his pulse pounded away at his temple. I wondered how high his blood pressure had climbed since he'd spied us like litter on his porch. "Isn't no one around here going to take those packs or anything in them." He turned to re-enter the B&B, then called after us, "Or anything else that has to do with that damned Appalachian Trail."

Part VII: The Company You Keep

Chapter Forty-two

"Violet's here? Damn!" The southern drawl spilled from Leroy Smith shelter.

I dropped my book to my chest and listened. Wind nudged through the birch leaves and a bee hummed low to the ground just outside the tent. At the shelter, gear rustled. Spork scraped against pot. Murmurs. I shrank into my sleeping bag but craned my neck and pressed my nose to the screen. Trunks and grass, a shelter wall. Unless I unzipped and poked out my head, I wouldn't know who was there.

It was my independence I was concerned about. Being on foot, with only one way north, meant it was hard to ditch other hikers, mostly yappy or obnoxious ones who hovered and droned, more annoying than the deer flies. One particularly exhausting day, I had trudged an unplanned five miles to avoid a couple who arrived early and set up their tent *inside* the shelters, crowding everyone else out. A bigger deal was the caregiver issue—often concerned older men who became self-appointed escorts. But, if I was being honest, I wanted space from my own caregiving, my tendency to lean into mothering other hikers, whether it was concern about loneliness, physical challenges, or even their nutrition. It was too easy for me to slip into a pace based on codependence rather than my daily mileage goal. Tuning in again to the shelter conversation, I decided this guy seemed different from what I had encountered before.

I caught the newcomer's trail name. Ragweed.

"She's signed in for the night." I heard. He was looking at the register. "Purple ink, like always." He didn't sound like an Indestructible. Older. Likely a thru-hiker though, that drawl out of place in Pennsylvania. The register smacked the wood floor. "You guys seen her?" he asked.

An Indestructible belched.

I watched a daddy long legs pick his way across my rain fly while I tried to warp Ragweed's interest into situations I'd encountered. Maybe he needed a doctor? I never signed *that* in the shelter logs, but trail gossip travelled like smoke, sometimes hundreds of miles, and I often heard about myself. Once, as I rested against my pack in a shelter's shadow, two older men hobbled in, and one immediately loosened his boot and rubbed his ankle. His pal offered, "I heard there's a lady-doctor out here walking. Maybe she'll come along and help ya." Another time, I encountered a group of Indestructibles sprawled by a lake, surrounded by backpacks and Skittles wrappers. One young man saw me approach and jumped up. "You're the doctor, right?" He dropped his Pop Tart, then dropped his shorts, baring a friction wound on his left buttock. "Will you look at this?" he asked, over his shoulder.

I slid my bookmark between pages and weighed my options. Hunker down and continue reading, hoping Ragweed would move on. Wait until shelter occupants settled into their bags, although neither my bladder nor my stomach would likely tolerate that. Emerge and claim I was someone else: Wobbles or Tinkles-on-Trail, or one of the other rare women hiking that section. I wasn't scared, just uncertain. You're more likely to meet an eccentric hiker on the AT than a violent one. Like Jesus, for example, who had wandered the trail in Tennessee, wrapped in a blue tarp and saving souls. Or Walk-On, who completed the AT in one direction, turned around and headed back. Over and over. For years. Still, I would have been more likely to pop out to investigate if Ben were there. But he was meeting me in Delaware Water Gap (DWG), at the New Jersey state line, to accompany me to Stormville, New York.... He had little interest in Pennsylvania's rocks, neighborhoods, and farmland.

"There's no girls here," said an Indestructible.

"There's a tent," another said, in my direction.

"So she *is* here," Ragweed sighed.

Busted. Time for dinner, anyway. I slid out of my sleeping bag, pulled on my fleece, beanie, and purple crocks. Zipping the screen, I wondered about this guy, hiking behind me and annoyed to catch up. As if I wasn't putting enough pressure on myself to push miles. Now I had a pit bull nipping at my heels.

"Violet," I said, offering my hand and issuing a steady, low pitched voice: *doctorvoice*. I looked Ragweed right in the eyes...which had the undesirable effect of disarming me instead of him; his blue eyes looked back, amused, but also kind. He was in his late fifties. A father, probably, and maybe a grandfather.

"Did you say your trail name was Stalker?" I asked.

Before I could pump his hand a second time, Ragweed slipped his palm from mine, pointed his forefinger at me, thumb in the air, and announced, "This is a stick-up. Hand over the book."

I took my first steps on Springer Mountain with Bilbo Baggins as he entered the Misty Mountains. Since then, I had crossed the French Broad with Inman, and Huckleberry Finn had run away somewhere in Tennessee. In *The House on Mango Street,* which had sprung up among the wild ponies in Virginia's Grayson

Highlands, I sat with Sandra Cisneros and embraced my otherness. Tramping with Whitman, stomping with Strayed, and bearing witness from the summit of Mount Washington as the angel Gabriel fell to earth, I gladly toted them all...friends, enemies, teachers, villains, and heroes. They waited for me in camp each night and greeted me in the morning more steadfast than the sun. Indispensable company. No matter how many miles, or how heavy my pack, I never walked without a book.

I chose *The Hobbit* as my first, not because of any kinship I felt with Bilbo, but because I viewed it as disposable, unaware at the time how important books would become during the journey ahead. As a teen, I had read it, and picked up this copy for Ben in a used bookstore. He'd never read the story, a fact I heard slack-jawed, similar to when he reported he never watched baseball. He was from *Oregon*, he said, a progressive and culturally rich state, but one lacking a professional baseball team. *How culturally rich could it be if he hadn't read* The Hobbit? I wondered, searching a dusty corner box, after the bespectacled shop keeper had pointed without looking up from his ledger.

The gilings and loess billowed as I rummaged, finally spying the tattered edition through a fit of sneezing. It held perhaps 150 pages, and the penciled price announced *50¢*. This was long before Peter Jackson had recreated Tolkien onto the big screen, first sensationalizing the *Lord of the Rings* trilogy, and then generating an epic, multi-year production of *The Hobbit* from this tiny book. Back then it was just a tale I had read growing up...and secretively. Not so much to avoid being classified with the Dungeons and Dragons crew, but to avoid notice by them. Three of those boys had bullied me relentlessly during junior high and high school, with name calling, taunts, thefts of text books and supplies. One morning, in hopes that I would be late for a first period exam, they had placed a padlock on my combination locker. To avoid their notice, I enjoyed *The Hobbit* inconspicuously. And here I was again, I had realized in the mist of those first few nights, sequestering myself to read it in the remote Georgia mountains.

Books I brought needed to be disposable because my reading material would fall victim to my quest for lightness—I shed read-pages like a snake sheds its skin. Each morning as I packed up, I tore off the enjoyed section and left it on a shelf or in the register bag. As with many trail practices, I got the idea from Aunt Bonnie and Uncle Don. Aunt Bonnie had brought parts of books, a half-inch of orphaned pages, no beginning or end, no cover, or even cover page, naked spine bound only by the thin strip of yellowed glue.

"Lighter," she said, shrugging.

"What's the title?" I asked, wondering what she deemed worthy to tote.

"Don't know," she answered, flashing her whimsical grin. "Left it home." She said she didn't read much on the trail, only as she fell asleep, and maybe a few pages on rainy days.

I like to know what I'm reading, so I kept track, but, like my Aunt Bonnie, I discarded my covers, as well as spines, and any extra pages. Packing for each leg, I pulled and ripped, thinking of the warning I had so often read: *if you are reading this book without its cover, the author and publisher are likely receiving no compensation*...Perhaps the pirate-division of the FBI was wrong. Perhaps it was harmless, cash-paying, long-distance hikers who created all those naked tomes.

Eventually, I developed a taste for trail books. Engaging, but not so gripping that the story delayed me in the morning. Not dark or scary, as *Geek Love* or *Dracula* had been, affecting my mood during long stretches alone in the woods. This year, I started from Boiling Springs with Kristin Hannah's enchanting feral child Alice from *Magic Hour*, and chugged over the rough ground, eager to spend more time with her in camp. Humor was good: after Hannah, Celia Rivenbark's *Bless your Heart, Tramp*: *And Other*

226

Southern Endearments lifted my spirits through Lehigh Gap, past the zinc mine's bare trees and devastation. But really, anything that would make me think, occupy my mind while meandering between trunks, ferns, and bramble. I mulled for days over abortion accessibility while reading *The Cider House Rules*. I would find myself standing and pulling at my lower lip, oblivious amidst a bustling wilderness. By that time in my career, the hospital's daily emotional trauma had piled up—bleeding emergencies, violent deaths, CPR patients dying under my hands—with no time to recover before racing to the next crisis, and I understood why Wilbur Larch needed escape.

But, in the beginning, I brought *The Hobbit* simply because I wanted a book I wouldn't miss when it didn't come home. So, I grabbed it from a stack on the floor by my bookshelf, pulled off the tattered cover, and tossed it my pack. Despite my hasty choice, Bilbo was great company. I burrowed into my tent each night with halflings, elves, and wizards. After a few days, I identified with this humble creature who embarks on an unexpected and impossible journey. I commiserated with his longings for the comfort of home, and yet, like him, didn't quite fit in, as alienated as I was by the culture of men and medicine. I longed for warm food and a full belly. And while I wouldn't call my fellow hikers dwarves, I often found myself looking around and thinking that these folks were not quite like me. I saw The Indestructibles—before or after college, or on summer break—also retired men, and the occasional woman as part of a couple. Rarely did I meet a hiker my age. So, Bilbo and I, we plodded together, limiting ourselves to "first breakfast," and suffering through the dark, cold, and rain—and a trail that seemed at times to rise up like an adversary. Some evenings I felt certain I would remove my boots and see a hobbit's oversized, hairy feet. I felt grateful that Bilbo's adventures made the Appalachian Trail seem tame: no goblins or trolls, or Volkswagen-sized carnivorous spiders...just mosquitoes, and maybe a snake or a bat. Perhaps most like Bilbo, this quest beckoned in some inexplicable way, and I marveled at the instances of bewildering beauty, and how the world seemed so much bigger than me.

Chapter Forty-three

"What happened with Dr-Kimodo-Dragon-or-whoever?" Ragweed asked as I mixed rehydrated peas into mac 'n' cheese. A piece of beef jerky clung to his beard. Disappointed by the lack of drama, The Indestructibles entertained themselves hurling food and insults at each other. They all ate the same thing: hard salami and sleeves of bagels. And Pop Tarts. I caught a whiff of marijuana. Two sat outside smoking, and one spit tobacco juice into a rusty can.

"Did the finger belong to the missing boy... ; Did a witch doctor get it?" Ragweed had been reading Alexander McCall Smith's *The No. 1 Ladies' Detective Agency* behind me. He knew where to look for the next section because I had written, "Next section Leroy Smith shelter," inadvertently revealing my identity with purple ink. I'm not sure when I started identifying locations for subsequent pages and reading to a point that seemed stoppable—the end of a chapter, story, or essay—attempts to be considerate, and assuming a *next* reader.

The fact that other hikers might read behind me helped avoid the initial haunting, like a draft around my shoulders, that accompanied damaging books. I was tempted to classify myself with Adolf Hitler, Pol Pot, Joseph Stalin, or any of the modern-day despots. I would read these books, as would others who came along. And others behind them. I imagined each aliquot of text to be like an orphaned silver button, catching the eye of a passerby, who stoops to pick it up, examines and admires the shiny object, then slips it into a pocket to carry along. And it came to fruition that these books were treasured on the AT even more than they were at home, where like food they existed as plenty.

One evening I read in the Sam Moore shelter log, "Thanks to whoever left the slices of Pi (referring to the *Life of Pi*, I presumed). Much enjoyed during the long Virginny miles." The reader must have picked up the sections and unknowingly walked past me, leaving the note when he finished. At one campsite, I placed a few pages of Charles Frasier's *Nightwoods* (mostly blank ones from the end) by the fireplace. A thru-hiker caught me later in the day, and handed over the pages, gently chastising me in his Tennessee drawl, "Charles Frasier don't never end up in the fire."

I imagined other hikers reading as I did, snugged inside puffy sleeping bags, savoring words, re-reading. Sometimes I whispered a section to myself, enjoying the cadence. I became far more emotionally engaged with literary characters I met in the forest than at home, where reading was often relegated to just before bed, and where I struggled to get through a few pages before my eyes forced themselves shut.

Apparently on this trip, Alexander McCall Smith had developed a loyal following, literally. Ragweed had been lassoed in, unsuspectingly, first enjoying Precious Ramotswe's backstory and the genesis of her pioneering goal: to become the first lady private detective in Botswana. Then enduring her trials, from confronting the Botswana's "traditional" views of women, to the audacity of chickens who took up residence in her office. Ragweed, like me, had become enamored of the usually mundane, and yet somehow fascinating, day-to-day conundrums Mma Ramotswe endeavored to solve.

"It's Dr. Kimoto," I corrected Ragweed, "I can give you some pages now." I took a bite of my dinner, popping the peas between my teeth...enjoying the texture they gave to this mash of processed cheese and macaroni bunnies.

"There can't be many chapters left," Ragweed said.

"I'm stretching it until DWG. My husband's bringing me the series' second book."

"I'll take what you got. This trail in Pennsylvania—honest to God—if I wouldn't a been reading this book, I woulda gone crazy," Ragweed said.

Pennsylvania had been difficult for me, too. I missed climbs and meditative walking. I found it hard to get lost in my thoughts when I was focused on hopping between jagged eruptions from the dirt, at times teetering like a gymnast, single-footed on a balance beam before I launched forward to the next one. During the smoother stretches, images of my mom crept in—my efforts to cope with her worsening drinking, and her intoxicated antics at my Aunt Bonnie and Uncle Don's fiftieth anniversary party.

I had been optimistic, despite Ben's misgivings, when she had called to ask if I would share a room at the Syracuse gathering. I pictured us dressing together, sharing her cosmetic-hound collection, watching late night TV and news in the morning, struggling through hotel-room coffee. Maybe we would go out to breakfast with my cousins, and she'd order "french toast with *real* maple syrup," like she used to.

My flight had landed late afternoon, the earliest I could get to the east coast. I rushed down the hotel hallway, eager to see my mom and to surprise my aunt and uncle. When I pushed open the door, my mom stood red-eyed, between the queen beds, swirling a glass of Dewar's and engrossed in a talk show.

I forced a smile and tried to halt judgment, tried to prevent myself from reacting out loud and tainting the evening.

"There you are," she said, clinking her ice and slurping. "I wondered if you were going to make it."

"Nice to see you, too," I said, moving her Dewar's jug from the counter so I could set down my bag. "Everyone here?"

"Everyone but you," she said, raising her glass to me. "So here I am."

My face reddened. When I was a child, I hadn't folded the sheets right; let shirts wrinkle in the dryer; hadn't guessed my brother needed a ride home from somewhere; made the wrong dinner. Like then, she wouldn't acknowledge what it took to get to the party: time, expense, or even my excitement. Instead she found her excuse, the millstone she could exploit to rationalize her early drinking. I finally recognized the addict-behavior in real-time, but I still couldn't force the gut-roil to vacate my body.

Over dinner I congratulated my aunt and uncle and caught up with my cousins, trying to ignore my slurring mother circling the room like the arm of clock, and repeating herself over and over. "What I can't understand is why aren't we dancing? Where's the band?" Or demanding from the bartender, each go round, that he name which teams played ball on the TV behind him. To his credit, he politely answered, every time.

After the party, we headed to the wing where most of the out of towners had rooms. Exhausted, I hoped to crawl into bed. But my mom barged in, drink in hand, and kicked off her heels. She wedged the door open and called up and down the hall if anyone needed a room for the night. I slid out to corral her just in time to see her corner two strangers and offer them a place to sleep. When they politely declined, she pointed the index finger of her drink hand and her stockinged foot at the woman and said, "Oh come on, you don't want to stay with him! Come into 403!"

I must have looked horrified because my cousin and his daughter quietly flanked me and invited me to go home with them. Guilt descended as I contemplated abandoning our girls' weekend. My internal dialogue whirled: my mom had ruined the weekend, not me, but shame still squeezed itself in, like a cockroach flattening under a door. Even a year later, on Pennsylvania's Appalachian Trail, I struggled with aligning my emotional response with my clinical understanding of addiction and my psychological understanding of its effects on loved ones.

I'm not sure if I somehow willed it to happen, or the trail was looking out for me, but about then I slipped sideways on a rock and rolled over on my left ankle, which yanked my thoughts back to the serrated track. I hobbled forward on my stinging foot, jarred but grounded, and recommitted to my emotional boundaries. The rest of the day, I allowed the rocky earth's unlikely reprieve to command my attention.

Pennsylvania had some high points, the halfway landmark, for one. I loved Boiling Springs, a tiny and quaint town, and the Hawk Mountain Center for Raptor Research just north of Port Clinton. The cornfields and back yards in the Cumberland Valley felt homey. I visited a cousin, then living in Philadelphia, who had provided a respite just north of Lehigh Gap. But I was happy to cross into New Jersey.

"Maybe I can get a book in Delaware Water Gap," Ragweed said, rolling out his sleeping bag, making sure to put his headlamp on his bunched-jacket pillow. "Before this I never carried a book," he admitted.

It was all I could do to avoid spitting a pea at him. I thought of books to the trail like one of those esoteric comparisons from the high school SAT tests. "Pickup truck is to banana, as umbrella is to...." Except it was more obvious: books are to hiking, like truffle oil is to french fries, like chocolate is to peanut butter, like sunshine is to summer. Not only did I enjoy books *on* the trail but selecting AT books had become part of my preparation ritual. I planned a bookstore trip like my trip to REI. But it was often unnecessary, since a stack of potential choices waited expectantly on the floor next to my overflowing book shelf. I picked them up all year as I encountered them... . *That looks perfect for the trail.*

Chapter Forty-four

I popped to my feet from the curb outside my DWG hotel, two hands in the air, hot drink in both, and shimmied a little, hoping not to spill but mostly hoping the approaching maroon minivan was Ben's airport shuttle.

"Excuuuse me!" Ben said, flapping a map out the open window. "I'm looking for the Apple-aay-chian Tray-el." I laughed so hard I splashed coffee anyway.

The next morning, we set out hand-in-hand following the AT blazes across the water gap, the border between Pennsylvania and New Jersey. The I-80 bridge practically bowed with the volume of cars and semis roaring by, vibrating under our feet, exhaust wafting into our faces. We finally gave up talking, and hustled, eager for the forest's gentler atmosphere.

Finally, green light closed around us. Segments like the Cumberland Valley and Delaware Water Gap bridge would inevitably interrupt a footpath running the entire eastern seaboard, but each disruption seemed to occupy disproportionate place despite being a mere cobblestone in the 2000-plus forest miles.

"An appalling start to New Jersey," Ben announced as we climbed up Kittatinny Mountain, since he felt liberated to skip sections he perceived as subpar. He was doubly miffed at the DWG I-80 bridge.

But the traverse along Kittatinny Mountain met all expectations, affording unexpected views of rolling

235

green hills punctuated with open fields and farm houses. Even being raised in neighboring New York State, even though New Jersey held the title of "Garden State," I was always taken aback by its un-urban nature. Our first overnight was an easy ten miles to the Mohican Outdoor Center (MOC), so we lunched for two hours at Sunfish Pond. I was happy to ease up on the pace, plus we chomped on new food: tofu and salmon jerky with nut-flour crackers. Novel tastes and textures broke up monotony. Ben stretched out his long legs and I contemplated dunking my feet while we caught up.

Ben had finally made peace with the senior physicians' club's sabotage of the kidney transplant service. Our community seemed unwilling to wrench free from outdated paradigms, unwilling to embrace new people and new ideas, and potential brought by change.

"Hey, you know what's different?" Ben asked, propping himself up on his elbows. "Scuttlebutt around the hospital about the new residency program director."

"What are people saying?" I asked, watching pond skeeters zip across water.

"The program needs to quit being so myopic," he said.

For the first time since I'd started, I looked ahead with optimism about educating the next generation of doctors. Maybe I wouldn't feel squelched every time I introduced something new, like shifting the schedule to allow consistent hospital coverage, or designing curriculums in women's health and medical ecology. Tiny insects hovered over a ripple on the water's surface while I considered possibilities. A frog croaked rhythmically to my right, then *splash*! Insects vanished, leaving me and my thoughts and the crumbs from my novel lunch.

"So what's ahead?" Ben asked, as he extended his collapsed hiking poles. New Jersey's seventy miles held High Point State Park. And in New York, we would remove our packs to navigate the well-known Lemon

Squeezer, a narrow passage between two boulders, then pass through Harriman State Park with its view of the Manhattan sky line, and Bear Mountain where we would cross the Hudson River.

At Mohican Outdoor Center, while I set up camp, Ben investigated the shelter and found Snickers and M&Ms...really, he was more like Bilbo than I was. We finished up our evening routine and curled up together in our bags.

"You brought a hardback?" I asked, watching him extract *The Girl with the Dragon Tattoo* and set it on his sleeping bag. "That must weigh pounds!"

He shrugged.

"Well, you're not going to leave any sections of that behind," I said. "Unless you have a hatchet." I rooted around for the next Mma Ramotswe novel, *Tears of the Giraffe,* and realized that I hadn't mentioned Ragweed.

"It works, leaving parts behind," Ben said, cracking open his tome.

"Not always."

"Oh, hogging?"

I pulled my camp towel over my face.

The year we walked through Virginia, I carried *Scoot over Skinny: The Fat Nonfiction Anthology,* a collection of essays about being overweight in America—personal experience, as well as sociologic and medical perspectives. A friend had gifted it, probably because she knew I was perpetually working on two things: being thinner, and not thinking about being thinner. Despite my education, I had been enslaved like most American women by the culture of thinness and dieting.

The first essay, "Letting Myself Go," described Sallie Tisdale's efforts to achieve contentment, regardless of the number on the scale. I wanted to burst free, too, like a soft, luscious belly popping a button, liberating my mind to make room for intellectual and philosophical ruminations. The subsequent essays, including pieces by David Sedaris, Annie LaMott, and Atul Gawande, appeared equally sage, so the book became trail approved. Thinner, of course, as it shed its cover and excess pages.

"What about Atul Gawande?" Ben had asked, as we shoveled in double portions of black beans and rice at Manassas Gap shelter, just outside Shenandoah National Park.

"Bariatric surgery, such a brainiac," I said.

"And David Sedaris?" he asked. Ben is a devout fan.

"It's called "A Shiner Like a Diamond," about his father's size-ism...Whatever you call it," I said. We thought about it.

"Hate," we said at the same time.

A voice interrupted from behind us. "Are you the one who left the article on hogging?"

I stared straight ahead for a beat, then turned slowly. *Damnit.*

The Indestructible emptied a tuna pouch into Raman noodles. A leaf poked out from his overgrown blond hair. In my head, I declared him "impressionable," at the same time realizing that, if he was out here walking alone, he was probably more worldly than I gave him credit for. But he looked so young. To make matters worse, he called himself Cricket.

"The essay about having sex with larger women?" I asked, hoping there had been some mistake, but knowing there wasn't.

"Is that real? Doing that?" Cricket poked and stirred his dinner, then let his tiny alcohol stove burn out. He wore shorts and sandals, and a ripped, filthy blue t-shirt, looking emaciated after so many miles sustained on ramen and tuna.

The ninth essay was called "Big Game Hunters." I had read it two nights before and left it—without thinking, obviously. The author, Sarah Fenske, had interviewed men who pick up large women expressly to degrade them during sex and used the despicable term "hogging." If the essay itself had upset me, the idea that I had introduced this young man to such misogyny made me physically ill.

Hikers had responsibilities to each other. I took this seriously, as I'm sure other hikers did, packing out garbage, leaving the privy clean, sweeping the shelter, warning about hazards. When asked, I provided medical advice, and shared rides, and sometimes paid for meals, since I knew the younger ones had tight budgets. So how had I left that pile of crap in a shelter? What a flail. My Virginia-AT carelessness stayed with me even beyond Harper's Ferry. I usually toted upsetting events from home to the AT, not vice versa, and yet this had really stuck with me.

My consistent concern with younger folks was a manifestation of compulsive caregiving, one of the few lingering behaviors born of being the oldest child of an ill parent and an addict that I embraced. From a young age, I carried too much responsibility, whether it be cleaning, laundry, or hauling dinners out of the freezer to feed us. It's probably what drove me to become a physician and why I never considered *not* teaching. Patients, students, residents, more people to take care of—and, at times, more neurotic ownership of issues that weren't mine.

At work, what preoccupied me most, what I thought I owned as much as their medical knowledge and patient care, was trying to warp the intense, battering-ram work environment into one that didn't pile trauma upon trauma, undermining residents' future mental health. It was me versus Goliath, raging against decades and tradition, frenetic schedules and merciless deaths. I was set up to fail and too often left with an ache like a poorly healed bone.

One afternoon I worked with an intern who faced her first death, a cancer patient named Carl. The intern and I had walked to the floor together, quietly reviewing the steps to "pronounce." In the room, she leaned over

Carl's chest, her stethoscope in her right hand, auscultating Carl's still heart. The first death on the wards is hard, even when it's expected. And watching the intern, I had remembered the first patient who had died under my hands. I was a medical student, and the patient's name was MaryAnn. Bedside, I watched her last breaths through her dry, cracked lips, her chest's heaves. When I noticed the multicolored, crocheted blanket stretched across the foot of her bed, she became my grandmother who had died in a hospital a year before. Grief erupted into my body, and I vibrated at MaryAnn's bedside, desperate to wet her lips with the sponge lollies, my fingertips. With *anything* to comfort her. But my feet rooted to the floor, taking cues from the rest of the standoffish team. I surreptitiously rested my hand on her arm.

Afterward, I tagged along behind the residents, their shoulders straight, white coats trailing. I acted steely and clinical, afraid to appear unprofessional, volunteering to check another patient's blood pressure, stop in the library to look up treatments for hepatitis, and then finally to fetch burgers and frosties from the Wendy's across the street. It was one of many traumas I would tamp down, convincing myself that I was alright, traumas that would come up later as emotional fragility, irritation, sleepless nights. I had found a loving and supportive partner, who faced many of the same stressors, and I had found the woods, helping me heal and regenerate. I didn't know how others coped but at the time physicians had the highest divorce and suicide rates of any vocation in the country, so I suspect they didn't.

At Carl's bedside, the intern's pager sounded, and I watched red-faced, as she repeatedly reached down with her left hand to silence the ER calls about the almost-vacant bed. As she recorded the time of Carl's death, in my fog of anger, I pictured the bed careening to the wall, tilting up, sliding his body through a dumbwaiter to the morgue, and then empty, returning

240

to its place, flashing a green light to indicate availability for the next admission. The intern hurried toward the staircase to write admission orders for the ER patient. I stopped her to ask, "How are you feeling? You should take time to process this death."

"I've got this ER patient," the intern said, "And then there's a woman in labor on the fourth floor. Plus a C-section at four-thirty."

"Maybe this evening, or weekend, think this through. Really feel it," I said. Because if she didn't, it would stay with her, piled with other deaths, other fountains of blood, other lifeless eyes she is sure to see in her career. Maybe she'll bury it with alcohol or drugs, or maybe it will bubble up as anger or anxiety directed at her coworkers, or at her spouse or her family. The ones she loves the most.

She raced down the stairs, her voice echoing in the stairwell, as she called back, "I'll process later."

I couldn't force her, or fret about it. I needed to let it go, like releasing a samara—a maple helicopter seed—to the wind, knowing you might not see what happens after it begins its dance on the breeze, that it might or might not float past you again, might land and take root, grow into a mighty force, rot buried in mud, or dash itself against a boulder, as all the forces of the universe and the seed's own relationship to flight and gravity conspire to determine its path.

I was getting better at not assuming too much responsibility. At work. In my life. And I was finally releasing myself from my mom's choices, viewing her behavior as symptoms of her chronic illness. The young hiker who had found my discarded essay would have to spiral along, making his own relationship to women and the world.

At Manassas Gap, I watched Cricket finish a bag of jelly beans and crinkled the wrapper, throwing it in the fire pit. I felt conflicted. If he was adult enough to be walking the Appalachian Trail, he was adult enough to form his own opinions about women and sex. And he was on the trail alone, so maybe he operated independently of his peers' opinions. Regardless, here I was again, taking on too much responsibility for other people's reactions to the disturbing essay. My part: the piece was packed with disrespect and hate, and I had left it like litter, an eyesore, to impact other hikers' experience.

"I'm sorry I left that essay. I should have thrown it in the fire," I said to Cricket.

"No worries," he answered, shrugging as he hung his food under a tuna can on the shelter's line, laid out his sleeping bag, and crawled in. "I did."

Part VIII: Falling Down Is Better than Melting Down

Chapter Forty-five

The shuttle dropped me at NY Rte. 52, about twenty AT-miles from Connecticut's state line. I hoped to traverse Connecticut and Massachusetts, and then Vermont, to Rte. 11/30, near Manchester Center. I dug in right away, shooting for fifteen miles by late afternoon. I didn't plan to hurry the whole section but wanted time on this day for a stop around mile twelve. After that, I had three miles to the Appalachian Trail Train Station, where hikers could hop aboard to chug thirty miles straight into New York City. But not me. I was shooting for the garden center nearby that allowed camping. By trail-overnight standards, it seemed luxurious, tucking in among shelves of marigolds, petunias...and maybe some violets.

My reaction to New York's ninety miles had been subdued, though it was my home state. No nostalgia, no unique connection to the land. The most intense emotion I experienced was frustration, and it had been the year before, on what I had assumed would be an "easy" ten miles between High Point and Pochuk shelters. Instead, the track had been maddening, climbing through and over rocks, at one point leading me to a precipice. I stared over the cliff, walked methodically around the edge, backtracked, and finding myself at the same spot, felt so outraged that I hurled my pack over the ledge with a primal scream. It turned out to be the right direction because I heard a hail from below, "Fore!" And then another voice, "Fangs or no fangs, I'm not carrying that up for you!" I peered down to see two men climbing, demonstrating the way down.

Maybe I had processed my thoughts and attachments amidst vivid Maryland memories. Or maybe the proximity to NYC made this part of state seem unfamiliar. The city had always been foreign geography—a crowded, complicated behemoth that we braved on rare days to see Yankee games, and eventually evolving into the daunting abyss where my father vanished when he received cancer treatment at Sloan-Kettering. Whatever the reason, in the two seasons I walked in New York State, I recall only my usual exhale into the forest, and—excepting my melt down—surprise at the boulder obstacles.

Until now. Today I would encounter the Dover Oak, a remarkable three-hundred-year-old tree, reputed to be the oldest on the Appalachian Trail, who stood her ground perilously close to West Dover Road. I arrived with enough time to admire her weathered trunk, twenty-foot girth, and fanned branches. Logs rested around her base, and I sank down to take her in, using all five senses. At home, spending twenty minutes forest bathing had been hit or miss, work, exercise, family, pets, always pulling me away. But on the AT, it was easy, with only occasional road sounds to disrupt my experience, and, even then, I was simply reminded of how a single tree can remove 4.5 kg per year of car pollution, otherwise known as particulate matter (like dust, soot, and smoke), which according to the WHO increases incidence of asthma, lung disease, cancer, heart attacks, and strokes. I imagined this sprawling, ancient oak removing far more.

The afternoon advanced with the sun edging west through the mass of leaves. I rested my back against a log to eat a late lunch. An hour passed quickly, probably more like a blink to a three-hundred-year-old tree. The acorn that birthed the Dover Oak had fallen when the Mahicans, part of the Algonquin tribe, had

245

traversed and worked this land, missing the seed as they foraged for stew pot or coarse flour. It had germinated when the British viewed the eastern seaboard as a colony; sprouted as British and French skirmished with each other and the indigenous people for control. The sapling survived quests for firewood and shelter material, and watched as George Washington, in 1778, set up his Fredericksburg blockade to contain the British in New York City. Offered shade to local soldiers who took up muskets to join the Union Army's Fifth New York Regiment. This tree had survived how many peoples? How many conflicts for this terra? Conflicts for rights to claim food, water, fuel, resources from the earth in which its roots condignly reached and spread.

The battle is insidious now, and the tree is warrior, absorbing particulate matter from the army of cars and filtering swarms of carbon dioxide, carbon monoxide, nitrogen oxides, and ozone molecules, releasing the oxygen we breathe. Defending soil against floods and withstanding assaults of heat and drought as the climate warps with increasing speed. I followed a leaf as it dipped and swerved, descending its circuitous, unhurried journey to earth, thought about the oak's web of roots, of life. Despite its struggle, the Dover Oak persisted—persists—steady and sturdy, yet gentle enough to offer a lone Appalachian Trail hiker solace and shade on her sojourn north.

Chapter Forty-six

The next day, I ambled alongside Connecticut's Housatonic River where rushing water masked my footfalls and elegant foliage hung like soothing décor. I wished Ben had been there. Several months before, his sixty-two-year-old pristinely healthy, meticulously disciplined, yoga-performing mother had died. When he received the call, shared the impossible news, I croaked in reply.

Ben's parents had awakened late during a resort getaway, a welcome break from the long hours spent running their small business. Dennis had gone to the kitchen for coffee, amidst Susan's jokes about his sluggish pace, and when he got back, bearing a cup in each hand, she lay unresponsive. That was it: fine when he left, gone when he returned.

Since then, Ben had drudged through his days mired by grief. He wore exhaustion home like an article of clothing, weighting his shoulders, and rarely shed his darkly circled eyes and tight mouth. I worried he would become sick.

Forest would be the best setting for Ben, time away from the undertow of hospital, dialysis unit, clinic, phone calls, meetings. A novel place that would be absent familiar images and reminders. Moving among trees lowers cortisol levels which would alleviate feelings of stress and anger, decrease brooding, and elevate his mood. It would also increase his immune function since cortisol is a steroid which suppresses white blood cell activity. White blood cells, in particular natural killer (NK) cells, fight infection by attacking viruses and harmful bacteria. Studies in Japan have shown that NK cell activity increases by as much as fifty percent after forest bathing, an effect lasting up to thirty days. This immune boost is likely augmented by a combination of other, less understood terpene effects. Ben frequently remarked how rarely I caught colds or other viruses, and I had attributed it to running. I now suspected *trail* running kept me healthy, the nearly daily break to breathe deeply among leafed and needled trees.

None of this convinced Ben to accompany me from New York to Vermont, but he was a hard sell. Medicine's bustle helped him bury his grief, and he worried that psychic down time would allow his pain to flood like a river through an abandoned beaver dam. And he struggled with the mental energy it would take to wrench himself from his autopilot routine. Eventually I convinced him to join me for my last days, into Vermont.

We had each lost a parent, and under different circumstances. Ben's mother without warning—without words her family would have no doubt wanted her to hear—transformed from wisecracking and vital to pale and still, in less time than it took to pour a cup of coffee. My father under lingering illness, months of struggle against the inevitable march of his disease, cruel stretches of uncertainty, equally cruel flickers of hope. I sat by his hospital bed in his last days, after the blood clot to his lungs had stolen his breath, his consciousness, his comfort. In the shadowed room lit only by the slatted window, events of the last eighteen months replayed... . What should I have done differently, to make it easier for him? With each strained inhalation, the stuffed bear I had brought jerked up and down on his chest, his skin grayed, melting away from his once robust face. I wished the room didn't reek of hospital. Wished the morphine delivery worked better. Wished the oxygen mask didn't cut ugly red welts into his cheeks. I adjusted the plastic, hoping the skin would re-plump and banish the assault, banish my torment.

My brother came and went from the dark room, pacing at times, calling nurses and doctors, insisting on procedures, blood transfusions, labs, and studies, any last action that would prolong my father's life, help him breathe easy and go home with us again, so we could laugh at Seinfeld re-runs. Complain about the Yankees. Crunch peenits.

Bedside, my own pain hovered at times, but more and more it rose and evaporated from my skin, like pool water off the macadam when I was a child, and I knew that we should let go. If my father woke, he would face weeks of agonizing bone pain, wasting, incontinence, confusion, the tortuous death that metastatic cancer brings. A good doctor would want to spare him that. Would a good daughter? I watched my brother, wondering if he was loving our father better. Was my mother, sipping coffee by the window, harboring silent indictment, thinking I was checking out to walk the dog again? I treaded water, my toes straining for a place to rest. I wanted to want what a good daughter would want. Could a good daughter and a good doctor want the same thing?

Was this better? To have time for thought, for process, for preparation, as sorrowful as it was. To say what you needed to say, or what you needed your loved one to hear. Or was it simply an opportunity to make mistakes, second guess, judge myself for disappointing both parents, for everything else I was sure I had done wrong. Despite his abrupt loss, I suspected that Ben allowed himself flashes of relief that he was spared months of dread, of waiting.

But both losses had something in common: surprise. My father's unlikely cancer recurrence, and Ben's mother's cardiac arrest. Two parents, too young and healthy. It struck me, that both of us physicians, experts in life and death, could not have predicted or prevented either event. But then I started to climb, over Silver Hill and Bread Loaf Mountain, ground falling away behind my metronomic steps, and my thoughts left for wherever they go when my poles and legs and breaths all synched, and I inhaled forest. The afternoon slipped away.

Chapter Forty-seven

After two days in Connecticut, I climbed Bear Mountain and crossed into Massachusetts. I waffled about whether to stay at Sages Ravine Campsite or push farther. According to AT guides, Sages had tent platforms which I avoided because the wood pushed against my hips and heels despite my upgraded inflatable ground pad. I relished sleep on the AT, where my puffy sleeping bag called to my tired muscles and joints, and night sounds lulled me. Where I rarely woke before dawn.

At home, anxious thoughts, alternating between simmer and gush, often woke me. Some nights, waking to vague worry-sensation, causing me to mentally grope to haul up the issue like a fish, so it could then flop around. The thought-thumping would spread to my body so that, despite my pillow top mattress, I lay sleepless until about thirty minutes before my alarm would sound. Obviously, fewer causes for worry existed on the trail, and intense exercise mitigated anxiety and just-plain made me tired, but the forest itself contributed to my circadian coma.

A forest walk of one to two hours increases sleep time and quality, especially if people walk in the afternoon. Many factors contribute and among them are exposure to natural light rather than LED, screens, or fluorescents, and bathing in green, a relaxing color. Plus, both chemicals released by plants and trees, and contact with soil bacteria *Mycobacterium vaccae* cause relaxation by activating the vagal nerve. So I tucked in with a lower pulse, blood pressure, and anxiety level. Sounds also make a difference, since people tend to turn inward (as in brooding and self-criticism) when listening to urban sounds like sirens and vehicles, and outward (as in relaxation) with natural sounds like wind, birds, and especially water. At Sage Ravine, Sawmill Brook spilled through.

The lush, mossy gorge split by cascading mountain water, and populated with original-growth timber convinced me, wooden tent platforms or not. Descending Bear Mountain, I pushed away projections about sore hips and heels. But by the time I saw the campsite sign I was still worked up—or at least as worked up as I get on the AT—only to learn that there are some things I never learn. Expectations. In this case, too pessimistic: some tent spaces allowed me to set up on dirt. Small comforts.

By late afternoon, I rested in the shady, magical ravine, among a rich community of mosses ranging from dark greens to neons, and sometimes with tiny, orange antennae. Mosses make me think of pillows, spongy and settling, and I ran my fingers over reachable patches, inhaled the smell of ancient. Mosses were the first plants on earth, about 450 million years old. They don't have much nutritional value for humans, but reindeer eat them because they contain a substance that generates an exothermic (radiating heat) reaction in their blood, helping on frigid days. The old adage about placing moss on wounds has merit because mosses have antiseptic properties, and collectively, mosses remove more carbon dioxide from the atmosphere than trees. All this oxygen was surely pinking my cheeks.

I wandered, looking for old growth and spied spectacular beech, white pine and hemlock, ancestors tending a forgotten place. Dense trunks stretched around and above. I stared up for so long my neck cricked, but the spasm didn't diminish my awe-generated connectedness. When the sun lowered and mosquitoes began their irksome whine, I retired, certain to sleep like a log, which sounds cheesy, but completely setting-appropriate. A few days would bring me to Dalton, Massachusetts, where Ben would join me, and hopefully awe would crowd out his grief.

Chapter Forty-eight

We headed out as the sun rose, aiming for Bascom Lodge on the summit of Mount Greylock. The day held climbs: Crystal, North, and Saddle Ball Mountains, and finally Mount Greylock which crested at 3500 feet, practically alpine compared to the last few states. Passing through the lobby, the motel's owner offered warnings.

"Be careful out there, yes?" he asked in an accent that suggested the Indian subcontinent was his birthplace. Ben mentioned we were doctors. The man ran his fingers through a mop of black hair.

"Predators don't care what you do for a living. Or snakes."

"Predators?" I asked. "Mountain lions? Bears?"

"Or like those guys?" Ben pointed to photocopied mug shots tacked to a bulletin board, identifying the three men convicted of sex crimes in motel residence.

I leaned in, squinting.

"No mountain lions in Massachusetts," the man said. "That is for sure. But we do have bears." He raised his hands like claws, maybe trying to get our attention away from the mug shots. "Always hungry, those bears."

254

"Has it been like you expected?" Ben asked, carrying his poles in one hand on a flat section along Crystal and North Mountains.

"You know how that goes," I said. "It's always harder, easier, wetter, hotter, buggier, rockier, steeper, flatter than you expect," I said.

Ben nodded. "Expectations sneak in the back door."

"Or under the house," I said. "Rattlesnakes that slither and lurk and bite your ankle when you least expect it." We stepped over a log that had fallen across the trail. "Sometimes it works out great." I told him about Sages Ravine.

On the north side of Chester, the woods began I earnest, properties appearing less and less groomed, wilding with each step north. I admired the leafed out maple and oak, and undergrowth grew thick. It looked and smelled like late spring where I had grown up. Except for the long, tawny body that slinked from the west edge of the trail, about a dozen yards ahead. She slid low to ground, almost liquid, flowing through a ray of sun. Her paws fell noiselessly. Sinew and muscle flexed under her shimmering gold and tan coat. She never turned her head. Majestic is what she was. As I lifted my hand to point, the graceful, swaying, impossibly long tail vanished into the verdant brush.

"No mountain lions," I whispered, hand still in the air, feeling puny yet cataloging the sight, so I couldn't talk myself out of it later.

"None," Ben whispered back.

We stopped for a late lunch at Mark Noepel lean-to, where I had expected I would need rest given the climbs, and my expectations were right on this time. I tugged off my boots, peeled off my already filthy socks, and elevated my feet on my pack while I ate trail-mix and downed a liter of iodinated water. Ben flipped through the register.

"Didn't expect to see a mountain lion," I said.

"What mountain lion?" Ben said.

"On that subject...I plan to focus on situations that turn out better than I thought," I said, scanning trees and bramble outside the lean to. Since not-seeing the mountain lion, I'd been more vigilant. They seemed more formidable than the raccoon-like black bears; a lion conflict could be more about me-as-food, rather than stealing my food.

"Like Sages?"

"And like the mountain lion. In particular, I have been thinking about the new residency director. I didn't see this coming."

"You mean he's an outsider?" Ben asked.

I pulled my feet from my pack, bent my legs under me and twisted to look at Ben. "I didn't expect a change in leadership. Didn't expect a guy as experienced and forward-thinking choosing to work outside a big city. Didn't expect to be appreciated." The new program director, Clark, had experience in medical economics, injected new ideas and energy, and his booming voice seemed to underscore his enthusiasm. He had poured over my curriculum work, organized by year, subject and location. He whistled under his breath, and a few weeks later offered a promotion to associate director.

"Did he say when you'll get your new position?"

"He said he needs to work out pay and details of the Kaiser partnership." The program was partnering with a local Health Maintenance Organization (HMO) to expand the patient base to include insured patients. And for the infusion of funds. "I'm not in a rush. It's just nice to be treated with respect."

Ben nodded, then pointed to an entry in the log. "You can see Bascom Lodge when the trail zigs and zags along the ridge," he said. "Every time you re-zag it's closer."

"Let's get zagging," I said, as we headed for another night with a shower and a bed. "What a cushy hike."

Chapter Forty-nine

I face planted a quarter mile shy of Story Spring shelter. A gnat had been buzzing my nose, diving and hovering, until, cross-eyed, I tripped over a root and pitched forward into black, sucking mire serving as the Appalachian Trail. I lay sprawled, at eye level with a pile of moose dung. When I extricated myself, my hands, forearms, torso, legs all wore greasy sludge.

"My face is covered with mud, isn't it?" I asked Ben.

"Yup," he said, swatting a mosquito on his neck. He extracted a stuck boot with each step.

"How does such a large animal make such tiny little poops?" I asked, squatting to wiggle my caked palms in a puddle, scanning the marsh for one of the giants among the bony trees and reeds. "I mean, the piles are moose-sized, the height of traffic cones, but the pellets themselves, they look like a rabbit left them." I wiped my hands on my butt, the only swatch of clothing not covered in muck. "Maybe they *are* piles of rabbit pellets," I added. "Maybe huge, one-ton were-rabbits are stalking us right now." Mud on my chin and cheeks tightened and cracked when I smiled. I hung on to the happy facial expression in case it improved my mood.

June in Vermont is termed "mud season," a phenomenon I had clearly underestimated. The path, a generous term, stretched mucky and dark for as far north as we could see. Ground cover of mossy stones and downed trunks stretched on either side, preventing detours which is why dark goop had covered me to my knees even before I fell. My hip flexors ached from lifting sodden boots.

In the last few miles, we had passed several stagnant basins caused by beaver dams, hosting swarms of black flies and mosquitoes like little dive-bombing planes. I sang, cracking facial clay, but it disrupted the maddening whine around my ears. I wedged my hiking poles under my arms, leaving my hands free to swat at the eyeball-swooping insects.

Ben wore an uncharacteristic scowl. "We're done," he said, "We're sleeping in town. Bed. Hot shower. Tomorrow night."

"Expectations like that," I warned, "Could be disastrous." In the last day, we had spent as much energy fending off fatigue and crabbiness, as we had hiking. Nothing makes a trail-day worse than a bitter, angry final few miles. Resentment gathered like the mud on boots, each stride falling heavier onto earth, feeling heavier wrenching out of earth.

"I mean it. Tomorrow night. Promise." He nodded and slogged off. I squished behind, swatting and slipping after him.

At Story Spring shelter, before I even sat down, Ben had reached into my pack's outer pocket for the maps. He perched on the shelter's edge and pulled one knee under his chin. He scanned map to guide book, guidebook to map.

"The Appalachian Trail goes through Stratton Mountain Ski Area. It says on weekends the gondola runs down to Stratton Village." Ben tapped his finger on the map. "Tomorrow's Saturday! What luck!"

I seethed around camp, hating the trail and hating myself for hating the trail. My fingernails ached as I pried at my swollen, hardened laces. Ordinarily I would have loved sitting by the adjacent gurgling stream, loved cool water on my face, soaking my feet, and rubbing mud off my legs, pulling my "clean" camp clothes. Instead, I sat next to the water and stewed, swatting at mosquitoes, and wondering how I let myself slip into this gloomy dungeon. *Listen to the stream and the quiet. Smell the pine.* I was lucky to be able spend this time in the wilderness, to have this time with Ben. I would feel better in the morning. And especially after a hot shower, full belly, and bed. But if I expected town tomorrow, and we were stuck out here, I would feel even worse. If that was possible.

I handed Ben his camp mug filled with steaming corn chowder, kernels floating. Calories would help.

"We climb Stratton Mountain tomorrow—What is that? Eight miles?—then we'll be home free." Ben beamed. "No problem. Tomorrow. Shower." He nodded with each word. "Pizza. Beer. Bed...Did I mention beer?"

Ben's confidence was contagious, and I watched the sun set through isolated, fluffy, pink clouds, feeling like a child drifting off under a rainbow comforter and unicorn mobile.

At 3:30 AM my eyes flew open to thickening air: I instinctively knew. *One Mississippi, two Mississippi, three...rumble, boom, grrrooowl. Shit.* At the next flash, I counted again. Cold creeped into our snug space. I imagined gray sky and gusts, and sheets of rain. "It's going to rain," I whispered, pressing my nose into Ben's shoulder. "Not just rain. Storm. Bluster...Challenge us to walk even an inch, much less summit Mount Stratton."

"How can you tell?" he whispered back. He was always so patient when I woke him.

"I'm *from* here, from right next door to Vermont," I answered. "I know when it's going to rain. Drizzle. Dump." Ben's sleeping bag rustled. "It's going to dump."

"We like the tent in the rain," Ben said. "Let's curl up and enjoy the next few hours."

"We should take it down and load into the shelter. I don't want to carry the extra pounds of wet gear," I said.

"Who cares?" Ben said. "Eight miles to the summit? Two thousand feet? No big deal. Then we'll ski-lift down and be inside."

I sniffed the air and shook my head. "You don't get it. It's electrical. The gondola won't be running."

Shortly after, hammering rain woke me and I peeked out. Water pooled and a small stream flowed around and under us. Our floor and walls were saturated, and puddles formed in the corners. I nudged Ben.

"Whoa," he said.

"I'll start breakfast," I said, rolling onto my knees.

"Hot chocolate for me," Ben said, already moving.

"You take down the tent and fill water bottles," I chattered. A completely unnecessary conversation—we had regular tasks—I was calming my nerves. Routine helped. It wasn't mileage that made me nervous; I was worried about another emotionally disastrous day.

All the "how-to" Appalachian Trail books warned against getting angry. Sound advice. How the track snaked through the hills, and how the terrain rose up, was always unpredictable. The best days came when we shed expectations, taking the day—and the trail—as it came. Emotional melt downs like one we had succumbed to the day before made hiking miserable.

"It's twenty-two miles to Rte. 11/30 into Manchester Center," Ben said, already studying the guide book. "That's less than eight hours hiking at three

261

miles an hour." Ben was serious, unfolding the map, already anchored to plan B.

Rain waterfalled off the roof. Ben ignored it and drank his cocoa. I watched it and drank my coffee. We passed a pot of polenta and berries back and forth. The pot felt warm in my hands and on my lap.

"Eight hours plus breaks," I added.

"You'll lead," Ben crooned. "You can crank out four miles an hour when you're determined."

"No pressure, though," I answered. Ben had that typical male self confidence that was completely out of proportion to the situation.

"Forest service road by 8:00," Ben said, looking at the map. "Then climb. Four more miles and two thousand feet to the top of Stratton, so that'll take, say...ninety minutes max. You'll gun through."

I pictured myself wielding two six shooters, pelting mileage signs like Calamity Jane, and felt the pressure of his high expectations. The track would be wet and slick at best. Hopefully less mucky, the higher we got.

"The top by 9:30, and we'll probably take a break. There's a cabin hikers are supposed to be able to use, so we get under a roof," he continued, undeterrable.

I sipped. Maybe I could convince Ben to stay under the summit cabin's roof. Hot tea, sleeping bags, books. Warm.

"Stratton Pond Shelter is another three miles," he said, and I turned to stare at him. "And the halfway point. There by 11:00, take a break, eat an early lunch. Let's say we're leaving there before noon."

I watched Ben fall into the process that had helped him achieve: setting and attaining goals. In a familiar, predictable environment he was great at it, his talent and focus almost always guaranteeing success. Increasing average hemoglobin values in dialysis patients. Decreasing rates of hospitalization. Seven minute mile pace. I compared the circumstances between his attempt to qualify for Boston and now. He had been physically capable but too ambitious...Hmmmm.

"Five miles later, we'll hit William Douglas shelter...Say 2:00. Break. Then 3:00 the Spruce Peak shelter." Ben strategized like a coach. I imagined him pacing back and forth through puddles, whistle hanging around his neck. I resisted being swept up, resisted fishing out the violet pen and cementing my commitment by drawing arrows and estimated times at the different landmarks on the map.

"If we're beat, we can sleep there," I offered, donning my chipper voice. "Then the next day would be a nero-day to Rte. 11/30, and into town." I felt better having a soft landing.

"Spruce Peak is only three miles from the road. Since when is three more miles too much?"

I watched him over my mug. *The question was, would I want to?*

"We'll be there by 4:00, then in town and cleaned up by 5:00," Ben said. "Shower. Bed. Pizza. Beer."

"Ben & Jerry's," I said, watching him with narrowed eyes. *Phish Food. Chunky Monkey.* The ice cream would feel cold on my tongue, and I imagined running the cool spoon across my cheeks.

Chapter Fifty

I hit the trail using all four limbs, pulling and pushing, leveraging poles for maximum propulsion. Ben's job was to keep up. For me, the trick to longer days was to get as far as I could as early as I could, when my mental and physical energy were highest. Despite the driving rain and sticky trail, and my achy elbows, we hit the forest service road in about forty-five minutes, and I wondered if I might sleep in a bed after all. I burst across, searching for the white blaze.

I stopped.

A faded, blurred sign stood where the AT continued north, indicating a detour. We could make out "BRIDGE WASHED OUT," and "UNSAFE CROSSING," and "FIVE MILES." We thought we could make out "Big Branch." Was that between us and the road? *Five mile detour*? Was it now *twenty-seven* miles to Rte. 11/30? Was this weather-assaulted sign even from this season?

"Old sign and we're on the usual AT?" Ben asked.

"Beats me. Did you see 'Big Branch' on the map?" Rain whipped, stinging my cheeks. Our thoughts whipped with equal intensity. Uncertainty felt like a bigger barrier than Stratton Mountain.

"Nowhere to go but forward," I said. "When we start climbing, we'll know we're headed up Stratton." A gust shoved me sideways. "Let's move."

Climbing was good. Both the rain and my thoughts calmed. **I relaxed into a sense of recognition. This was familiar—the universe's shake 'n bake approach to plans. But then I darted away from that sinkhole, better to cling to a clear mind, if that was possible. Behind me, Ben, head down, doggedly push-pulled up the mountain.**

On Stratton's deserted peak, the weather doubled down. Water cascaded and wind howled. The cabin was locked. I rattled the door and peered through windows. We pressed under the narrow overhang, sheltering as best we could. My rain pants clung to my skin, tugging my knee caps, causing an ache. Ben looked at the map. Water ran in muddy streaks across the weather-resistant paper.

A brown sign in front of us directed left to Stratton Pond shelter, and I could have sworn that the arrow's shaft flashed like neon between horizontal and right angle toward the valley.

"Down," we said together, using the cabin wall to shove ourselves up. I avoided looking at the time, superstitious, worried that if I fixed on a schedule, we'd face an earthquake or fire or tsunami, or more likely a catastrophic accident to foil us.

I knew the exact moment the sun broke through because I was looking right at it. No choice, trapped as I was on my back, wedged between two boulders flanking a small break across the trail. Below me, a creek cut through the rock. I waved my arms and legs like a flipped tortoise, scraping my pack's canvas against the rocks squeezing me. I smacked my left elbow and howled.

Ben, then leading, turned, did a doubletake, and hurried over.

"Are you laughing!" I squawked which caused him to shake, trying to stop. I resisted laughing along with him, unwilling to relinquish jurisdiction over my mood. What else could I control out here? Plus glee might invite the universe to inflict more mayhem. Instead, I formulated a plan, patting the ground for my hiking poles. One lay next to me and the other lay bent in water below. Casualty of the trail. I reached for the closest pole.

"This is a *turtle*," I said, pointing to myself. "Famous AT fall." Using my elbows to pivot my shoulders up and my legs down, I scrambled out. Ben hooked my wounded pole's wrist strap and lifted it. I grabbed the pole and scuttled forward, fleeing my impending meltdown as much as aiming for the road. An alarming image intermittently forced itself into my thoughts: me at dusk, wheezing forward toward distant diesel sounds, in torn clothing, dragging one leg, an eyeball dangling and slapping against my cheek.

"Maybe three miles left," I said, after we'd regained momentum. "Looks flattish-downhill-ish on the map. Shouldn't take too long."

Apparently, I never learn.

The well packed, rock-free, slightly downhill trail slanted cruelly against the hillside, one edge elevated at least thirty degrees. My world tilted, like I'd just stepped off a boat. And my hips ached. My feet burned, convincing me that upon exposure to air they might spontaneously combust.

"There's no control," I said, as a car's hum reached my ears. The road's proximity had given me courage enough to acknowledge and vocalize my thoughts. Town was near enough to let my guard down. In my head, I catalogued accomplishing another impossible task, one step at time. I would store this moment, add it to a tattered list, to resurrect in case of future dauntings. Right then, I wouldn't be able to judge the exertion as worth it until hot water hit my back, and my squeaky clean feet hit the squeaky clean sheets.

"This day?" Ben asked, drawing next to me.

"Yes. This day. The trail," I said, too exhausted to head off the sinkhole thoughts. "But everything, too. Diagnosing a forty-two-year-old, never-smoker trail runner with lung cancer. Or when a twenty-five-year-old's kidneys fail from lupus."

"Like my mother," Ben said. I quieted, allowing mountain air to surround him and open space for him to speak, but all I heard were our footfalls.

"Your dad," he said, eventually. "His whole routine, prayers, church, reading the New Testament every night." We walked side-by-side. Ben continued, "Low carb thing, gym every day. He was protecting himself."

"He had it all figured out," I nodded. "And he seemed so lost at the end. Confused.... *Hadn't he done everything right?*" I watched my right arm swing, plant, push; I had unconsciously placed the trail's slope exactly where the crippled pole could gain purchase and propel me forward. Memories of my father's lopsided golf swing emerged, his floppy arm as he jogged, the way he curled all his fingers to use a fork.

"The Utah arm," I said, remembering one of our last conversations.

"Didn't he decide on the old-fashioned, mechanical one?" Ben interrupted me.

"He did. He loved the Utah team, and the speedy way Uncle Bob's family arranged the team's visit to measure him," I said, snapping my fingers, unable suppress my smile. "Amazing." I lifted my arm and inched my shoulder around, moving my fingers in imitation. "Like Star Wars," I said. "He thought it was too expensive. So absurd, we would have wanted him to have anything." I tromped forward again. "But that's not why I brought it up."

"His rules," I said, as the road sounds crept around us. "Like he couldn't spend too much." I recognized his worry: treating himself would cue ominous events. More road sounds wafted up. "He

loved to chatter about the technology. Brilliant people."
My father loved status, his children's proximity to
innovation added to his pride. We stepped faster, close
to our goal; I'd never anticipated traffic so keenly. I
glimpsed pavement through trees. My dad viewed his
life like a giant jigsaw wall map; pieces would never fit
into undesignated slots.

"One day he sat down across from me on the
patio," I said, stopping to face Ben. "Reading glasses in
one hand, crossword puzzle pinned against his stomach
with the other. He had wedged the situation into one of
his rigid rules. He said, 'That's why you go to a place like
Stanford, JoDean,' and he pointed his cheaters at me.
'Because you meet people like that.'"

After pizza, beer, and Ben & Jerry's, I waddled to
the B&B's back porch, listened to the crickets chirp. A
bullfrog's intermittent yawp cut through the peaceful
evening like my dad's last breaths cut through the
hospital room's stifled air. I tried to redirect. Anything:
work, my book, my dogs, but fatigue jabbed at my
defenses. I leaned straight into the punch.

The screen door opened and shut behind me.
Boards creaked. Ben sat with me under the white
gingerbread eaves. "What's the next goal?" he asked,
wrapping his arms around my shoulders, tugging me
into the present. Frogs became frogs again.

"New Hampshire and the White Mountains, next
year. Then Maine. Summer after next you'll be shooting
for Katahdin," he said.

The words *next year* fell on me like a mighty
chestnut. I was ready to hike again tomorrow, not fly
home. "It's not the miles, or how far we get anymore," I
said, as Ben swirled his bottle, and we watched the sun

sink behind maple trees. "Because you never know...what the trail ahead will look like."

"Smell the balsam," Ben nodded.

"Or the moose shit," I smiled. "Walk without a goal," I noticed the eaves' silhouette against the night sky, fresh cut grass scent, a rare in California. I settled into the summer evening's peace, next to the love of my life, and surrendered to feeling fortunate.

Part IX: Path Less Traveled

Chapter Fifty-one

I leapt across the boundary between road and dirt like it was the wardrobe, and I was destined for Narnia, then forged up Bromley Mountain, my crooked insides struggling to straighten themselves with the trail as it stretched behind. I wasn't used to boiling over during a climb, since it was when I usually felt so...Zen. But I had been holding it together for months, wandering lost at work, something that never occurred in the forest. For too many days, I had yearned for the company of trees, the protective ancestors that buttressed my journey north, yearned for miles carrying weight, for the section's rhythmic half-million steps. Finally, as trees enveloped me into their magical world, I strode, building momentum, stretching with each swing of the hip, working my arms so that my shoulders burned, willing the ache to vanish with my glycogen stores.

My roots burned under my sunhat, face reddened, pores opened to release heat. Sweat ran from my scalp to my knees. When fatigue weighted my boots and I stumbled, I paused to lean against my poles but re-started when my breaths slowed, hoping to exhaust my muscles and my sadness before first nightfall, exhaust the second-guessing that accompanied me. I courted every permutation of exhaustion, even screaming—at boulders, at treetops, at startled chipmunks who scurried away into fluttering brush—until the words came hoarse, at which time I would halt my progress to stomp and gyrate in place, stopping just short of hurling myself onto the dirt...anything to accelerate my escape into the simplicity and peace I had come to expect on the Appalachian Trail.

Coping, or thinking-over-feeling, is developmental. Children, before the basics emerge, rely primarily on adults to manage distressing situations. A kid with fever for example, will tantrum unselfconsciously: scream, cry, pout, and refuse to eat. In clinic, this sick kid, curled against a parent's body can be alarming, because that level of helplessness in adults would indicate grave illness. But that's because as adults we buck up, comfort ourselves by acknowledging we will feel better soon, and in the meantime strategize about self-care: fluids, rest, anti-fever medication. We ask our partners for household support, attempt to work from home, or call a supervisor for time off and to reassign essential duties.

Coping at a higher level, whether it is simple (like taking steps to feel better) or advanced (like attending to work duties) develops over adolescence, and certainly by adulthood. Or one hopes it does. And if it doesn't, it behooves us to fake it, which is what I did one Thursday morning faculty meeting, when upon adjournment, I methodically collected my materials, sauntered to my desk, and held the phone's receiver to my ear, pretending to be engrossed in a conversation rather than the dial tone. On the outside, I exemplified a professional attending to her responsibilities. On the inside, a demon-possessed hummingbird fluttered furiously, scrambling my composure.

That morning, I had beelined to work, strolling into the conference room with my curriculum report and cup of tea. Good leadership generated relaxed atmosphere, and meetings were now collegial affairs, filled with productive discussion and even laughter. Our new director Clark welcomed my ideas and had offered me a promotion to associate director. This was finally the job I had strived for, and I was the faculty member I thought I should be.

About three quarters through the meeting, the new director said he had an announcement. Optimistic faces turned to him; I got out my pen to record my thoughts.

"As you know, we have partnered with Kaiser—financially beneficial—but also offering our residents a wider range of patients," he said, picking up his papers, tapping them, setting them down. The Kaiser HMO seemed like a wild card, with a mission at odds with our commitment to underserved patients. And the doctors had chosen different careers than we had, fulltime clinical care rather than teaching. But the partnership could be mutually beneficial: for Kaiser, it meant an influx of doctors, since residents tended to stay where they trained, and for us, much needed resources, both economic and specialty services. Despite our differences, we were willing to try the alliance.

"To facilitate this partnership, and because, frankly, I need help," Clark said, and we all nodded in support, "I have appointed a new associate director."

I looked up, surprised he was announcing my promotion. A small thrill raised goose flesh, then worry because I hadn't yet thought about what to say to colleagues. I couldn't wait to call Ben. Our Thursday date night would now be an unexpected celebration. The director's face reddened as he looked down, and I felt affection at his humility, his embarrassment that he hadn't cued me in.

"Please congratulate Dr. William More, our new associate program director," he said, tilting his palm toward a largely unknown physician Kaiser had sent to work part time with us.

The director scanned every face but mine. A familiar vibration spread to my chest, and my arms felt weightless. Disorientation displaced calm. Did this just happen? I second guessed myself: perhaps I had misunderstood the offer, or he had rescinded it, and I missed the memo. Or he had been joking. I watched the meeting from outside my body, betrayal hanging like a veil between me and the room. Chatter ricocheted, but I couldn't interpret the words. The clock over the door showed too much time between now and eight o'clock. How had I never noticed its relentless ticking? The fluorescent lights buzzing? I forced the corner of my lips up, hoping for better than a grimace and shifted my gaze from one person to another while my concentration disintegrated. Finally, the clock succumbed to my will. My colleagues exited as I remained, collecting my papers under the glare of naked bulbs.

Midday sun blazed at Peru Peak shelter, where I stopped for lunch. I welcomed the shade, dropping my pack, stretching and twisting, pulling and expelling long conscious breaths. My vagal nerve activated, my body released a bolus of the workplace deceit, tension evaporating, jaw relaxing and gut unwinding. I hadn't eaten since darting from the road, so I rummaged for trail mix with mango and chocolate. Sugar would burst into my system and calories would brighten my mood. I glanced at the sun and wondered what kind of downer-person didn't appreciate a day like this.

Downer-person, I thought, chewing. *But that was five minutes ago.* I felt better already: sweat and distance and woods and chocolate and leaving it all at the bottom of the hill. I filled up with fresh water, restuffed my gear, and started for Big Branch Shelter, but not before I put my sunglasses on.

Chapter Fifty-two

In late July, the Vermont Appalachians grew lush and lovely, a seasonal biorhythm I should have paid more attention to the year before. Maple, oak, and birch populated the lower altitudes, with spruce and pine dominating higher. As I ascended, balsam fragrance floated in discrete patches, as if I walked through scent clouds. Biting insects had thinned. Daily temps ran in the 70s, the nights cool. Fair weather was a valuable ally for my ambitious section from VT 11/30 to Gorham, New Hampshire. It wasn't the 250 miles that posed the challenge; it was the terrain. New Hampshire's White Mountains, in the second half of my hike, garnered awe for height and beauty, but garnered angst for steep slopes, boulder fields, and slick rock faces under spilling water. Signposts, guidebooks, and official personnel offered ominous warnings about exposed stretches above tree-line subject to year-round capricious and extreme weather.

Could it be more difficult than the planning? I had wondered, as I worked out mileage, supply boxes, weather gear, overnights. I surveyed my calendar and designated camp spots. In northern New Hampshire, I would have to stay on a strict schedule. Camping wasn't permitted above treeline in the Whites' Presidential Range, certain sections particularly fragile, so hikers had to reserve coveted spots in official huts run by the Appalachian Mountain Club. Greenleaf Hut, Zealand

Falls Hut, Carter Notch Hut. I had pulled out my maps the autumn before to make sure we got spots, and left wiggle room to stay on schedule, given the reputed rough, mile-an-hour traverse.

Just before the Big Branch shelter, I crossed a suspension bridge over the Big Branch River and recalled the faded, barely readable sign from the year before. So this was Big Branch. I wasn't sure what year the sign had been posted, but I imagined the water swollen, rushing and unruly, forcing a detour. Not this year. I stopped midway and watched the current, clear and smooth in deeper sections, sliding over and around rocks and fallen branches, foaming where turbulence introduced air. The swirling, white patches chilled me, as if the spray touched my bare arms. Water had no choices, governed by obstacles and forces like surface tension, heat, pressure, and gravity. I, too, succumbed to pressure and gravity, but I could choose, could look for clear and smooth.

After the faculty meeting, a fog had settled over me, a numbness. I showed up on time, tended to my patients and teaching, completed curriculum projects but without the same energy. Plus, the atmosphere changed with the new allegiance, a disconnect developed between faculty and training. Changes were announced, rather than discussed, and my curriculum adjustments had morphed into reactive, rather than thoughtful and planned.

I stared at Big Branch over the railing, watching and listening to the water. Leaves quivered on the bank. A mule deer stepped lightly to the northern edge and reached to drink. I ran events through my head and seesawed between second guessing and congratulating myself. Initially, Clark moved forward with the organizational partnership, not addressing what had happened. Conflict arose during the next one-on-one curriculum update.

"I can't believe you're reacting this way. This decision was in the program's best interest," Clark fired at me over the table. "You apparently don't care about that."

The room tunneled and spun, seemed to be sucking me backward. Facts scrambled. I struggled to order my thoughts, and shame rose from my stomach like flies from a decaying deer carcass. They swarmed and hovered, blocking my windshield. *Yes, yes. The best interest of the program was paramount.* I was too entitled, adjusting my tiara, arriving to hike in a limo. I sank into my seat, somehow smaller, and turned my gaze to the broad window comprising Clark's office wall where two massive blue oaks dominated the narrow space between the building and street. Intermingled, verdant branches pressed the glass, riot of leaves like a filter, forcing me to look through them to see landscape beyond. A scrub jay lit on the nearest branch, hopped toward the window, stared as if looking at me, and tilted its head right and left. A bulky Burrtec Waste Management truck rumbled by, rolling between openings in the foliage. Ground debris rose in its wake, circled, and settled. The leaves persisted against the window, unperturbed.

I sat straighter and looked again at Clark. "That's not the issue here," I said, giving him a few moments to speak. When he didn't, I collected my papers, this time with genuine calm and returned to my desk.

Eventually, and unexpectedly, Clark asked if I would co-associate direct, with Dr. More handling the Kaiser interface. It had felt wrong right away, as if he had been pressured to add a home-turf leader and because the faculty didn't seem to trust Dr. More. Given what I had seen, and the subtle nagging that flopped around like a beached fish in my prefrontal cortex, I should have said no.

On Big Branch, the deer's front hoof slipped forward, and she sprung back, pushing with both feet, butt-first up onto dirt and grass. She sniffed at the water, twitching her huge ears, and searched for a firmer place. She wove through shadows cast by trees and brush until she vanished altogether. That left me, the water, and the trees. I inhaled deeply the scent of wet earth. The trail had been mostly dry, but dryness magnifies forest aromas, and I had been aware all day of pine and moss, lifting my mood.

In the last year, wet earth and eucalyptus had been frequent scents on my longer than usual trail runs, as I logged miles hoping to find resolution. That was the hardest part, carrying the wounds with me, up hills, along fire roads, through stands of eucalyptus, live oak, and manzanita. Some days, I hesitated, reconsidering my urge to run despite the usual benefits, because daily activities would no longer hold my attention and my mind would sink into the unbreakable, obsessive patterns rehashing whatever had happened that day, or that week.

I stood still as the bridge slightly rocked, as if it breathed with me. I closed my eyes, listening to the water chatter, chortle, sigh. Whisper *settle*. Settle into this open space that doesn't see insult, compliment, good, bad, right, wrong. Doesn't *tax lives with forethought of grief*. When I opened my eyes, the forest seemed to rise around me. Trees stretched toward the sun like lazy cats and boulders swelled. Rolling summits drew themselves into a circle, funneling light. Brush tangled and thickened. Vastness consumed me and granted perspective. Now buffered and safe, I allowed images to flash through, in the way that events replayed themselves on my hikes, as if to give me one last view before I left them behind.

First to flutter by was the ranty letter William had sent to Clark, in which he announced my under-qualification, and his refusal to share authority with me. Then meetings where they sat shoulder to shoulder and installed me across the table. Patronizing words and grins. A local fellowship director stalking into the residency, spitting words through gritted teeth about William foisting unethical choices on her, leveraging his Kaiser resources.

One scene played longer, as if dangled by flickering winged insects. I sat at a round table, speaking about curriculum to Kaiser physicians. Core topics stacked on the white board: hypertension, diabetes, atrial fibrillation, and methodologies for teaching during "in between" moments in their overbooked clinics. Then William barging in announcing that he wanted to introduce me, relegating me to the *Sutter* associate director position.

"You've been at the residency for what...just over five years?" he announced, placing a hand on my shoulder. "And you all know me, the associate director, teaching and mentoring residents for twenty-five years."

I fought to control my emotional reaction to his powerplay, as if he had a right to introduce me, and the way he installed himself above me in his imagined hierarchy. I wondered where exactly he had been *teaching and mentoring for twenty-five years,* since ours was the only teaching program in the area and none of us had heard of him before this alliance. I imagined a cartoon-thought-balloon inflating behind him, and inside a star expanded, twinkling, pressing the rest of us into a corner.

Then I was perched in the front row at the most recent graduation ceremony. Clark stood at the podium, introducing speakers: William, the associate director, and me, a faculty member. Surrounded by colleagues, I sat alone in my new suit, feeling like a pig-tailed school girl who had been grudgingly invited for dodge ball but whom the boys elbowed to the sideline.

The question was, did I truly want to play? I had accepted the faculty position, *clung* to the faculty position, because teaching compelled me, drawn as I was to support the young people through training. The advice, direction, opinions I had heard marched by like ants to spilled trail mix: "To make biggest impact, you want to be at a residency," one physician had said during my own residency as I discussed a clinic patient with her. Another time, moonlighting at an urgent care, a senior doc pulled me aside. "You should have a group of residents following you around," he had said. "What are you doing here?" A mentor had insisted that someone with my "insight and perspective on medicine should be at a residency, front and center, training the next generation." I had dived into a faculty position because it's what others had expected me to do. But these faculty positions, all consuming, occupied by the old boys, weren't constructed for people who looked like me, and who were concerned with reaching a hand behind for those who came after, rather than clawing up an artificial hierarchy. Stymied by expectations again, not mine, but those of well-intentioned people in my life. I never slowed to think whether other pathways existed and what might be right for me. But if I listened to myself, honed in on what I wanted, what would medicine look like?

Thousands of miles in the mountains had helped me reconnect with buried skills: a sensitivity to subtle scents, discernment of sounds, and what I was finding most important now—the ability to recognize a place I had been before. I recognized this place, where I struggled to engage in a passion, stay a course, despite the unhealthy environment. At Woods Hole shelter, eight years and 1700 miles earlier, I committed to the confidence that my skills and dedication would carry me forward, that I deserved a respectful work environment. I had traversed hundreds of peaks and hollows since then, tumbled and risen, stepped through exhaustion and fear to continue my journey north. I would stay on my journey, continue to teach, but on my own terms—trusting myself to make my own way forward. And this unhealthy position, where politics, sexism, and egos trumped education and progress, I would leave behind like a muddy footprint.

A lone cloud moved across the sun, dousing the spotlight. Show over. I took a few more breaths, inhaling must and mud and fresh leaves, searching for and spotting the doe up the bank on a sandy, gentle approach to the water. The sun's returning warmth soaked into my skin. I turned to where the bridge's railings ushered me north and strode across to settle for the night.

On day three, I climbed Killington Mountain, the highest traverse in Vermont. By then, the climbs had normalized, and I floated comfortably in my mostly empty head. Pine scent dangled and worked its magic, easing my mental and physical fatigue and supporting my sense of expansiveness, my membership in the forest's web.

Cooper Lodge, a large stone shelter, sat atop Killington, nine miles from Big Branch. I had chosen this day as a "wiggle," thinking I could stay at Cooper if the climb wore me out, or head down to Pico Camp or Churchill Scott shelter. I summited around noon and plopped down, annoyed rather than tired. When had I ever only walked nine miles? I had underestimated myself, unable to claim my identity as accomplished long-distance hiker.

Or accomplished doctor, faculty member, daughter, runner...anything. I could claim my worth at certain times, like leaving an unhealthy faculty position, but still consistently underestimated myself. Why? There was maintaining a beginner's mind which I thought was important. And, again, I recognized my ingrained thought-pattern that if I claimed good things out loud, the universe would snatch them away. But that didn't seem like the whole picture. I had always internalized negative comments, and not heard positive ones. Before Maryland, Ben had pointed out that I minimized my accomplishments as couldn't-be-that-hard.

I faced the obvious challenges, my treatment by Clark and William, and medicine's entrenched hierarchy and ubiquitous sexism. But the undermining had started early. My high school guidance counselor suggested nursing when I expressed interest in medicine. The surprise on my college physics professor's face when I appeared at his office after he asked the person scoring the exam's high grade to stop by. The subtle bullying in the hospital when colleagues "doubled checked" my treatment suggestions, or knee-jerked to propose an alternative plan. No wonder I had difficulty claiming my identity as expert in health and wellness, and the uncertainty had spread like a tuber—impacting writing, teaching, running—sprouting hesitation about the nine miles to Cooper Lodge.

I chewed my lunch and ruminated. On the slope above, a single oak towered tall and unapologetic among the conifers, limbs extended, accepting and thriving under the sun's nourishing rays. I traced the oak, from roots to tallest leaf, studying how it stood solid and unique among the firs. Then I packed up my lunch, donned my sunglasses and started out. I would let the terpenes sharpen my focus, invite my observations to loop, and replay, inch toward accepting my intelligence and competence. My self-image should be sturdy as an oak, undistracted as it stretches toward the sun. And put-downs should be rolling off me like water around rocks in the Big Branch River.

Chapter Fifty-three

I staggered into Hanover, New Hampshire with stinging quadriceps and dragging boots. Dirt caked my calves. A blister between my left thumb and forefinger smarted as I worked my poles. To keep myself huffing forward, I pictured a hot bath scented with Japanese cedar oil (hinoki). Hinoki, unlike terpenes, is distilled from wood. It soothes aches and pains, and my bones and muscles throbbed from crown to toes.

I burst into the sparkling lobby of the Six South Street Hotel, telescoping my poles and declaring my reservation. When the desk clerk looked up, I balked and took a step back, imagining only the whites of my eyes to be visible under the dirt.

"Two nights, Ms. Nicolette?" he asked. Should I correct him to *Doctor* Nicolette? I decided in this place, claiming my professional identity was irrelevant. This internal struggle would go on for decades. He asked if the room was for one person.

"Two. My husband also arrives today."

I alternated between looking up at the trail and down at the scrawled list of questions, brought along to discuss in the White Mountains. I ducked and swerved.

A spruce branch reached like a hand, almost snagging my hat.

"This one is from July 16th and the question is *Are you wearing socks?*"

"Who hikes without socks?" Ben asked.

"The Indestructibles. In their Tevas," I said, reading from *Q&A a Day, Five-Year Journal*, a tiny diary with a question at the top of each page. Besides *Are you wearing socks?* other questions read *What's the last number in your cell phone? What's your hair style?* and *Whom do you miss?* The book has 365 questions, but 1,825 answers, because each page is divided for five years' worth of responses. I tried to jot my thoughts without peeking at what I had written before. That year I had copied a few to carry north.

"Is it your socks I smell?" Ben asked. I looked down at my two pairs: sweat-stained liners and grimy tan hiking socks. My relationship with my socks had not improved since Tennessee. Light rain began as we approached our first big climb in the Whites, Mount Mooselauke.

"*What is your favorite piece of clothing?*" I asked, flipping the page.

"Not my socks," Ben said. "On the trail, or off?" he called forward. After a pause he said, "It doesn't matter. It's my red hat."

I turned with a look only a wife can give. "You're becoming that middle-aged husband who needs his wife to cull his frayed and moth-eaten closet."

Ben had purchased the hand knit hat two decades before, from an elderly woman sitting roadside in Ladakh, India's northernmost province, where we had shoestring travelled after our first year of medical school. The Ladakhi woman, wrapped in the same wool, smiled toothlessly at Ben, as he held out his rupees. She swept her hand over the colorful array next to her. Without hesitation, he picked vibrant brick red, adorned with a robust pom-pom. We had no idea then that the hat was enchanted, would survive several moves and several continents in addition to the years. I thought for sure it was finished the autumn before when Chase, our greyhound, snatched it from Ben's bedside table and ravaged the already emaciated top strands, leaving only a few strays, reminding me of the Vandeventer emu when he wore it, which was while reading or dragging the recycling bin to our driveway's end, and traipsing on the Appalachian Trail. I contrasted it with the pricey, layered synthetic beanies worn by other hikers, including his wife. Now Ben's three-rupee hat had made it from Georgia to New Hampshire, offering him warmth, and, I guess, memories. It endured like we did, weathered, bedraggled, frayed at the edges...but always present to accompany each other's journey.

"Here's proof that these question-writers are somewhere cushy!" I called to Ben over my shoulder. "July 28th: *Does anything hurt today?*"

Chapter Fifty-four

At the base of Mount Mooselauke, the southernmost White Mountain, I paused and studied the rocky face. Here, it started: one of the legends. I tucked my uncertainty down deep, near my cooking pot. Ben nodded, and I dug in. But the climb required only a pleasant exertion, and struck me as so lovely I was moved to unfold a scrap of paper, uncap my purple pen, and write:

> We climbed Mt. Mooselauke in the rain. Scents of balsam and soaked stone accompanied us, and pattering drops applauded as we ascended to the sky. In the quiet, I noticed our breath and the metallic clink of our poles, often in time with each other. Steady. Strong. When the sun broke through at the southern summit, we were almost disappointed; rain had been a fleeting but fine friend that day, easing the climb, and cooling verdant air.

What all the fuss was about? I was so full of myself, strolling along the ridge's old carriage road, that I swaggered to a cliff's edge and challenged the north-reaching range, "Is that all you got?"

The Whites answered back: stony and silent. The climb up Mooselauke had been a cruel joke and the worst thing I could have done was allow it to stoke my expectations. Two miles farther, the descent into Kinsmans Notch humbled me. Our conversation halted as we slipped, crawled, scrambled, and rolled down the next 3,000 feet. We picked down waterfalls, cascades parting around us. Bare, steep rockfaces had forced trail workers to bore rebar and fix logs for hand and footholds. Occasionally, one would dislodge, leaving two holes to stare as if pained at our poor choices. We grabbed at trees and roots, still skidding several feet at a time. I pictured a step giving way, tumbling and bouncing next to me to the bottom where it landed with a splash, and I with a splat. I wanted to squeeze Ben—hand, wrist, ankle, anything—for reassurance.

The next nine miles consumed seven hours, and we made it to Eliza Brook shelter at dinner time with barely enough energy to heat water for instant, prepackaged chicken fried rice, and, even though it wasn't Italian food, I imagined my father shaking his head and asking me why I couldn't see the Whites like normal people. By car.

The next day we scrambled through fifteen breathtaking miles, above and below tree line, along a buff-colored, dusty trail, to Mount Lafayette's summit, and our first experience with the huts. Greenleaf Hut is a rustic structure with log and plank surfaces, and spectacular views of the Franconia Range. Mountains spiked with rich green conifers sprawled in all directions. As with all the huts, it was spartan because supplies were carried in and out by staff-on-foot and rare helicopter drop. No napkins, paper towels or toilet paper. Scents of fresh bread and savory dinner greeted us from the industrial-type kitchen. A few hikers lingered in the central room, perusing books, or playing board games at long, benched tables. Staff, busy with kitchen tasks, called greetings and checked reservations. We investigated, finding sleep rooms with bunks stacked four levels high. We set up head-to-head on rubber-covered mattress, the closest to each other we could get, and stretched out before dinner, intermittently reaching past our heads to hold hands.

At the 6 PM chime, we squeezed along a bench, elbow to elbow, conversing with other hikers. A father and daughter chattered about their first backpacking overnight, and retired man described his goal to visit each of the huts. Staff settled pans piled with chicken breasts, hearty homemade bread (enchanted, and clearly made in Fae), vegetable, and salad. Not a scrap of food remained after this or any of the hut dinners. Afterwards, the staff introduced themselves and the hut's history, then held a Chewbacca sound-alike competition, and encouraged tips. I cleaned myself and my bandana using the icy water from the bathroom's metered push faucet and turned in early.

For the next seventy miles, we tramped along gradual ridges and in and out of notches, equal parts hiking, twisting ankles on loose rocks, and sliding on marble-like scree. We descended slowly, at times tortuously. Gusty winds pelted us with pulverized stone and debris. During climbs, I stored my poles, alighting four-limbed, from crack to crag like a bighorn. My tenacity rose with the peaks, escalating on the most arduous miles. Despite the turbulent wilderness, the way ahead remained clear and my progress north steady, almost automatic, leaving stretches where my mind could engage elsewhere, noticing rugged summits and dense forests that filled me with wonder. Or my mind could be tugged more remotely, which is why another situation involving a cyclone parting for my quiet determination entered my thoughts.

Magazines, crumpled fliers, pencils and pens, and the TV's remote control zinged around me, bouncing off the carpet or my head as I sat on the floor of my mother's Florida condominium, clicking and swiping at my brother's tablet. I splayed my legs, as if forming a barrier to defend the pill bottles, weekly pillboxes, and mixing bowl filled with colorful tablets and capsules gathered between.

"You are NEVER to enter this house again," my mother yelled from the couch, before hurling a Sudoku book. The door slammed, and John stalked in.

"That's enough, Mom," he spoke with authority, reminding me he wasn't my little brother anymore. He surveyed my mother's cluttered couch-side table and picked up a mug, tumbler, and shot glass, shooting me a sheepish look.

"Elder abuse!" my mother screeched. "You're doing this because I'm old."

"We asked her to do this, Mom," my brother said. He and my sister-in-law had asked me—more times than I wanted to admit—to collect, identify, and organize the havoc of medication scattered throughout my mother's condo. I dodged the task hoping to avoid this exact scene. But, when they reminded me their children stayed there regularly, I caved. On the pill identifier screen, I entered the shape, color, and number of the pill between my thumb and forefinger.

John dropped to his hands and knees, sweeping loose pills like marbles from underneath the couch. He scooped with both hands and dropped them into the bowl.

"That bottle's the benzos," I pointed. "That one, hydrocodones. And those, I have no idea." I indicated a small bowl with brown granule-filled capsules, like dirt. "They're not marked, so maybe supplements." I plunked the blood pressure, thyroid, sleep, and various antibiotic medications in the corresponding containers.

My mother stormed out, and we heard cabinets and doors slam in the kitchen. Then quiet. When no one followed her, she returned to stand in the archway, mug of scotch in hand. She stabbed her finger at my brother and said, "When those kids are here, I watch them like a hawk."

A passed out hawk, I thought, ruffled and snoring after ingesting too many fermented juniper berries comingled with its snagged rabbit. My brother lifted another stash of assorted pills from the shelf under the end table.

"What are these?" He held them up to the window.

"Put those back!" my mother screamed. "I know what each and every one of those pills is and if ONE is missing, I'm calling the SPCA."

We looked at each other, then at her.

"AARP!" she corrected herself. She looked from John to me, and back to John, her faded green eyes filled with rage. The red rims sagged, so tired they rested on her cheeks. I didn't argue that it was addiction robbing her control, not her children. It had robbed our control, too, with late night phone calls to alert us about falls and ER trips, disrupted parties and celebrations, rages about depleted scotch stashes. We excluded her from important events now, to avoid inevitable scenes. It caused my brother guilt; I viewed it as logical consequences. She refused to address her chronic illness. If she had diabetes, and never took her medication, allowing her blood sugars to skyrocket, especially on holidays, always landing her in the ER, she would face a similar choice: treat your illness or you're not invited.

I surveyed the jumble of pills. This would take time and effort, but I'd get through it. I filled the AM and PM compartments in her pill box with her daily medications, set it on the coffee table, then restarted sorting the various bottles, bags, bowls, and loose tablets.

Chapter Fifty-five

Mount Washington is reputed to have the worst weather on the east coast, and as we headed out from Lake of the Clouds Hut at its summit, docents and Visitor Center staff warned us that this was a day to take the cog railroad down or try to catch a ride. The forecast predicted rain, and winds that would reach gale force by afternoon. They laid it on thick, telling tales of failed rescue attempts, five-figure rescue bills, and dead and frozen hikers. Since Madison Hut was only six miles north and almost 1500 feet down. We figured we could be there before lunch, shelter briefly for hot soup and fairy-bread, then hike off the mountain before the storm. We snuck out the door.

The forecasters were wrong. The sixty to seventy mile/hour gusts picked up by mid-morning, knocking me over several times, my rain gear acting as a sail. Ben took the lead, hunched and trudging forward, stopping intermittently to wait for me to crawl upright, using anything available, shrub, tree, or rock. During the worst of it, we crouched behind boulders, until the bluster slowed, then staggered along as quadrupeds, using feet and poles, no fewer than three points of contact with the rocky ground. Twice, I crawled on my hands and knees, low like a soldier avoiding shrapnel which came in the form of branches, dust, and small, sharp stones.

On the bright side, we made it to Madison Hut uninjured except for a cut over my right eyebrow that leaked down my face, staining my t-shirt and lavender bandana. After prying open the door against the gusts and slipping in, we skulked, humbled, into the central room, enduring staff's eyerolling when we said we'd come from Lake of the Clouds Hut. The disapproval didn't hinder me from helping myself to too much bread or from draining the hot water carafe for my tea. But it prevented me from rationalizing that because we made it, our actions had been reasonable. Why I had stubbornly attempted this traverse between huts, forced myself on this obstacled path when I had other options. Simply to keep on schedule? Stick to a rigid plan? *Because it's what I always wanted to do?*

Adults coped. And re-evaluated...Knew how to re-assess choices when the status quo became suboptimal. Hadn't I done that with my job, maneuvering a contracting position and only showing up to work with the residents? I came and went without political rocks in my path, high velocity projectiles, and spectacular Superman face plants, leaving my brain and heart with more space to engage in better things.

Wind slammed against the hut windows like a shove to the shoulder, daring me to bring it outside. I watched, aloof, sipping tea, unwilling to be goaded into another defiant move. We alternated between quiet and discussing the afternoon, weighing the options: hunker down here, or head down to Joe Dodge Lodge and summer weather, either by short cut or the Appalachian Trail long way.

"Staying is an option," I said, looking around, proud of myself but also noting physical discomfort at abandoning my plan. "Most hikers won't make their reservation tonight; they'll have room." Ben stood to inquire, knees scraping the bench back, and I silently worked with my inflexible goals. Then, abruptly, the sky lightened, and the sun cut through, illuminating my map. The air around the hut settled like gently falling leaves. I took it as a sign.

We arrived at Joe Dodge Lodge after a two and half hour descent. For the next day, we read, snacked, and lounged in the sun. A kind soul in the kitchen kept me supplied with iced tea. Only the Wildcat and Carter Ranges, about twenty miles, stood between Pinkham Notch and Gorham, and we were light, thanks to food and water provided by huts. At first, apprehension hung around me: not there yet and some gnarly peaks. But then I chased it away and allowed myself the confidence earned with achieving my section goal and completing the White Mountains.

"You're probably thinking the Whites aren't really that hard after all," Ben said, with familiarity and insight that comes of a twenty-year partnership. He handed me a tea and popped the top on his Sprite.

"Nope," I said. "They're butt-kickers." I lifted my feet onto my pack. "But I kicked right back." I jabbed a foot at the air.

"Your favorite part?" he asked. "The conquering?"

I thought about how male that sounded: conquering. Beating something else. I wasn't thinking about being better or stronger than the mountains, or the trail, or a work colleague, anything else. I challenged myself; summoned something from inside me. I had been a part of this huge expanse of land, moving over it and with it. Rolling with peaks and notches, walking among trees and boulders, breathing air and wind.

"I didn't conquer," I said. "Just experienced." I let my head tilt back to see the tops of the trees sway. "And I'm claiming it, claiming what I can do." A raptor's silhouette floated high above, barely discernable. My life, with its tight schedule and fluorescent lights and ticking clocks seemed too packaged to deserve this return to wilderness. I acknowledged gratitude for every time nature accepted me back.

"I don't think I've ever seen a place so...magnificent," I said. "That's my favorite part." I dropped my foot and looked at the slopes stretching north. "These peaks, the rugged edges, how we emerged above tree line and looked down." I paused to feel the goose flesh rise. "These aren't the same mountains I've walked in since Georgia. And yet I feel a part of them, too."

Ben set down his can and looked north.

"It's a new feeling. How hard it was, and emerging on the other side," I said, "I think it's majesty."

Part X: The Last Mile

Chapter Fifty-six

For long-distance hikers, the last mile can be the day's most challenging. Mental and physical fatigue combine with calorie deprivation to lengthen the track, warping distance, stretching it like a rubber band. Whether that mile leads to a campsite, a shelter, or straight into town for pizza and a shower, it can be interminable. We've all wondered if we missed our day's goal, staggered past the sign...or perhaps the sign was removed, and what appeared to be a faint deer track *was* the turn off to the ramshackle, three-sided structure—infested with mice, floored with adjacent baseball bats—now perceived as offering the comfort of a Thomas Kincaid cabin. We stumble and curse, consider pitching our tent right on the trail, and wonder why we ever decided to do this.

This is the longest mile I've ever walked ...definitely longer than the map says! The ATC is playing some cruel joke; I'm going to write them a letter! I've worried, even though I have *never* missed a shelter, about where I will spend the night now that I have blundered too far. And will I make it to the next spring or creek, to have water for cooking and washing? I resist temptation to pull out the map one more time, instead entertaining the idea of charging straight down the adjacent slope, dodging log, bear, and bramble, until I hit civilization, and never come back.

Despite the many "last miles" since Georgia, my concept of last mile changed as I experienced my final section in Maine, which surpassed even New Hampshire's White Mountains in its notoriety. *There ain't no huts. Nor helicoptered supplies,* was a frequent comment, punctuated with a cackle. Terrain remained untamed and resupply difficult. Man-eating insects outnumbered people, and weather assaulted the mountains in unpredictable, rapidly changing fits. Any time I dared express fatigue or frustration, a fellow hiker would affect a pitying glance, shake his head, and deliver the ominous warning, *Just wait until Maine.*

Looking back over the decade I journeyed the AT, I'm now struck by the seamless way preparation, travel, and hiking came together. One or both of us flew from the west coast, connecting without difficulty; our backpacks and shipped supplies arrived; shuttles met and delivered us on time; we walked without injury or illness. While it seems absurd to describe the AT this way, I see now that I coasted along. Little did I realize, as I eagerly planned my journey to Mount Katahdin, that my final section's hurdles would surpass hiker myth and legend and make me wonder how I ever got this far north. My last summer became a metaphor for every last mile: longer than it should have been, littered with obstacles, and assaulted by events more challenging than the peaks.

I planned for Maine in the usual way, calculating miles and blocking out time, mostly for Ben's schedule. Days off weren't an issue for me now that I taught as an independent contractor. I worked most days, filling in whenever the residency needed, but I wasn't confined to accrued vacation. This was one advantage of my new relationship to the program, which I reminded myself when I occasionally second guessed my choice to step away, missing peers and intellectual exercises like developing curriculum.

As spring approached, I planned in earnest, propping open trail guides during meals, marking campsites and shelters, estimating difficulty and pace. Scribble, erase, re-scribble. Just before Mount Katahdin stretched the daunting Hundred Mile Wilderness, for which I budgeted six days. Most hikers, including me, allotted an additional day after that to walk the eleven miles to The Birches shelter, at Katahdin's base, and then another day to summit and descend.

Thoughts of dense conifer forests, rippling summits, and energetic, steady climbs interrupted my days. I pictured exhausted evenings, lulled to sleep by burbling water, and waking by glassy lakes lit by peaceful sunrises. I imagined climbing White Cap Mountain, where hikers catch their first view of distant Mount Katahdin. After so many years and miles, I couldn't believe I would reach this extraordinary goal.

I worked out the last of the organizing on a Wednesday night in early April, set my pencil down, straightened my stack of maps and guidebooks, and thought, I am going to do this—stand on Katahdin's summit this year. I felt confident, and completely in control.

Chapter Fifty-seven

"We're not going," I said, twenty-four hours later, staring at Ben over saag paneer. A visceral ache spread, an almost tearing sensation at the disruption of my plans. This is what makes goal oriented people, I thought, psychologically and physiologically wedded to their course, reel from the unpleasant wrench that occurs with changing direction. I acknowledged the discomfort, then rode it; it would pass; this was the right decision.

We arrived at dinner after Ben's cardiology appointment, where he'd finally gotten his heart checked. Three years ago, after his mother's sudden death, he committed to an evaluation before his forty-fifth birthday. The deadline had passed, and with a nudge from me (okay, persistent nagging), he arranged it. I don't remember who drove to the restaurant; neither of us could have navigated the roads safely, both dazed and silent, unable to focus on anything but his diagnosis.

The news had been so bad, the cardiologist, who was Ben's closest friend, abandoned his usual professional demeanor, including his doctorface.

"I'm so sorry," Greg said, visibly distressed in his crisp white coat. "I thought I was going to walk in and say everything was completely normal."

With a pen, he pointed out Ben's Brugada pattern on EKG, sign of a rare familial condition predisposing patients to spontaneous, fatal heart arrhythmias—usually ventricular fibrillation, the bag-of-worms heart. He asked Ben about previous symptoms like fainting and palpitations, which he had experienced, but forgotten, and which I was forced to assert. Me, the pushy wife. As Greg explained about defective heart muscles and factors increasing risk, heat blossomed at my crown and washed downward, over my shoulders, then chest, and out to my fingers. My knee started jiggling. Ben listened without speaking or moving. Greg paused and reached for the chart.

"What are the odds?" Greg asked, re-reading the EKG, as if it might tell him something different this time. He swiveled to face us and dropped his hands to his knees. "I didn't see this coming."

But I did. There was my dad's unlikely illness. And my knowledge that crazy happens in the human body. But mostly I credit my specialty with birthing my intuition.

Family physicians are trained to integrate the effects of relationships—whether family, community, or environment—on health and illness. When Ben's impossibly healthy, sixty-year-old mother had died suddenly, and his family spun with shock and incredulity, I quietly accepted another example life's unpredictability, and immediately connected the tragedy to Ben's grandfather's sudden demise at age fifty. In 1958, the family had assumed he suffered a heart attack, but they wouldn't have known for sure. Sudden deaths in consecutive generations seemed ominous, so a few weeks after Ben's mom died, I cautiously raised the idea of a familial condition. He agreed to get a cardiac evaluation, but I wondered if he was humoring me with this future deadline, thinking I'd forget. Finally, when he was six months away from turning forty-six, and I was 280 miles away from Mount Katahdin, the cardiologist dealt us the blow.

"How can you think of not finishing?" Ben asked, reaching for naan. "I've watched you daydreaming." He chewed and swallowed. "We're hiking to Katahdin."

We.

Me. Ice in my water glass shifted and condensation slid down the glass. I could walk through Maine by myself. Finish. Remote or not, it was a tenth of the distance I had walked already, most of it alone. I rolled around in the idea of it, the way my dogs roll around in the grass: I could sleep where I wanted, rise alone. Leave camp early. Walk as long or as little, at my own pace. Would only have to worry about feeding myself (or not). Climb that last, behemoth peak on my own terms. I pictured myself, arms raised in triumph, at the famous battered sign. *Mount Katahdin, Baxter Peak—elevation 5767 ft, Northern Terminus of the Appalachian Trail.* What a feather in my cap. Bragging rights. Up over Bemis Mountain, the Saddlebacks...the Hundred Mile Wilderness. I toggled between my personal triumph, and how much it would impress others. Like my dad, who I yearned to share this with. It used to annoy me when he boasted about me, as if my successes meant more to his ego than what they would bring to me and my life. But I ached for him now, pictured him carrying the photo of me at the famous sign, scrolling, pulling it up, asking his friends if they knew what it meant.

Thoughts piled in and rushed by in an instant, like early morning dreams, and then suddenly I flushed under their weight, ashamed of my vanity. Ben had come to love the trail, too, love to hike, love to tell his friends about it, love to re-hash misadventures. I wanted to share the experience with him, especially summiting that last mountain. Could he meet me at the base and make the climb with me on my last day? Or maybe, after we sorted out this situation, whenever that was, we could hike through Maine. Or not.

I looked up and said, "It's okay if I never finish the Appalachian Trail. Having you around is the most important thing."

I spent the next few weeks shouldering our heavy knowledge. The days would distract me, and when the physical sensation of distress re-emerged, check in with myself about what was nagging. *Right*, I would think, *my husband and best friend of more than twenty years could drop dead at any time.* Since Brugada victims are at highest risk for dying in the morning, as his mother and grandfather had done, each day upon waking, I immediately reached for the reassuring rise and fall of Ben's chest. I startled every time my phone rang, sure it was the police delivering the news: my husband had collapsed at work, and despite being surrounded by physicians, had expired during a *code blue*. Images from his marathon returned again and again, my worry that he had collapsed on pine needles adjacent to the course, and I wondered if the scenario had been a cruel foreshadowing. Too many times, I imagined us hiking through dense forest, as we had done for years, and Ben halting, his face pale, dropping onto roots and moss. My shoulders would sting as I performed chest compressions on his bag-of-worms heart, on my bloodied knees until I dropped from exhaustion next to his lifeless body.

Even during this period of worry, the Appalachian Trail called. For a decade, every year, I had planned, trained, and then immersed in the forest to long distance hike. It was part of my seasonal rhythm, like spring sun chasing away winter rain, days lengthening, and in California, the hills melting from green to gold.

"We're finishing," Ben insisted, when I dismissed his questions about airports, shuttles, spending a few days around Bar Harbor before we headed home. Unrest haunted me, intensified, stalking quiet times in my days. But, intellectually, I accepted our change in plans, and redirected my thoughts to the process of documenting Ben's condition, which would lead to the only intervention available for Brugada syndrome: a defibrillator inserted in his chest. This device would sit just under the skin, bulging like a silver dollar, and if his heart fell into chaos would shock and reset orderly pumping.

Over the next two months Ben underwent study after study. We waited for results, waited for the next appointment, waited for the next consultation, waited for resolution. We drove to and from San Francisco hospitals, seeing cardiac electrical specialists. A Brugada specialist at Mayo Clinic in Arizona read Ben's EKG and asked us to travel to Scottsdale for a consultation. Each time we heard conflicting opinions about what studies should be next, what increased Ben's risk, and received "inconclusive" results, frustration rose. We recognized how it must feel for those who have less knowledge of human physiology, who weren't medical "insiders."

For me, the most maddening aspect of the emotional rollercoaster, was that every single doctor responded to Ben's inquiry the same way, including the cardiologist who had just administered a drug to document Brugada by deliberately inducing ventricular fibrillation.

"Absolutely finish the Appalachian Trail this year," he said, looking up from the red, portable "crash cart," the cabinet loaded with drugs and equipment designed to restart erratically beating hearts.

I glowered at him.

"Ben has lived with this condition for forty-six years, why should the next few months matter?" he softened his voice as he patronized me. Ben particularly liked this argument because it supported the illusion that we have time.

"It's probabilities," the cardiologist argued, "Even the highest risk patients are looking at less than 1% chance of death per year."

"Calling bullshit," I said, unconcerned with his annoyed expression. The pushy wife again. The statistical argument meant nothing; I believed in the probability of the improbable. I watched my father experience a bizarre illness. Ben's mother and grandfather had both dropped with sudden cardiac death. But these were doctors—left-brainers, I called them—their cognition limited by linear thought and their own constructs of logic. I replied with what seemed too obvious to ignore. "Here's your statistic: Brugada isn't batting less than 1% in Ben's family. It's batting a thousand."

Ben finally convinced me using my own words from my first AT section. I had made a hurried call home from Nantahala, North Carolina, just before meeting the rattlesnake atop Cheoah Bald. Ben had panicked because the machine had truncated my message. *Was I injured and in need of help? Should he call for search and rescue?*

"I didn't eat for two days," he'd said, when I called home again. "You can't be out there alone."

"It's my life and my risk," I had told him. "It's not fair for you to limit me with your fear." Despite his discomfort, Ben supported my subsequent solo hikes. He was asking for the same room to choose.

Chapter Fifty-eight

I assembled what we needed to trek from Gorham to Mount Katahdin quicker than a long-eared chipmunk could stuff its cheeks with acorns. Right away: ramp up exercise, make plane and overnight arrangements, call shuttles. Two weeks before: shop for books and food. One week before: pick up medications and first aid supplies, pack supply boxes, make final arrangements for cats and dogs. Four days before: setup tent for final check, inventory equipment, pack up pack. Three days: make last trip to outfitter, mail supply boxes, confirm shuttles. Two days: get haircut and clip toe nails. One day: bring pets to kennel, select book for first leg (tear off cover, recycle). Everyday: obsessively check Maine mountain weather. I stowed my worry about Ben like I stowed my rain gear, zipped into a pocket to be pulled out only when necessary.

As always, my ritual helped with anxiety. It was protective, like saying, "Lucky, lucky white horse—ding, ding, ding!" every time I stepped on a crack as a child. One of my most important rules before the trail was to never stray from routine. Deviations were bad luck and could cause delays, such as injury or fire or earthquake, or worse, trigger my neurotic brain to distract me while I hiked.

But this year my compulsiveness failed as talisman, we had a series of calamities. Three days before we left, my bay-and-white paint horse Jimmie and I fell during a lesson. Jimmie was fine, having my left knee to cushion him, but I was off my feet for two days. Despite wrapping, anti-inflammatory medication, and icing right up until landing in Maine, I limped for the first forty miles, using my poles as crutches, and swinging my leg sideways over rocks and logs. Travelling east, we faced canceled and missed connections. Ben's backpack was lost. A meticulously assembled supply box arrived battered and empty except for a small baggie of peanut butter malted milk balls—its food, books, maps, and clothing all mysteriously gone. Inside we found a note from the US Postal Service stating, "You have the right to expect your mail to arrive undamaged. We apologize for any inconvenience."

Despite the setbacks, we obtained what we needed, made do, and made up distance. Each incident seemed small, but together they became exhausting. As we launched into our final leg from Gorham in late afternoon, shooting for a spring atop Hayes Mountain to camp, we managed humor.

"Hey, Gimpy," Ben called ahead to me. "I noticed you gave me all the heavy food." He poked my backpack with his pole. "And that limp's not fooling me." He watched me struggle over a log by sitting on it, then lifting my left leg with both hands. I knew humor hid concern, that he cringed watching my canted gait in airports as we scuttled between juggled connections.

"You can just call me Grace instead of Violet," I called back. "Luckily, the judges aren't scoring us based on finesse." I stopped and posed with my arms out, left leg in the air behind me. "They're just looking for 'forward.' Plus, regardless of how far we get each day, our real measure of success is that your heart is still beating."

Crickets.

"This is my vacation. If I CPR you, I'll bill you for time and half," I said, hoping I hadn't stuffed my injured foot in my mouth.

Maine lived up to the legend. Rocks and logs challenged our path, streams and rivers crossed at regular intervals, necessitating hops from stone to stone. The scramble through Mahoosic Notch, an infamous mile-long boulder patch, took us almost ninety minutes, and involved crawling, shimmying, squeezing, and tossing packs ahead before flying leaps over gaps. Even the sunshine, for which I had been originally thankful, added to our toil. June had been one of the wettest months in history, with Maine receiving almost eight inches, and by three days into July the precipitation had already exceeded that month's average rainfall, as well. Only two weeks before our hike, the river crossings had been perilous; hikers found themselves setting up camp and waiting days for water levels to drop enough to wade safely. I imagined trudging through Vermont-deep mud, dragging heavy boots. But true to hiker lore, the weather abruptly flipped.

"Maine really *is* that bad," I said, to the ninety-plus degree air, and plopping onto a mossy patch, inching under a bramble's sparse shade. I peeled soaked shorts away from my quadriceps. My lead-like legs seemed to slam down onto the path. After traversing both Moody and Old Blue Mountains, we staggered into the campsite and sucked down water.

"By the time we topped Old Blue, I wondered if my aching muscles were in rhabdo," I whispered to Ben in the tent. Rhabdo is short for rhabdomyolysis, which is when your muscles get so stressed the cells break apart. The fragments clog up your kidneys and cause them to fail.

"The thought crossed my mind," Ben-the-kidney-guy said. "You peed once today." He pivoted his head toward me. "That's not enough urine for a day."

"Monitoring my urine output?" Laughter shook me.

"Mine, too," he said. "I kept thinking: AKI, my kidneys are doomed!"

"Geek," I elbowed him. You can get acute kidney injury (AKI), which I had worried about in the Smokies, when your rhabdo-busted-up muscles cells clogs up the tubes. It seemed our kidneys had a harder time climbing those mountains than our legs. Knowing the potential adverse outcomes from our sizzling hike...Ben could be both the best and the worst thing for my attempt at Katahdin.

"That last mile from Third Peak might just as well have been a marathon. Each step was a step too far," was the last thing Ben said before we drifted off, listening to a welcome breeze rustle leaves overhead.

Chapter Fifty-nine

I wasn't surprised to encounter my most-challenging-ever last mile in Maine, between Carlos Col and Full Goose shelters. We lingered at lunch, avoiding light rain. Finally, tucking away our jerky and wheat crackers, we set out around 2 PM for what looked to be an easy four miles. We would traverse the peaks of west Goose Eye Mountain, then east Goose Eye Mountain, before hitting north Goose Eye Mountain, none of which were substantial climbs, and finally the flat last mile to the shelter, called Full Goose. Although it sounded like a great many geese, we didn't actually see any.

What we did encounter were rocks, wet ones, both under our feet and in our way; we stumbled along, too often climbing...up, over, or, the worst, down. I slipped and skinned my palms and knees. We scaled a ladder secured to a sheer face by only a rope. Ah, yes...Maine, by now we should expect this. We'd misjudged yet again, apparently less able to learn than the alleged alpine geese. Overcast sky spit at us, and wind gusted, leaving the air just chilled enough to discourage rest. Although it seems unlikely at 3,500 feet where the terrain is mostly rocks and moss on rocks, and a few stunted trees sprouting from rocks, we also encountered several bogs, hindering our progress even more.

The Maine AT Club (MATC) is a conscientious trail maintenance organization. Workers strive to make bog-crossings safe for both hikers and the fragile ecosystem by placing parallel planks over mucky areas. We stepped widely atop the two wooden treads. We waddled, really, arms and poles out to the side, making me wonder if the ancestors who had named the peaks watched, chortling, at the hiker-geese. The planks intermittently ran under murky water, making foot placement a leap of faith. I used my poles to explore ahead, often glad I did, because between planks would be a hazardous spot to step.

Local geology provided a distracting conversation topic and got us through another mile. I squinted at moss and green shoots popping up. Bogs apparently are not limited to low lying areas. Since Merriam Webster's definition of bog, *wet spongy ground*, makes no mention of altitude, we decided these wet, spongy pockets resting in wind- and water-eroded rock qualified. But unlike low-lying bogs, they couldn't be very deep.

Ahhhh...but they could, which I learned as I missed a plank and sank to my right hip. My left foot still rested on a board in two inches of brown water, and behind it, my left butt cheek. My left knee bent to my chest, where I could rest my chin, and in fact had to, keeping my weight forward so my pack wouldn't topple me backward. My right leg was nowhere to be seen. I reached down with my right boot tip...nope, no bottom. I pushed my right pole down a little farther into the mud...nope, no bottom. Bottomless, the bogs. What if all of me had fallen in? Would I have sunk to China?

I struggled to gain leverage; mud had created suction around my leg. When I tried to push myself up, my hands sank, too. I wiped my palms on the front of my jacket. My left leg started to fall asleep but if I let myself sit, I'd lose my small amount of purchase. Rain started to fall, and I realized it made absolutely no difference how far the shelter was, I wasn't going anywhere.

Behind me, Ben belly laughed. I closed my eyes...tired, chilly, frustrated, impatient for the camp spot, and now mud-bound, but not alone. I tilted my head back and tried to see him.

"Okay, you be Curly and I'll be Mo," I said. Ben and I collected these moments, assigning them "re-tale value." I could already hear him telling his friends over a beer, "...and then JoDean plunged in, right up to her waist!"

Ben guided the pack off my shoulders, and with one foot on each row of boards, tried to hoist me up. The quagmire sucked at my leg. Gusts of wind blew raindrops against my cheeks, and I wondered if the earth was claiming me, after offering me so much in my life. Balance due. Then my left brain suggested I try to break the vacuum.

"Keep hold under my arms," I said and rotated my thigh, then tried forward and back, simultaneously scooping with my hand. Finally, I bent my right knee which allowed just enough air. "Lift! Quick!" And then I was on my hands and knees, the two halves of my body on different planks. I scrambled up and steadied myself against Ben as I lifted my wet pack off the boards, slid it on, and waddled forward again.

I won't say the walk into Full Goose shelter went quickly after that, but at least it wasn't boring. We clamored up a ladder to the shelter—which sat on a moss-covered rise—tired, wet, and muddy, so I made us hot tea right away. We alternated between silence and quiet chuckles, enjoying noodles and peanut sauce, then turned in, drifting off, hand-in-hand, shoulder-to-shoulder, with my mud caked rain pants draped over our tiny two-person tent.

Eventually we outpaced the complications and fell into the trail rhythm. At some point, my knee pain miraculously disappeared. Maine's rugged nature and splendor spellbound me. Scents of pine and balsam accompanied each step.

Absorbed in each day, I would forget how close I was to my goal. Ben loved to remind me. At campsites or rest breaks, he would reach into my pack, pull out the map and call out remaining miles. "Two hundred!" he would say, or "One fifty!"

The MATC trail work continued to wow us. We found steps carved into rocks, and stone staircases up mountains. My back ached just thinking about lugging and stacking. Hand holds steadied us on steep slopes. Blazes beckoned, clear and well-spaced. While the MATC has a "no bridge" policy to minimize impact, they had strung ropes across rivers and streams to make the traverse less harrowing. At the most dangerous crossing, the seventy-foot wide Kennebec River—where an upstream hydroelectric plant releases water at unpredictable intervals, tragically drowning at least two backpack-ladened hikers—the MATC pays a local paddler to shuttle folks back and forth in his red canoe. A white blaze on the bow designates the canoe-ferry as "the official AT route" across.

Before we left, I was convinced the worry about Ben's heart would sit like Maine rocks in my pack, dragging us both down. Instead, aside from the mornings, when I woke and immediately listened for his breath in our cocoon, I spent the days thinking about trail things.

I cried for the first time in Rangeley, a lakeside town where we stopped for supplies. Wandering, relaxing, and letting my guard down, complex emotions swept over me. I struggled to name them: excitement, anticipation...grief? The conclusion to a consequential part of my life.

I let the town library's used books sale distract me. One book's spine nudged out, and I pulled it free. My shoulders sagged, and tears fell onto the tattered cover of Maya Angelou's *I Know Why the Caged Bird Sings*. A woman appeared next to me put a hand on my arm.

"You're a long way from Georgia," she said. She had sharp blue eyes that stood out from her pale, lined face. Her white hair coiled loosely into a bun, and she wore peach lipstick. Glasses hung from a pearled chain around her neck. I felt certain she was the librarian. She added, "It's more than miles, they say."

"How much for this one?" I asked, holding up the caged bird like it was a mirror.

"You take it, dear," she said, closing her hands around mine. She tilted her head, studying me back. "You're almost there." She smiled with closed lips, nodded, and turned to mingle with the other browsers. She looked back and added, "Almost."

Chapter Sixty

In our hotel room, Ben dozed. Restless, I recalculated our food needs, transferred laundry, checked news stations. Finally, I picked up my phone and powered it on. My brother and his son had close birthdays, and the family was celebrating by "glamping" at Disney. I hesitated, then texted to ask how it was going.

"Can u talk?" was the immediate reply.

Gut punch.

I should have known better than to expose myself to the potential turmoil, given that I was closing in on a decade-long goal. My thumb reflexively reached for the off button. I touched it, lifted my thumb, touched it again. Thought of texting that I was on some isolated peak with sketchy service. Sat down, stood up, sat down. Stared at the screen. Ben snored softly, so I stepped outside. *You're being self-absorbed. Just call.* Dread pulled me down onto a deck chair as I keyed the number and watched my thumb hover between "send" and "off."

"Hey! How's every...".

"We had a bad rollover car accident; we're all in the hospital in Lakeland, and Mom broke her neck," John blurted.

The air hummed. My chest hummed. A weight like chain mail dropped over me. I tried to process the information. *All* of them hospitalized? With what? Punctured lungs? Ruptured spleens? Broken bones? He hadn't said anything about a trauma center or surgeries. How was he calling from his cell? Where was Lakeland? Was my mother dead? I stared up at the eaves, glancing from cobweb to bird's nest. I stood to wake Ben.

Seconds went by before John added in a calm voice, "We're all okay."

I imagined him savoring the impact. How soon before this was on Facebook? Anger started down deep, where the dread had been. Way to sucker punch your sister, who is in a remote part of Maine with no transportation.

"We were walking out of the ER, headed to Disney when the doc called us back to say the radiologist found a fracture on Mom's neck CT scan." I slumped against the wall of the building, my body in a tug of war between anger and relief. His wife and kids were okay. My mother was okay. It was especially obvious that he was okay when he started rapid fire explaining.

"I told Mom, just like I always do, put on your seat belt. We're not leaving until everyone is buckled in," he said. "The kids were in the back seat with her. They both called her out, 'Grammy-Sandy, seat belts for safety!'"

I saw my mom's stubborn expression, and her crossed arms. Yep.

I sank down onto the chair again. It wouldn't occur to my brother, when faced with breaking this news to his sister who is on the Appalachian Trail, to start the conversation with, "We're all okay, and still headed to Disney World, but I wanted you to know... ." Or perhaps to hold off telling me, altogether, given that they were all okay.

"So, when we started out, I assumed she had her belt on," he was still talking. "I told her. The kids told her..."

I had almost lost my whole family, in seconds, in a completely unpredictable life event. My hands shook.... Could I hike?

317

"...I'm pretty sure even Diane told her." He took a breath. "But you know Sandy, stubborn and never takes responsibility for herself or how she acts."

I transitioned to grateful, able to share my brother's fear and offer support, and at the same time, wished I'd never turned on my phone. *Which was it?* My outrage shifted to my mother. She refused her seatbelt, in front of her grandchildren—*nice role-modeling, Mom*—and her choice ruined their birthday trip. When I heard they were bringing her, I cringed. She would drink too much and make scenes. And then, wake at night in an unfamiliar place, stumble around and fall. Sheesh, they hadn't even gotten to the first night.

"So then this blacked-out sedan flies by, weaving in and out and cuts me off. So I swerved, but then...We were rolling and rolling and somehow landed right side up," he said. "There we were—sitting on the grass next to the highway."

I saw from his eyes, hands clutching the steering wheel, landing upright, rocking side to side, finally settling—the hot, humid Florida air pressurizing the minivan's interior. He's still shaken but turning, afraid of what he'll see. It's slow motion: Diane. Joe. Emma. Mom.

"Everyone around us stopped to help," he spoke quickly, as if he thought his time was up. "They were yelling at the police to go after the guy." John took a breath. His mouth sounded dry. "They told the police that he cut some of them off, too, screeching in and out of lanes. Who saw that coming?"

A pang rose in me, displacing anger, displacing fatigue and sore muscles. I wanted to take the guilt from him, tuck it into my pack like a grenade, and sprint north into the trees, where I could drop it into a pile of rocks to explode into a million pieces without harming him or me or his family.

"None of us has a scratch, can you believe it? Well, Diane has a bruise from the seat beat," he said. I could hear his relief as he said it. "Except mom, who had slammed against the roof." He was edgy again. "But as I said, she refused to put on her belt."

I grabbed the grenade. "You don't own Mom's choice's," I said. "And that was some heads up driving, avoiding a pile up." Did he relax a little? "Imagine how many people would have been hurt. I mean, seat belts or not, a crushed car is a crushed person." He needed someone to say he wasn't to blame. At least I could be an authoritative voice. Older sibling. Doctor. He certainly wasn't going to get any reassurance from my mother, who only thought about herself. Every time he paused, I repeated the message, as many ways as I knew how.

"Should I try to hitch a ride to the airport and come down there?"

I climbed onto the bed and waited for Ben to wake. Eventually, he opened his eyes and turned, noticing my face. He sighed. "You called your family, didn't you?"

Ben listened and I saw his concern, and his frustration with the summer's pile up of events. But also a subtle something else. Relief? And who could blame him? The focus was finally off his heart. He had my mother to thank for that. Currently, she was hospitalized until a neurosurgeon could consult. With my mother tucked in, my brother's family headed to Disney, trying to salvage my nephew's birthday.

"A specialist probably won't weekend-consult on a non-emergent case," I said to Ben. Not because he didn't know, but because I wanted to raise the possibility that we should stay in town to be reachable, even though it might cost us until Monday.

"Let's hangout here," he said. "Rest and refuel. We haven't even tried that ice cream place on Main Street." He shrugged and went back to his book. He was way too okay with this.

The more resting and refueling we did, the more exhausted I got. I fidgeted and paced, refused Moose Tracks ice cream and most food altogether. Katahdin somehow got farther away.

On Monday morning my brother called.

"How's Mom?" I asked, wondering if I really cared.

"She wants out of the hospital," he answered. "Here, talk to the neurosurgeon."

"Wait! Wha...?"

"Hello? Dr. Smithson here." I pictured a tall, African American man attached to the deep voice. "I hear you are hiking? Let's get you on your way."

Good, two doctors talking. Right down to business. The hospital whirred and beeped through the line. "Okay, shoot."

"We have three options with your mother's fracture," Dr. Smithson continued, describing her first cervical vertebral fracture, which occurred when she hit the car's roof.

"We can stiff collar your mother, which she would wear for twelve weeks. We can halo her, which would promote healing in less time. Unpleasant, though, as you can imagine." A halo collar sits on the shoulders. Rods connect bands on the neck and head. The head band is secured by bores into the skull. Practically a medieval torture device.

"Or lastly, we can do surgery right here and now, inserting a plate in her neck. All equally likely to promote healing. But with surgery, the plate will permanently limit her neck's range of motion," he said.

"Your recommendation?" I asked him.

"That's your decision," he hedged.

"Dr. Smithson, if it were your mother?" I asked. I know this game; I play it.

"I never feel that the halo is the best option," he said. "They are unwieldy, uncomfortable, and garner attention." I pictured this and agreed.

"Thank you so much for your time. We'll sort this out right now, so you can move on." I imagined him checking his watch. "Can I talk to my brother?" I heard him hand over the phone.

"What does Mom want?"

"She wants us to choose," John said.

"So *now* she'll take a suggestion from you?" I asked. "Put Mom on."

The receiver rubbed and clicked.

"Hi, JoDean," I heard, in a whiny voice.

"Mom, how are you?"

"My neck hurts," she said. "I was fine before. Now it hurts." *Don't act so pitiful*, I thought, *you did this to yourself.*

"What a hassle, Mom. What's your preference? Do you want the collar or surgery?" I left out the halo option.

"You guys decide," she said.

"Mom, I need you to buck up. Do you want to get a collar today and leave?" I asked. "Go to Disney World with the kids? Because you can do that." I knew my mother, and I knew she would want out. It would also be *way* easier on my brother to have her with him, rather having surgery and recovering hours from home, and during his vacation. "Or do you want to have surgery?"

"I could go home and see a doctor there, right?" she asked.

"Yes, you could get the stiff collar and follow up there," I said.

"I'll take collar," she said. I could picture her trying to nod in her temporary collar. "Then I can leave this hospital."

So you can have your scotch. "Okay, love you, Mom. Can I talk to John?" I did love her, but I felt sick. Angry. Guilty. *Pull it together.*

I sat on the bed and agonized over whether I should continue hiking or abandon the trip and head to Florida.

"Did she ask how you were doing?" Ben touched my arm and startled me out of my thoughts. "Or apologize for interrupting your hike?"

"You're kidding, right?" And it wasn't just me. My brother, my nephew. How many of their vacations had she ruined?

"Did she ask how far we'd gotten?" Ben continued, as if he couldn't believe it.

"Nothing about us. Not your heart. Nothing," I sighed. None of them had asked. All these years, working my way north, and except for my Uncle Don and Aunt Bonnie, no one seemed interested.

I knew what Ben was trying to tell me. My family had been at Disney that weekend, while I suspended my hike to be reachable. They were headed back to Disney, including my mother. In fact, they would be more comfortable "glamping" in Disney than we would be. Then they would return to Fort Myers and follow up there. Why couldn't I let it go? Take care of myself?

Brushing my teeth, I stared at my pale face in the bathroom mirror. I had bags under my eyes. Water circled and drained. *You don't own this.* Where was my alter ego, the physician, now? The white coat? Logical thought? I walked over to the bedside table and tore a sheet off the notepad. I wrote DR. JODEAN NICOLETTE and stuck it under my bra strap. Labelled, I returned to the mirror, waited for the transformation. I took it off, added a comma and then MD...nothing. I always told my family, "I am the daughter, not the doctor," and now it haunted me.

I did the only logical thing. I called my sister-in-law, Diane.

"Look," she said, in her rational voice, "Your mom is being discharged. We are going to Disney World. We're going for normal—for the kids—so Joe's birthday isn't ruined." She paused. *"Normal.* So don't come and make things not normal. For you to hike right now, that's normal."

My brother took the phone.

"John, we're gonna walk. We're heading out right now," I said. "And we won't have cell service. Enjoy Disney!" *Please, don't call me,* is what I wanted to say.

"Oh, and John?"

"Yeah?"

"Happy Birthday to you and Joe."

Chapter Sixty-one

Pack heavy, thoughts heavy, heart heavy, all of it anchoring me in the room. I hefted my resupplied pack to my back, and the weight pulled me down onto the bed. Ben laced my fingers in his, drew me up, turned me, and with his hands on my shoulders, guided me out the door. I squinted in the morning light, felt the impulse to shrink back, then refused to succumb to the old pattern. I clipped my waist band and started toward the road.

Our next town lay a hundred miles north: Monson, a famous trail town that sat on the southern edge of the Hundred Mile Wilderness. I stepped off Rte. 4 and into the heavy timber, using all the mental skills I had developed in the last two thousand miles: no obstacle is insurmountable; one foot in front of the other; have faith in progress; stay grounded in the present. By the time we hit Piazza Rock shelter and headed for Poplar Ridge, the density of trees and sheer remoteness had formed a buffer between me and my other life; I sank back into wilderness.

We charged over Saddleback and Spaulding Mountains, and along several peaceful lakes and ponds. Trail landmarks beckoned. Even the relentless rain that poured for ten miles into Pierce Pond shelter failed to slow me, as eager as I was to see nearby Harrison's Camp, one of the last remaining historic hunting compounds which lay a quarter mile east into the trees.

The contemporary place hosts non-hunting guests and offers hikers an all-you-can-eat breakfast if you're there by 7 AM. We sipped coffee as we waited for blueberry pancakes, examining the memorabilia and photos.

Next, we crossed the Kennebec River in the famous canoe "ferry." Goose chills popped when I first spied the white blaze on the red bow. I stowed my pack and teetered in. So many trail-legends: Clingman's Dome, Damascus, Shenandoah National Park, Harper's Ferry, Dover Oak, Lemon Squeeze, White Mountains, Mahoosuc Notch...now the Kennebec Ferry. Ben snapped photos like a tourist and for once I loved it. Gratitude shone on me with the August sun as the canoe returned with Ben leaning and smiling from behind the paddler; how could I have experienced this without him? Even thought of it? We thanked our captain and headed into the trees.

Still, at times my focus evaporated, and uncomfortable emotions slipped in. Guilt bothered me the most, when my caregiver-self emerged, drawing momentum from each year it dominated my personality. My mother had a serious, painful injury which would worsen without distractions from her grandchildren and Disney. And my brother deserved a break. It was an undertow, the urge to rescue. Do laundry, fetch groceries, dispense medications, prepare meals—all tasks ingrained in my youth.

Then I would remember my diagnosis: terminal helper syndrome, the compulsion to offer assistance, energy, support, even when it harmed me. I wasn't a child anymore; I didn't have to assume an impossible role in a dysfunctional home. I couldn't change my mother's choice to ignore her illness, or my brother's choice to enable, but I could change my response, limit the impact on my life. The person who needed— *deserved*—my care was *me*.

"Let's talk," I would say to Ben. We would pull from our stash of conversation topics or hash out more questions from my *5-year Q&A Diary.*

If you could have dinner with anyone, dead or alive, who would it be? Together, we said, "Fareed Zakaria," then chatted about our favorite interviews and columns.

When was the last time you went dancing? We both said it had been too long.

If you could be a literary character, who would it be? Ben said, "Sherlock Holmes," but I thought he was more of an Atticus Finch.

"You?" Ben asked, interrupting the rhythm of our steps. Faces shuffled through my mind like playing cards, conjured from many authors' artfully constructed protagonists. Mostly from my favorite books...*Signature of All Things, Color Purple, Prodigal Summer, Hundred Secret Senses, Thousand Splendid Suns...* . When "Sookie Stackhouse" escaped from my mouth like a cat out the front door, Ben stopped and turned, eye brows raised.

"I feel like her," I said, hands on my hips. "Like I got born unsupervised into this person I don't understand, alone, and challenged with conquering rapid fire surreal obstacles in order to self-actualize." I waved my poles to keep him walking. "Plus, she's brave. And she kicks some serious boogie-man ass, which is what I need right now."

"I meant," Ben said over his shoulder, "Would you consider her...literary?"

One day out of Monson at Moxie Bald shelter, I got serious about searching for moose. I had yet to see one, despite seeing moose droppings since Massachusetts. Our tent site rested above Bald Mountain Pond, and I was enjoying the sunrise and my first cup of coffee, scanning the pond's edge. I stopped and stared... .

Ben was on the ground, slumped against a log, legs splayed in front. His eyes were open. He wasn't moving.

I called his name; he didn't respond. I called again. A jay landed at his feet and hopped in the dirt, but he didn't move. Chill rose through my breast. Panic seized my body. My thoughts scrambled. *Only a day from Monson. One. More. Day. To. Town.* A mourning dove's eerie call floated from the brush as I stumbled from the bank. I surprised myself at how quickly I became a doctor, despite the frantic thoughts—*Thirty compressions, two breaths. Don't stop compressions except to change out rescuers. Another rescuer...Had anyone hiked in last night who could relieve me? How many minutes of CPR before he had anoxic brain injury? How long could I keep him alive waiting for helicopter? Who had a cell phone and could call for help? WHERE was my cell phone? Was there cell service?*

I watched myself from above, striding. Looking so calm. "Ben," I said his name softly but firmly. Then again, "Ben," slightly louder each time. How many times? Twice, three times...my doctorvoice, my doctorface. I donned my professional demeanor as easily as pulling on a lab coat.

"Is anyone here?" I called out to the woods. Step, step. Faster. "I need some help here!" After a few interminable seconds, during which I envisioned the whole horrific, worst-case scenario, Ben tilted his head toward me.

"Did you say you needed help?" Ben asked, with a glassy stare, emerging from deep thought, and oblivious to the dawn's sounds and sights.

"What is wrong with you?" I screamed, feeling my sweaty skin cool.

"Just thinking," he said, collecting his sleeping bag and mat. "Such a nice morning. Do we have any peanut butter left for the oats?" He smiled, then looked concerned. "And raisins.... . What's wrong? Did you see a moose?"

"He bolted through," I spit out, kicking his boots. "Plowed right over you." Then I stomped away, afraid saying it out loud would make it more real. "Yes, peanut butter. And you better eat all of it. It's seventeen miles into Monson." I refused to look at him as I finished our morning routine.

What makes up a perfect day? I read from my crumpled paper as we passed Marble Brook.

"Okay, where?" Ben asked. "Let's say on-the-trail."

"Sunny weather, but not too hot," I said, thinking about climbing Moody and Old Blue mountains.

"A great view...worth the climb," Ben said. To him, and to most people, view means a wide, unobstructed swatch of country, usually from altitude. In terms of biophilia, that's the view that produces calm and perspective. And trees, well they obstruct views. But to me, trees *are* the view. I surveyed the straight trunks flanking us on both sides. And in front. And in back. Various colors and shapes of needles and leaves. I inhaled, wallowing in the connectedness that arises in the forest.

"A great place to camp: tenting," I said.

"Next to a stream or pond," Ben added, then said, "How about cool fellow hikers?" We hadn't seen anyone for miles.

"You mean, like me?" said a male voice at our backs.

We turned. The man behind us who had managed to pad silently atop the Maine rocks introduced himself as The Professor.

"The Ghost, more likely," I said, "Heading to Monson?"

"Just past," Professor said, "Loaded to finish." He reached behind and patted his pack. "Had no idea the conversation would be so interesting." He fell in with us, no doubt slowing.

"Feel free to chime in. I was just going to add *a manageable trail*. Walkable, so you can make good time. Or at least the day doesn't feel like a struggle," I said, still trying to work out what I meant. The arduous terrain in New Hampshire and southern Maine had stuck with me, even though the going had eased up. "What I mean is, for a day to be perfect, you can't think it's going to be an easy nine or ten, but then it turns out to be a nightmare-marathon day, and you end up slogging through a boulder field and you're hating the trail."

"So you walk just about as long you think you're going to walk," The Professor said.

We nodded, thinking that part had more to do with that unlearnable lesson: curbing expectations.

"Even though I don't know you personally," The Professor chimed in, "And haven't really walked with a female... ."

"All hikers. Immediate community," I said.

"...I think I can add this," he chinned toward me, acknowledging. "A good solid evacuation at the start of the day, you know, a BM. That's important."

Ben nodded and raised his index finger. "Yes! You don't want to be hiking all loaded down."

I let the men share their moment.

Just south of Monson, The Professor peeled off, heading a few miles farther, into the Hundred Mile Wilderness. Ben and I were tired and hungry, eager for a shower, bed, and real food. The trees thinned and sunlight shone brighter. Road sounds and voices reached us. Despite our interest in exploring another famous trail town, I hesitated, never happy to leave the woods behind.

"There's something else that makes a perfect day," Ben said.

I waited. "What else?"

"A perfect day has a surprise," he said.

"You mean like a hiker stealth-gaining on us?"

"Sort of...something kind of cool like that. And not bad. Something special," he said.

"Today was close," I said. "Pleasant but not perfect." Frightening surprise just before breakfast. Past that now. I took my last inhales of wild and nodded to the dense conifers, took my last steps on the soft cushion of needles. Trees surrounded the small town but would exist mostly in the background for the next day as we resupplied. Wilderness had circled me again, like wagons, had offered me respite and a chance to claim perspective. I was right to step away from Rangeley and under their sheltering boughs; this wild place was where I was supposed to be.

Chapter Sixty-two

My phone beeped and buzzed in my hand. The screen displayed texts, voicemails, and social media notifications. My throat caught in a familiar way, flashing back to pager onslaughts during my intern year. Suddenly, the knot in my throat grew, became red hot, and swelled to my back and neck as I realized the likely origin. I turned the screen against my thigh and stared where my muddy boot toes had halted, at the boundary of trail and concrete. I had only wanted to give our hostel an arrival heads up. I looked up at Ben, wondering if my eyes looked round and pleading like SPCA-ad puppies.

Ben held out his hand. He studied the screen, then read out loud. "From Facebook we're supposed to pray for your mother due to her 'physical and mental deterioration.'...And transfer to the ICU." Ben tapped bubbles and read, "Here's another post from your brother about 'hoping my mother will pull through.'" He swiped and tapped a few more times.

"You've got texts from your cousins asking for 'real' (he made air quotes) information about your mom," he said, tapping throughs messages. "They're about your brother's drama-posts, but how he won't respond to direct communications."

We walked while I took deep breaths and tried to force the fog of despair to dissipate into the clear blue above us.

"How could your mother go from discharge-to-Disney to brink-of-death between Rangeley and Monson?" Ben asked.

"If this were my patient," I said, "I know what I would think."

In town, I called the Lakeland ICU. My mother had gotten confused in the hours between the neurosurgeon's visit and her discharge. Tremor and delirium started soon after.

"Wasn't she on your most aggressive CIWA protocol?" I asked the nurse. CIWA stands for Clinical Institute Withdrawal Assessment and offers nurses an objective scale to measure alcohol withdrawal and dose treatment benzodiazepines (like Valium). "She probably told you *one drink a night*, right? And even if it was only *one*, that means a coffee mug full of Dewar's," I said. Clinicians know that it's reasonable to quadruple however much a patient tells you. I listened for a few seconds.

"That explains it," I said into the phone, and cut my eyes at Ben. "Thank you for all you're doing."

"She didn't tell them one drink a night," I said to Ben as we kicked up dust. "She told them she doesn't drink. Period."

"They got behind the eight ball."

"Something else she did to herself. And to John and his family," I said. If she had been honest, her team would have CIWA'ed her on admission to prevent withdrawal. Further complicating the situation, she had thrashed around in her delirium, putting her neck at risk and necessitating transfer to ICU for restraints and a twenty-four-hour sitter. Alcohol withdrawal can look scary, especially in elders, although it's treatable, and she would clear eventually.

I watched Maine fly by through the windows of our Bangor airport shuttle, the blurred maple, spruce, and Douglas fir taking me back to my first section, the only other time I unexpectedly left the Appalachian Trail. I had retreated from Fontana Dam because past events ambushed my hike, and I needed time to process and grow stronger. Now? Now, I faced current events, but events buttressed by almost fifty years living with a parent's addiction. It seemed to culminate here: guilt, shame, self-indictment, the need to please, to assume responsibility when I wasn't responsible. Was I doing this for my mother? My brother? Myself?

"I'll fly to Lakeland and stay with her," I had responded when my brother explained he and his family had returned to Fort Myers. My words seemed to circle around my gut, like vultures anticipating the upcoming evisceration.

"I have to work," he added, as if he needed to justify why he couldn't keep his family away from home indefinitely. "Can they transfer her to Fort Myers?" he asked, "If I find a doctor here?"

Obviously, he felt guilty, too, and his struggle tore at me. I wanted him to set better boundaries, not feel responsible for her messes. Convince him to stop buying her Dewar's jugs and propping up her lifestyle. But I couldn't heal him, yank him out of co-dependence. He'd have to take the steps himself.

"Not medically necessary," I said. "Think of it as logical consequences. You've done more than enough for her. Be home and be happy about it."

My own guilt now originated from a different place, out of my indifference, it lingered like a shadow adjacent to the healthy boundaries I had finally erected. Was I taking a step backwards into the co-dependent behavior, allowing her to steal another important event from me? If I was supporting my brother's co-dependence, was that co-dependence once removed? Small towns dotted our progress, each marked by cafes touting lobster specialties: lobster po' boys, lobster bisque, lobster mac n cheese, lobster wraps. Instead of the usual deep hunger that punctuated my sections of the Trail, the signs prompted a mix of nausea and resentment. Addiction keeps a cruel tether on loved ones.

Waiting for our flight in Bangor, I answered texts and phone calls. No, my mother was not "deteriorating." Yes, alcohol withdrawal is a disappointingly common condition, requiring patience while she rode it out. No...ICU simply to protect her neck. Ben and I settled into our seats, welcoming the flight's isolation, and for a while, suspended over the mountains, we flew free. In Philadelphia, we hugged good-bye amidst throngs of hustling travelers. He boarded a flight west, and I stumbled numbly against the flow, zigzagging and bumping shoulders, to board a plane heading south. I wondered if I would return to the Appalachian Trail.

My Mom snored in a dimly lit ICU room, sedated by carefully titrated benzodiazepines. I paused at the foot of her bed and watched her breath, waiting for a familiar feeling to spread through me, the same pang and dread I experienced in my dad's hospital room. It didn't come. My mom had choices my dad didn't have. I felt sad for her, disappointed for me, as I remembered her vibrant creative self, the one who took up tap dancing at age forty. The one who smuggled home achievement tests and "played school" with me, administering them early, so I would score higher when I took them—a leg up in a tiered educational system. She was a highly functioning alcoholic then and had been for my childhood, but the waterfall of booze, combined with aging had sucked her into dysfunction. I thought of the times we had tried to reason with her, suggest rehab, and she had crossed her arms and shut down.

I tugged a cord to light the bedside, sat in her chair, and read, watched TV, watched her. She intermittently woke, sometimes lucid, medication slowly leaving her geriatric system. One afternoon, she fixed her once vibrant green eyes on me, and I explained what had happened.

"What do you mean they left?" she asked. *Really, Mom. That's your focus?*

"No one could predict how long it would take for you to recover from the alcohol withdrawal." I named it for the second time, surprised at the shame that accompanied speaking the truth. "I flew down from Maine."

"I want to go home," she said. "Get me home."

You're welcome, Mom. Yes, it has been quite an upheaval to accommodate your behaviors. For all of us.

"We'll see about getting you discharged and home when you wake up more," I said. *Yes, they got home safely. Yes, your choices cut Joe's birthday trip short, but he got some Disney time.*

"I want to go now! My neck hurts," she said.

Ben is fine, thanks for asking. Yes, the hiking was going well, before I got yanked off track by your antics. I have the Hundred Mile Wilderness left, and the additional miles to summit Mount Katahdin.

"Let's call the nurse for pain medication so you're more comfortable," I said.

"I can't believe you guys stuck me here," she said, then turned away and closed her eyes. *You're welcome, Mom.*

335

"Ummm...your brother's on hold about transferring your mother," said the nurse who had come in with her portable.

"Yeah, he gets like this. It's how he manages anxiety," I said, thinking of how he had called every doctor he knew, and some he didn't, when my dad's cancer recurred, hoping for a different prognosis. He called my dad's oncology office to tell the doctor about "new" medications, which of course the doctor knew about, and in fact weren't even new. "It helps him feel he has control. He bails her out of her alcoholic messes. Please be patient with him." I put down my book and stood to take the phone.

"I understand co-dependence," the nurse said, then hesitated. "It's just that usually doctors arrange a transfer—if it's medically necessary—not the patient. Or patient's family."

"I know," I said. I hesitated before adding, "I'm a doctor." A doctor who is a family member can make a team practice defensively, or prompt over-treatment, which can mean too many tests, and too many therapies that are meant to demonstrate how dedicated the team is, but don't improve care and sometimes worsens it.

"You are?" She leaned against the door jam. "You're the one who hooked him up with the helicopter transport?"

"The what?"

"Helicopter transport," she said, staring at me in disbelief. "He found a doctor to accept your mother in Fort Myers, but he had to get your mom there."

I fell back into the chair. *How was he paying for this?*

"He hired his own transfer. It's scheduled to land on our roof-pad in 60 minutes," she said, looking both sympathetic and amused. She came into the room and put a hand on my shoulder, offering the phone.

It was time to kick some boogie-man ass and be the heroine of my own life. I waved the phone away. The Appalachian Trail was calling.

336

Chapter Sixty-three

The gold-framed sunglasses clung like memories to my nose as we entered the Hundred Mile Wilderness, striding past Spectacle Pond, Bell Pond, North Pond, and over Little Wilson and Big Wilson streams. On a whim, a week before we had left to hike through Maine—so long ago, yet just a few weeks—I purchased the cheap shades with huge, square frames, aiming for a piece of celebratory gear. Hunched over at the kitchen table, sunglasses in one hand and glue-gun in the other, peering through cheaters at various rhinestones and baubles in my craft tackle box, I'd reminisced about my mother; I must look like her. She had a similar set up, spread across a dedicated table where she created broaches from antique memorabilia, beaded purses and jewelry, repaired porcelain, and arranged dried flowers which I now realized were littered with small violet petals. The images stomped through my brain as I stomped north, and I lifted a hand to slide my fingers over the gems—hopping rocks in the stream of memories—shades of purple interspersed with yellow.

I wanted to keep hold of that mother: creative, reaching for new interests, fun, stubbornly unwilling to miss a good time. I allowed this person into my final leg, perched on my nose with a bird's eye view. I found her lingering presence a comfort, despite intermittent, fingers of grief poking into my thoughts. And despite the amused looks and occasional guffaws my glitzy glasses prompted from other hikers.

We collapsed our second night at an unofficial site on East Chairback Pond, as if we'd been fleeing a pack of wolves for two days. But, by the next morning, as I perched on a partially submerged boulder watching the sun rise and fog float off the pond's glassy surface, events from the past weeks had faded into another life. The Hundred Mile Wilderness was my own eco-psychology, where I immersed in simpler life, removed triggers, and distanced myself from addiction, albeit someone else's. We cut short the next day to stay at Sidney Tappen campsite because I heard that a bull moose lumbered through at dawn and dusk to drink and graze at the spring. We met another couple, Wildstyle and Chafage, when they sidled over to sniff at our noodles with prawns, vegetables, and peanut sauce, learning they had stopped for the same moose.

Ben and I drifted into sleep with ears tuned, accompanied only by crickets and bullfrogs. Eight uneventful hours later, the first gray light gently nudged me awake, like a dog's soft nose, as if to confirm my camaraderie with the wilderness. Mother Nature must be rooting for my moose sighting. I listened. Birds chirped; leaves rustled. Dew dropped onto the tent. No crash, no branches snapping, no plodding dinner-plate hooves. No slurping water or snuffling and chomping grass. Ben stirred. Scents of wet grass drifted in. I pressed my nose against the screen and scanned. No moose.

I slipped out of my bag and into the warm air, minimizing clatter and whine. Tying my boots, I caught a white flash partially buried under loam and needles. Litter? Seriously? I reached and unearthed a package of temporary tattoos, buried and then offered up. I examined the icons and slid the slim gift into my pack.

That day we sprouted wings for the climbs: West Mountain, Haystack Mountain, and finally White Cap. From atop White Cap, we gawked at wide views of lakes, wooded valleys and mountains. We picked out prominent peaks, knowing one must be Katahdin but unable to identify it. The trail curved around the summit before heading down to the lowlands and to Cooper Falls' lean-to. Disappointed at missing Katahdin, I led at a hustle, rounding the last curve, eager to get past the sustained downgrade and the protest that would arise in my hips.

I yelped and scuffed to stop, spraying scree and planting my poles to keep my feet from flying out in front of me. Then I teetered like a huge pine before dropping to my knees, oblivious to the gravel that puckered and abraded my skin. Or that's how Ben described it. A fountain of energy expanded from my breast and spread as an electric charge to my shoulders, arms, thighs. Buoyant, I float above the trail, feeling altered by the sight. Again, this immense, unbounded space made me feel small and limitless in concert, intertwined with wilderness and the expanding ripples of life.

To the north, an immense, rhomboid land mass rose through flat layers of cloud like Saturn's rings. It dwarfed the surrounding peaks...actually, every peak within eyeshot, so that it seemed to stand alone with Maine kneeling at its base. Katahdin, meaning Great Mountain, received its name from the indigenous Penobscot people, and I could see why. Mountain among mountains.

My tears welled and fell to the dry earth I front of my knees.

After a decade, and 2100 miles, my goal was in sight.

Chapter Sixty-four

"Today was a perfect day," Ben said, as we dried from our dip in a downstream swimming hole, curtained by delicate brush. We tugged on camp clothes, and I slipped into my sleeping bag liner to nap before dinner. The Cooper Falls Brook lean-to sign had appeared on our right about an hour earlier than we expected, complete with flat tent areas, and a bubbly Cooper Brook fed by a spectacular waterfall. Half reading and half dozing, I listened to Wildestyle and Chafage traipse in. They chattered with Ben, and I caught snippets about staying the next night at the White House Landing, another old hunting camp about a mile off the AT. If hikers can find the lake and the dock, they blow an air horn, and the owner boats over to pick them up. I drifted off thinking about our day: views from White Cap summit, our lunch on a small rise overlooking Crawford Lake while a gaggle of Indestructibles splashed and cackled on a sandy beach below, the way-more-than 350-ft climb over Little Boardman Mountain.

A fingernail scratched on the screen, then a whisper slipped in, "Hey, baby...hungry?"

"So what was the surprise?" I asked, as we sipped our steaming split pea soup, and I stirred mango, vegetables, raisins, and pistachios to create Moroccan couscous. I shifted bags and utensils, looking for my packet of cinnamon.

Ben looked up and raised his eyebrows.

"The perfect-day-surprise." I found the cinnamon and sprinkled it into my banged up camp pot. After 2100 miles—jammed into packs, dropped, sat on—my pot looked like a used car: dinged, scraped, and dented. The lid no longer fit properly, but it still boiled water, and occasionally simmered pasta, so it remained a much-loved component of my gear.

"It was probably my singing, right?" I suggested, still in disbelief about my spontaneous Donna Summer rendition, as we descended White Cap after seeing Katahdin, when energy from my chest burst out my mouth. "Baby, there ain't no mountain high enough! Ain't no valley low enough! Ain't no river wide enough..." I had caught myself and glanced back, red-faced to see if Ben had heard my screeching voice.

"To keep me from getting to you, Babe," he had answered, in his rich, trained alto.

"Katahdin. Katahdin was the surprise," Ben said, as I scooped fragrant couscous and handed him the pot. "I hoped we would see it, if we had clear weather." He took a spoonful and sniffed. "It's just that it was such a...behemoth."

He stopped eating and looked up. "And you cried. I guess I should have expected that, but I didn't."

Me either, I thought.

About seventy-five miles remained between me and the northern terminus of the Appalachian Trail. Those miles, the same distance the AT stretches through my very first state, Georgia, and greater than its length in each West Virginia, Maryland, and Connecticut, seemed like baby steps after my decade-long journey. The land spilled flat before us, the small hills, bogs, and shorelines gesturing, almost funneling me in the direction of my goal.

We stepped out of the long green tunnel at Abol bridge onto the first developed road for a hundred miles and celebrated another milestone by relaxing in the sun and swimming in the Penobscot river. I floated next to shore, surveying the group that had assembled over the last several days. Roadrunner, a former pizza restaurant owner and Tennessee, a veterinarian from outside Gatlinburg, played cards at the picnic table. Space Cadet languished on the grassy bank. Honk snored softly, bare feet sticking out of his tent. All of us sported dirt, bumps, and bruises from the long trail miles. A relentless, abyss-like hunger from limited calories. A need to continue north despite the fatigue and pain, driving both to and away from the peaks elevated by our lives. Clocktower and I could walk farther, into the evening on this long summer day, overnight at The Birches backpacker camp at the base of Katahdin, then wake to summit tomorrow... . Or stay here, splashing and basking in comradery. The idea of staying—using time for playful interaction—bumped against my nature. Panged like changing a part in dry hair, or swimming against the Penobscot river's flow.

I dunked my head, wetting my flashy sunglasses, then hauled myself up onto the bank. Warm grass tickled my knees and a bee buzzed from one purple clover to the next. I noticed my reflection framed by gold and sparkling purple gems as I camp-towel dried my lenses. Until now, no sunglasses had ever survived an Appalachian Trail section. One pair had plunked into the Sook branch of Dicks Creek in Georgia as I dipped water, another had rattled down a craggy rock face in Virginia when I leaned to retrieve my Nalgene's cap. I lost some bright blue ones in a Cumberland Valley cornfield as I ducked off the trail for a pit stop. I sat on a pair of high-end specs during my flight to New York State. But these gold ones, despite being completely untrailworthy, had made it through all of Maine including the unexpected detour to Florida, and would summit Katahdin and fly back to California. They had grit, persevering like Monarch butterflies, far too fragile to migrate between Canada to Mexico. Or a middle-aged doctor, determined to hike through mountains from Georgia to Maine.

"So, you wanna move on?" Ben asked, looking up from his book, as I dropped down next to him and rested against his pack. We sat shoulder to shoulder, watching the water move.

"Let's hang," I said, reaching for a handful of peanut M&Ms from the Abol camp store. Wildstyle and Chafage whooped and cannonballed into the river which made me think I needed more of this in my life.

The next night at The Birches, I pulled out the temporary tattoos, pasting a stylized purple flower on my right arm while each of the bedraggled crew selected their own icons.

"Did you haul these all the way?" Tennessee asked, as he applied an anchor. Someone else took the rainbow. Another, the spider. Ben stuck a lightning bolt on his pectoralis muscle which looked suspiciously like an EKG tracing, and it gave me pause.

Where would I be now—how would this last state have gone—if Ben hadn't insisted on accompanying me? Maybe still stuck hip deep on the no-Goose Peaks. Or wedged in a crevasse in Mahoosic Notch. Or seething in Florida like an angered grizzly. Would reaching Katahdin mean as much? Would it mean more? I couldn't force my thoughts to imagine the trail alone: the stumbles, twisted ankles, rhythmic climbs, awe-inspiring views, restful lunches, sore shoulders, cool mornings when mist rose from the waters, parting to reveal the day ahead. When I closed my eyes to summon the dirt track and trees and mountains the way I'd seen them for so many miles—alone—I became small, like Bilbo again, in a humbling world. I missed that solitude, and the wonder that came with connecting with the mountains without distraction, letting the branches and brambles close around me, claiming me as part of wild space. But I also noticed a twinge behind my breast bone when I heard my single footfalls among the rustles and chirps, as if wrenching Ben from the trail wrenched away a part of me, as well.

Chapter Sixty-five

Ben and I climbed Mount Katahdin like we traversed the Hundred Mile Wilderness, without a mishap, mis-turn, misstep, or even a hiccup, comfortably achieving the five mile climb to 5300 feet as if it were a day hike, which it sort of was, since the rangers let you exchange your large pack for a smaller one before ascent. Even obstacles that might have otherwise vexed me, like cold rebar or narrow ledges seemed like another step in the journey. I hadn't worried about Ben or my mom, the unexpected events before and during my Maine section serving to contribute to the final leg's triumph.

As last miles go, the last Appalachian Trail mile wasn't the most challenging of the day, or even the longest. The final approach to Baxter Peak—the summit of Mount Katahdin—rambled across a gently sloping ridge, in sharp contrast to the hand-over-foot progress that led there. But I would describe it as the longest mental mile: a roller coaster. A time during which so many miles flashed through my mind: my first steps on Springer as I fled the trauma of my medical education, conquering my panic at Fontana Dam, grieving my father in Tennessee and through the long Virginia miles, stumbling through my relationship with my mother and her addiction alongside Pennsylvania and New York rocks, finding my place in medicine on my euphoric climbs and agonizing descents in the Whites.

And finally, enduring the personal tumult that made all of Maine a metaphor for every last mile in the thirteen states, and despite it all, ascending to the summit.

I stood atop Katahdin, in the same dense fog that swaddled me on Springer so many years before and ran my hands over the battered sign marking the northern terminus. A stranger snapped the iconic photo that the Appalachian Trail hikers claim, the triumphant pose behind the barely legible words:

KATAHDIN
BAXTER PEAK-ELEVATION 5269 feet
NORTHERN TERMINUS OF THE
APPALACHIAN TRAIL
A MOUNTAIN FOOTPATH EXTENDING OVER
2,182 MILES SOUTH TO SPRINGER MOUNTAIN, GEORGIA

I felt excitement, pride...but also loss. So many steps, so much preparation, so much of my life—a decade of summers—I was saying goodbye to an old, dear friend.

I reached behind me, into the curtain of mist for the hand that I couldn't see, but knew would always be there...for comfort, for reassurance, to complete the circuit that might allow some of the emotional charge to travel from my body to the earth, and back again. I felt the tug on my arm as he moved close, and I edged sideways to make room on the rocks propping the sign. Ben stepped up and posed next to me for the photo I would frame for our book shelf: the two of us, a wounded doctor in whom healing and grace had germinated during her sojourn among the sheltering trees, and her partner, a reluctant backpacker dedicated more to supporting her than to the miles.

346

As I look back over that last summer, I view it as a success, although not really a triumphant one. First, my husband's heart is still beating, and second, my mother is alive and functioning independently, and perhaps better than before. And third, unfortunate for its personal ranking in my life, I completed the Appalachian Trail.

Over the years, I've invited friends and family to share the trail magic, walking sections like the Hundred Mile Wilderness, in particular, two granddaughters of my Aunt Bonnie and Uncle Don, the ones who took me on my first backpacking trip and who started me on this journey; one young woman has since moved to rural Maine. This year, I brought a nephew and his partner. We're already discussing, Ben and I, when and where our next hike will be.

Earl Shaffer, the first thru hiker, and a man who intuited biophilia before it had a name, was the first to write about this unassuming dirt track through the woods. He, a better poet than I, writes what I have come to understand, that the Appalachian footpath is always there, stretching forward in its humble and yet magnificent way, "calling us back to the hills."

I'm older now, gray peppers my hair, and I carry reading glasses for maps in an outside pocket of my pack. My hips are sorer on the downslopes, my back tighter, and the ground less forgiving. But the shimmering leaves and whispered words among branches still comfort me, and nudges offered by the gentle breeze soften the miles. I still feel the draw to wild-up, inhale terpenes, step with the trail's rhythm: rising with the sun, sleeping with the dusk. The fatigue, the amble, the beauty.

I will always feel a kinship with the mountains, and with the other travelers, connected in a primal way to a place we evolved in—continue to evolve in— a place that persists in beckoning me home.

About the Author

JoDean Nicolette is a writer, physician, and teacher. A graduate of the Stanford University School of Medicine and the Pacific University Master of Fine Arts Program, she believes in the healing power of both nature and the written word. She sits on the Board of Directors for the Missoula Writing Collaborative, an organization that teaches love of writing in rural schools, and she partners with Pacific University to produce The Body Chronicles, a program designed to help authors write about the experience of wellness and illness. Her work has appeared in such publications as the *Sun,* the *Chicago Tribune's Print Row Journal,* the *Tishman Review, Sugared Water, Inscape,* and the *Rappahannock Review.* A Pushcart nominee, JoDean has been awarded Top Finalist in the Kenneth Johnston Nonfiction Book Contest, the Grand Prize for Prose in the *Maine Review*'s Rocky Coast Contest and the Scribes Valley Publishing Prize for Short Fiction. She is currently working on her memoir *Medicine Horse* and a collection of essays entitled *Trots the Air.* She lives in Montana's Bitterroot Valley with her dogs and horses. *Trail Magic* is her first book. You can learn more about JoDean on her website jodeannicolette.com.

Judge Jacquelyn Shah's Comments

Though it's challenging to take leave from the everyday stresses and trials of a physician's working life, the writer of *Trail Magic* manages to do so by giving herself over to the Appalachian Trail. A 2,200-mile hike from Georgia to Maine, the trail is a grand test of commitment and endurance. As such, one can only feel, I presume, the magic of it by paying close attention to it, despite expenditure of effort and the resulting exhaustion at times.

The writer describes a section of the trek: "I climbed Killington Mountain, the highest traverse in Vermont. By then, the climbs had normalized, and I floated comfortably in my mostly empty head. Pine scent dangled and worked its magic, easing my mental and physical fatigue... ." There was an instance of her much-needed magic.

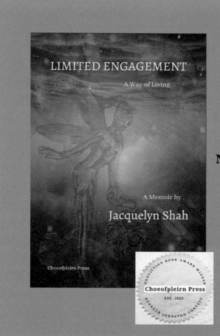

Jacquelyn Shah's memoir, *Limited Engagement: A Way of Living*, won first place in the first annual Kenneth Johnston Nonfiction Book Award in 2022.

Life is a limited engagement. Live it to the fullest and on your own terms.

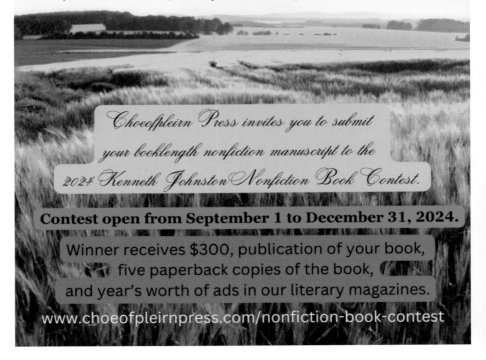

Memoir; Personal Reflection; Literacy Narratives; Expository Essays; Personal Stories

Choeofpleirn Press invites you to submit your booklength nonfiction manuscript to the 2024 Kenneth Johnston Nonfiction Book Contest.

Contest open from September 1 to December 31, 2024.

Winner receives $300, publication of your book, five paperback copies of the book, and year's worth of ads in our literary magazines.

www.choeofpleirnpress.com/nonfiction-book-contest

Choeofpleirn Press publishes four annual literary magazines: *Coneflower Cafe* (fiction), *Glacial Hills Review* (nonfiction), *Rushing Thru the Dark* (drama), and the *Best of Choeofpleirn Press*, which showcases winners and finalists of our five creative contests in fiction, nonfiction, drama, poetry, and art. See www.choeofpleirnpress.com for submission details and digital subscriptions.

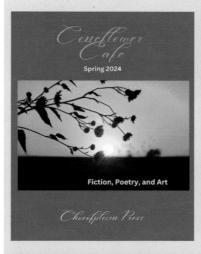

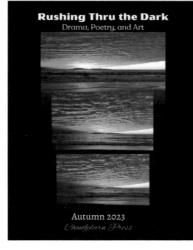

FUN
FACT

CHOEOFPLEIRN

IS A COMBINATION OF OUR
SURNAMES BY ALTERNATING
LETTERS

www.choeofpleirnpress.com
choeofpleirnpress@gmail.com

354

Made in United States
Troutdale, OR
05/22/2024

20055842R00217